The Wealth Inequality Reader

3rd Edition

Edited by Daniel Fireside, Amy Gluckman, Smriti Rao, Alejandro Reuss, and the *Dollars & Sense* Collective

DOLLARS & SENSE — ECONOMIC AFFAIRS BUREAU
BOSTON, MASSACHUSETTS

D1115868

THE WEALTH INEQUALITY READER, 3RD EDITION

Edited by Daniel Fireside, Amy Gluckman, Smriti Rao, Alejandro Reuss, and the *Dollars & Sense* Collective

Copyright © 2009, 2008, 2004 by the Economic Affairs Bureau, Inc. All rights reserved. No portions of this book may be reproduced in any form except by prior permission from the Economic Affairs Bureau.

ISBN: 978-1-878585-53-0

Published by:

Dollars & Sense
Economic Affairs Bureau
29 Winter Street
Boston, MA 02108
617-447-2177
www.dollarsandsense.org

Cover: David Gerratt, www.nonprofitdesign.com
Illustrations: Nick Thorkelson
Production: David Gerratt, www.nonprofitdesign.com
Printed in the United States

CONTENTS

SECTION II   THE CAUSES OF INEQUALITY

SECTION III   THE CONSEQUENCES OF INEQUALITY

SECTION IV   STRATEGIES FOR CHANGE

PREFACE

The United States approached the precipice of the current economic crisis with the most unequal distribution of wealth since the eve of the Great Depression. This sorry fact forms the kernel for *The Wealth Inequality Reader*. The authors here analyze the issue of wealth inequality from the multiple points of view informed by sociology, economics, and social activism.

Most discussions of economic inequality focus on income, not wealth, for the simple reason that data on income are more readily available. But wealth has its own dynamic, and its distribution has unique causes and consequences. More than income, wealth both tells us about the past and foretells the future. A family's wealth today reflects the asset-building opportunities open not only to this generation, but also to parents, grandparents, and great-grandparents. Likewise, parents use their wealth to position their children for future economic success in countless ways—moving into an excellent school district or giving an adult son or daughter money for a down payment on a house, for example—that are out of reach for those who may earn a middle-class income but have few assets.

Given the country's severe wealth gap, proposals for asset-building as a solution to poverty have recently come into vogue (although the chief policy incarnation of this idea, a matched savings plan known as an Individual Development Account (IDA), has yet to become more than a minor pilot program). This approach is in line with the individualist ethos that dominates U.S. politics. This volume describes IDAs and a range of other policies that can help individuals accumulate assets. But more important, several of the authors here argue that the wealth gap cannot be addressed unless our commonwealth of shared public assets, which form the foundation of individual wealth, are expanded and more equitably distributed.

The Introduction documents the worsening landscape of wealth inequality. Here are just a few items:

- Between 2004 and 2007, the median net worth of the poorest 25% of U.S. households *fell* by 37%, while for the richest 10% of households, median net worth *rose* by 20%.

- The racial wealth divide persists: In 2007, the median net worth of families of color was $27,800, just 16% of the median white family net worth of $170,400.
- In just 15 years, from 1992 to 2007, the average net worth of the wealthiest 400 Americans more than tripled in real terms, from $937 million to $3.85 billion.

Although systematic data are scarce for many other parts of the world, the trend in the United States is clear: over the last 30 years wealth has become more and more concentrated. Recent fluctuations in the stock market have pushed the share of total wealth owned by the top 1% of U.S. households up and down at different times. But the sub-prime mortgage meltdown is putting the wealth of many average Americans—whose home is their single largest asset—at risk. There is every reason to believe that wealth concentration will continue to grow, given the current direction of so many of the political-economic vectors that shape wealth distribution.

Since the first edition of this book was published in 2004, the U.S. and global economy have gone from a boom that greatly benefited the few to a bust that has pushed billions of people to the breaking point. Section I looks at the forces that led us to this point. The authors not only ask how we got here, but who benefited along the way, and who the losers are now. Although it will take some time to assess the full measure of the devastating impact this crisis has had on wealth inequality, the authors have begun to highlight the damage, and call for urgent actions to turn the crisis into an opportunity to level the playing field in favor of those currently on the bottom.

Why is the wealth gap in the United States widening now? Section II tackles the causes of growing wealth inequality. For nearly 30 years following World War II, both government and organized labor acted as counterweights to the power of corporations. Building on the legacy of the New Deal years, a range of government policies and a relatively stable business-labor compact moderated the excesses of the market, and as a result, a broad swath of Americans shared, at least to a degree, in the prosperity of the time.

But since the mid-1970s, determined efforts by conservatives and corporations have succeeded in dismantling parts of the New Deal legacy and crushing the labor movement. These efforts have both contributed to and benefited from the country's history of race and discrimination. Playing "the race card" has been a key piece of the GOP's strategy for enlisting low- and moderate-income white voters against their own economic interests; meanwhile, conservative economic policies worsen the racial wealth gap, an artifact of centuries of slavery and post-slavery discrimination.

The consequences of the growing wealth gap are dissected in Section III. As we noted, people usually think about inequality in terms of income. But wealth inequality matters at least as much as, if not more than, income inequality. For one thing, incomes are volatile, subject to the domestic business cycle and deepening global competition. In contrast, assets like a home, land, or savings offer a more stable form of security and allow families to survive financial setbacks without seeing their standard of living permanently undermined. Ownership and control of assets may be particularly important to members of historically disadvantaged groups; for example, a study in India has shown that women who own land or a house in their own names are, other things equal, far less likely to be victims of domestic violence.

Furthermore, wealth inequality is self-reinforcing and worsens over time in the absence of proactive efforts at redistribution. Wealth allows parents to give their children a wide range of advantages that position them to build even greater wealth as adults.

Extreme concentrations of wealth do not only hurt those far down the economic ladder. Concentrated wealth distorts democracy by giving a small elite both the motive and the means to buy the policies they want from contribution-hungry politicians. Concentrated wealth bites the hand that feeds it, too: evidence suggests that extreme inequality actually undermines economic growth. And concentrated wealth spawns a culture of excessive consumption that subverts all of the nonmaterial values people find difficult enough to sustain in a modern capitalist economy.

While the picture up to this point may seem dismal, we need only look back to find the cause for optimism. Throughout U.S. history, periods of excessive wealth polarization have been followed by mass movements for economic reform. The Gilded Age was followed by populism and progressivism; the 1929 crash was followed by poor people's movements and the New Deal. These movements for change succeeded, however unevenly, in getting working people and the middle class a larger piece of the ownership pie (although, to be clear, wealth has never been divided near equitably, even in the country's most egalitarian eras).

Likewise, today, a movement is beginning to grow to restructure the economy and reorient government policies so that wealth will be more widely shared. The plural—movements—might be more appropriate: countless activists, scholars, unions, and a few politicians and business leaders are engaging this issue from many angles. Section IV sketches out some of these potential solutions, from the nuts and bolts of specific asset-building programs to visionary proposals for institutionalizing an overall more equitable distribution of wealth—for example, by collecting rents and fees from private interests who use common assets like the sky and the airwaves, then paying those revenues out to all.

For those who believe that human beings can vary so widely in merit—however merit is defined—that one may deserve to possess billions of dollars and a surfeit of mansions and jets while another deserves to sleep on a sewer grate, the authors here will have little to say. But for anyone who is convinced that inherent in any definition of a healthy and just society are some limits to the unequal distribution of wealth, this volume provides a roadmap through—and, we hope, beyond—the current political economy of wealth inequality.

Wealth Inequality by the Numbers

N ot since the Gilded Age has this country seen such a yawning gap between the very rich and those with little wealth. Global wealth disparities are even larger. The following pages capture this polarization with facts and figures on the distribution of wealth in the United States and, to the extent possible, worldwide.

THE WEALTH PIE

The wealthiest 1% of households owns more than a third of the nation's household wealth. The next tier, those in the 95th through 98th percentiles, claims another 27%. While the top 5% holds well over half of the wealth pie, the bottom three-fifths make do with the crumbs—holding a meager 4.2% of total net worth.

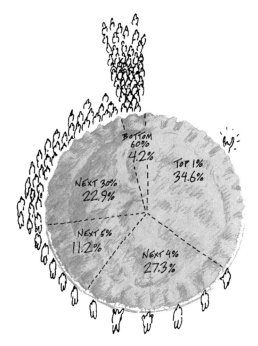

Source: Edward N. Wolff, professor of economics, New York University. Based on 2007 Survey of Consumer Finances.

Illustrations in this section by Nick Thorkelson

WHAT IS WEALTH?

A family's wealth, or net worth, is defined as the sum of its assets minus its debts. In other words, wealth is "what you own" minus "what you owe." Assets are all resources that a household holds in store—the bank of reserves a family has available to invest in its members and their futures. Many assets grow in value and generate income. Just as important, asset wealth provides a cushion, protecting families from the vicissitudes of the business cycle, as wealth assets may be drawn down during periods of crisis (a job loss, for example). Financial assets include savings, bonds, certificates of deposit, stocks, mutual fund investments, retirement pensions, and the like. Nonfinancial assets may include homes, other real estate, vehicles, ownership in a privately held business, and all sorts of other property—from rare baseball card collections to jewelry or hobby equipment. Debts are liabilities—credit card balances, mortgages, and other loans—that are owed.

One way to think about wealth, as distinct from income, is to picture it as a pool of resources—much like a pond. Income, by contrast, is more like a river. Most adults receive an income stream of paychecks, entitlement payments like Social Security, child support, or pensions that pays for housing, health care, food, clothing, consumer goods, and miscellaneous expenses. If any trickle of income remains, it is set aside as savings—becoming wealth. People with large "ponds" of wealth typically receive streams of income in the form of interest, dividends, or rent from those assets. The very wealthy have "lakes" of assets that spring substantial rivers of income.

Looking at information about wealth can tell us a lot about people's lives, and it can tell us things that income statistics fail to reveal. The bottom quartile of U.S. families has a mean net worth of *negative* $2,300—an average family in the bottom quartile carries a debt burden greater than all of its assets combined. From this, we can surmise that such a family most likely does not own a home, or if they do, all

Different researchers use slightly different definitions of wealth. For example, some exclude those retirement pensions that an individual cannot currently access, while others include the estimated present value of pensions. And some scholars consider automobiles a form of wealth, whereas others exclude the value of automobiles from their calculations.

Data on wealth is far scarcer than data on income. The primary source of information on private wealth in the United States is the Federal Reserve's triennial Survey of Consumer Finances, which collects household-level data on assets, liabilities, income, use of financial services, and other household financial behavior.

of its value has been mortgaged or its market value has declined. If such a family owns any asset, it is probably a car that they had to borrow money to purchase. By contrast, a family in the second or third wealth quartile is likely to own a home as its largest asset. Families in the top quartile probably own not just one or more homes, but also stocks and other financial assets.

While private wealth is an important source of security in our society, social wealth can reduce the need for substantial individual wealth. For instance, an adequate social safety net that includes income support and health care would reduce the need for individual savings to ensure basic economic security.

THE SUPER-RICH

Over a 30-year period beginning in 1970, the richest 1% (as ranked by income) accrued a mounting share of the nation's private wealth. Throughout the 1990s, the top percentile held a larger concentration of total household wealth than at any time since the 1920s. Its wealth share declined somewhat during the 2001 recession, thanks to falling corporate share prices, but then resumed its climb, reaching 34.6% in 2007 (since 2007 the fall-off in stock prices have no doubt pushed the figure down somewhat).

PERCENTAGE OF WEALTH OWNED BY THE TOP 1%

Source: Edward N. Wolff: [1] "Recent Trends in Household Wealth in the United States: Rising Debt and the Middle-Class Squeeze," Levy Economics Institute Working Paper No. 502, June 2007; [2] unpublished data, 2009.

The past two decades have been kind to the super-rich. From 1992 to 2007, the average wealth held by the nation's wealthiest 400 people more than quadrupled, rising from $937 million to a whopping $3.85 billion in inflation-adjusted dollars. Within the top 400, the highest ranked saw the largest gains.

THE WEALTHIEST 400 PEOPLE IN THE UNITED STATES

Wealth by Rank and Average Wealth (in millions of 2004 dollars), 1992–2007

Wealth by Rank in the *Forbes* 400	1992	1995	1999	2000	2001	2002	2005	2007
1st	7,746	17,002	89,716	64,318	54,000	42,361	51,000	59,000
10th	4,303	4,940	17,943	17,356	17,500	11,723	15,400	17,000
50th	1,537	2,068	4,222	4,798	3,900	3,152	4,200	6,300
100th	984	1,034	2,533	2,654	2,000	1,773	2,500	3,500
400th	326	391	660	740	600	542	900	1,300
Avg. Wealth	937	1,025	2,731	3,057	2,366	2,148	2,813	3,850
Number of billionaires	92	107	278	301	266	205	374	400

Source: Calculated from *Forbes* 400.

HOUSEHOLDS WITH NET WORTH EQUAL TO OR EXCEEDING $10 MILLION

The number of households with $10 million or more (in constant 1995 dollars) has grown nearly sevenfold since 1983, from 66,500 to 464,200.

2007: 464,200

2001: 378,400

2004: 344,800

1998: 239,900

1995: 190,400

1983: 66,500

1989: 64,900

1992: 41,600

Source: Edward N. Wolff: [1] "Recent Trends in Household Wealth in the United States: Rising Debt and the Middle-Class Squeeze," Levy Economics Institute Working Paper No. 502, June 2007; [2] unpublished data, 2009.

THE WEALTHLESS

The 1990s were supposed to be economic good times, and the brief 2001 recession was followed by six full years of economic expansion. Yet the share of Americans with no wealth at all was larger in 2007 than it had been in 1989, and the poorest quarter of U.S. households saw a 36.8% *drop* in median net worth between 2004 and 2007. Moreover, data from 2007 are too early to reflect much of the fall in housing prices and other asset values in the current crisis. Federal Reserve Board economists estimate the median net worth of all U.S. households to be nearly 18% lower today, in 2009, than it was in 2007.

HOUSEHOLDS WITH LITTLE OR NO NET WORTH, 1983–2007

	Percentage of Households with Zero or Negative Net Worth	Percentage of Households with Net Worth Less Than $5,000*
1983	15.5%	25.4%
1989	17.9%	27.6%
1992	18.0%	27.2%
1995	18.5%	27.8%
1998	18.0%	27.2%
2001	17.6%	26.6%
2004	17.0%	26.8%
2007	18.6%	26.6%

* Constant 1995 Dollars

IN 2007—

26.6 PERCENT HAVE UNDER $5000 NET WORTH
THE HAVE-A-LITTLES

18.6 PERCENT HAVE ZERO OR NEGATIVE NET WORTH

THE HAVE-NOTS

Source: Edward N. Wolff: [1] "Recent Trends in Household Wealth in the United States: Rising Debt and the Middle-Class Squeeze," Levy Economics Institute Working Paper No. 502, June 2007; [2] unpublished data, 2009. Excludes automobiles.

CLASS MOBILITY

LIKE PARENT, LIKE CHILD

In the United States, a pretty sure way to secure a high income is to be born to parents with high incomes. Only 7.3% of children born to parents with incomes in the top 20% grow up to have incomes in the bottom 20%. Likewise, just 6.3% of children with parents in the bottom income quintile earn incomes in the top 20% as adults. So much for the myth of meritocracy.

If anything, these figures actually overstate the degree of income mobility in the United States. This is because it takes much larger increases in income to enter the top quintile from the others than it takes to move up one, two, or even three quintiles from the bottom. In 2006, for example, the mean household income of the lowest quintile was $11,352 (2006 dollars), compared to $28,777 for the second quintile (a difference of $17,425). By contrast, the mean household income of the top quintile was $111,536, compared to $58,163 for the next highest quintile (a difference of $53,373—a much larger distance to travel). Although a large percentage of children born to parents in the bottom 20% move up a few quintiles as adults, their mobility is less striking than the *lack* of mobility into the top quintile.

Figures on mobility by wealth don't exist, but if they did, they'd probably paint an even bleaker picture.

CHANCE OF CHILD ATTAINING INCOME LEVEL AS ADULT, BY PARENTAL INCOME

Parents' Income Quintile	Child's Income Quintile as Adult		
	Top 20%	Middle 20%	Bottom 20%
Top 20%	37.3%	18.4%	7.3%
Middle 20%	17.3%	25.0%	15.3%
Bottom 20%	6.3%	16.5%	42.3%

Source: Thomas Hertz, "Rags, Riches and Race: The Intergenerational Economic Mobility of Black and White Families in the United States." In *Unequal Chances: Family Background and Economic Success*, ed. Bowles, Gintis, and Osborne, Princeton Univ. Press and Russell Sage, 2005.

Note: These figures are based on total family income for black and white participants in the Panel Study of Income Dynamics who were born between 1942 and 1972, observed as children in their households of origin, and later as adults (26 or older) in their own households.

THE OWNING CLASS

While upwards of 90% of people in the United States make their living by working for a wage or salary, a small number gain their incomes from the ownership of property. These large-scale property owners may have jobs (usually high-paying ones), but they do not *have* to work for a living. They own businesses, which yield profits; stocks, which yield dividends; real estate, which yields rent; and money, which yields interest. Unlike the houses and cars that are most Americans' primary assets, these forms of wealth typically yield income and, when their value increases, capital gains as well. They also give their owners, in varying ways and degrees, some control over the nation's economy.

Some of the 90% also own these kinds of property: a triple-decker or a small stock portfolio, perhaps. But ownership of income-accumulating property is even more highly concentrated than ownership of wealth overall. The income from such property is considerable—nearly $3 trillion in the United States in 2003, or over one-quarter of gross national income (even by the most conservative estimate). This is the tribute the owning class extracts each year from society's total production.

Profits and other private property income have ranged between one-fourth and one-third of U.S. national income over the last 45 years. This variation may not

PRIVATE PROPERTY INCOME (PROFITS, INTEREST, RENT, ETC., BEFORE TAXES) AS A PERCENTAGE OF NATIONAL INCOME, 1959–2006

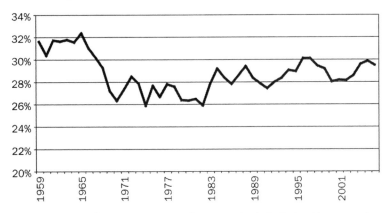

Source: U.S. Dept. of Commerce, Bureau of Economic Analysis, National Income and Product Accounts, Table 1.10 Gross Domestic Income by Type of Income. Percentages equal "Net operating surplus, private enterprises" divided by the sum of itself and "Compensation of employees, paid."

seem like much, but when the private-property share of national income declined sharply in the mid-1960s, as a result of high employment and rising worker militancy, U.S. capitalism went into crisis. The "recovery" beginning in the early 1980s coincided with property ownership garnering an increasing share of national income, as attacks on unions and social welfare programs eroded workers' bargaining power. In short, capitalism "functions" as long as the owning class can take a satisfactory cut of the national income.

THE STOCK OWNERSHIP PIE

If the distribution of wealth overall in the United States is very skewed, the distribution of financial assets such as stocks and bonds is far more so. A home is the single largest asset for most American families who have any wealth at all; most other kinds of assets are heavily concentrated in the hands of the wealthiest few percent of families. The chart shows the distribution of the nation's publicly traded stock that is directly held—in other words, outside of a managed account such as a mutual fund. The richest 1% of families owns over half of all directly held stock; the bottom 50% owns one-half of one percent. Assets not directly held, such as those in IRAs, are more equally distributed—but only among the wealthier half of the population. The bottom 50% owns almost none of those assets either: only 0.7% of the value of mutual funds and 3.4% of the value of retirement accounts such as 401(k)s.

SHARE OF STOCK OWNED, BY WEALTH CLASS (2004)

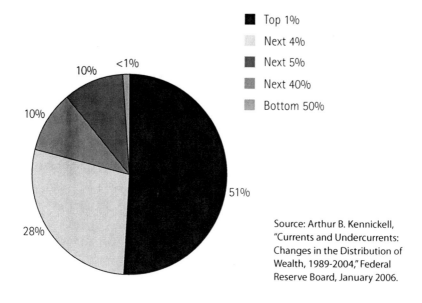

Source: Arthur B. Kennickell, "Currents and Undercurrents: Changes in the Distribution of Wealth, 1989-2004," Federal Reserve Board, January 2006.

THE RACIAL WEALTH GAP

The United States has a racial wealth gap that far exceeds its racial income gap. This wealth gap persists even during periods of economic growth. In the 1990s boom, the median wealth of families of color (nonwhite and Latino) actually fell, although this drop was reversed in the 2000s. This intransigent wealth gap is the product of a long history of discrimination in the United States, and is perpetuated by family inheritance patterns that pass accumulated advantages and disadvantages from one generation to the next. The median net worth of families of color is just a fraction of white families'. The racial wealth gap is far larger than the racial gap in income and, as the table below shows, the wealth gap between families of color and white families has grown wider over the past decade even as the income gap has narrowed somewhat.

WEALTH VS. INCOME BY RACE, 1998-2007

(thousands of 2007 dollars)

		1998	2001	2004	2007
Median Net Worth	Families of color	21.2	21.0	27.2	27.8
	White families	121.9	143.0	154.5	170.4
	Ratio	**5.75 to 1**	**6.81 to 1**	**5.68 to 1**	**6.13 to 1**
Median Income	Families of color	29.7	30.1	32.7	36.8
	White families	48.6	52.9	54.3	51.8
	Ratio	**1.64 to 1**	**1.76 to 1**	**1.66 to 1**	**1.41 to 1**

Source: Brian K. Bucks, Arthur B. Kennickell, Traci L. Mach, and Kevin B. Moore, "Changes in U.S. Family Finances from 2004 to 2007: Evidence from the Survey of Consumer Finances," Federal Reserve Board, February 2009.

Racial disparities are found across all categories of asset ownership. For nearly every kind of asset, whether financial or nonfinancial, white families are more likely to own the asset in any amount *and* have larger holdings in the asset, as the following table shows.

FAMILY HOLDINGS OF SELECTED ASSETS BY RACE, 2007

		Certificates of deposit	Savings bonds	Stocks	Pooled investment funds	Retirement accounts	Primary residence	Privately-held businesses
Percent of families holding asset	Families of color	8.2	7.8	9.4	5.8	39.1	51.9	7.4
	White families	19.4	17.8	21.4	13.7	58.2	75.6	13.9
Median value of holdings for families holding asset (thousands of 2007 dollars)	Families of color	10.0	1.0	8.0	30.0	25.4	180.0	60.0
	White families	20.0	1.0	19.0	64.0	52.7	200.0	112.5

Source: Brian K. Bucks, Arthur B. Kennickell, Traci L. Mach, and Kevin B. Moore, "Changes in U.S. Family Finances from 2004 to 2007: Evidence from the Survey of Consumer Finances," Federal Reserve Board, February 2009.

WOMEN'S WEALTH

WOMEN AND WEALTH IN THE UNITED STATES

Women own less wealth than men, but the gender wealth gap may be shrinking. So suggest the most recent data on wealth ownership in the United States. Virtually all data on asset ownership is by household and does not distinguish among people living in the household. So, the only gender comparison that typically can be made is between single women and single men.

Data from the 2001 Survey of Consumer Finances show a dramatic gap between the net worth of households headed by single females and those headed by single males: the median net worth of the latter is 69% higher. Data on young baby boomers —those born between 1957 and 1964—from the National Longitudinal Survey of Youth, however, show a much smaller gap between these two groups; this snapshot of the young boomers does suggest a promising trend.

MEDIAN NET WORTH AND FINANCIAL ASSETS OF ALL HOUSEHOLDS (2001)

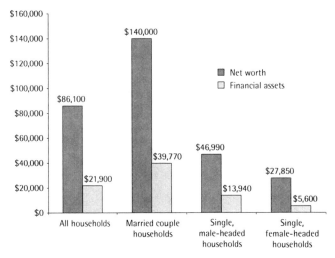

Source: Jeanne M. Hogarth and Chris E. Anguelov, "Descriptive Statistics on Levels of Net Worth." Paper prepared for the Women & Assets Summit, March-April 2003, Brandeis University. Data from 2001 Survey of Consumer Finances.

MEDIAN NET WORTH OF YOUNG BABY BOOMERS (2000)

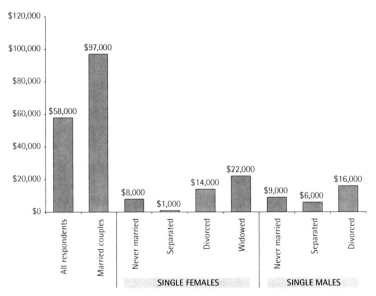

Source: Lisa A. Keister and Alexis Yamokoski, "Single Females and Wealth." Unpublished paper, April 2004. Data from the National Longitudinal Survey of Youth, 1979 Cohort. The sample contained too few widowers to include.

WORLD WIDE WEALTH

Data on wealth ownership and its distribution are scarce compared to data on income. This is particularly true on an international scale: only a handful of countries systematically collect information on individual or household wealth holdings. In the absence of such data, two World Bank economists have estimated the per capita wealth in different world regions using national-level data. They derive total wealth by adding the monetary values of a nation's natural resources (for example, oil, timber, and cropland), its produced assets (for example, goods and factories), and its "human resources" (the wealth inhering in people's projected lifetime productivity, computed as a function of GNP with some adjustments). The authors acknowledge that these are rough, preliminary estimates.

Poor countries tend to have lower per-capita natural resource wealth than rich countries. But it's notable that the natural resource gap is much smaller than the gap in the other components of wealth (the Middle East excepted). This suggests that a country's natural endowments are less important than how it deploys them and how the international rules governing trade and financial transactions shape its economy.

GLOBAL WEALTH DISTRIBUTION (2000)

	Population Share	Wealth Per Adult	Wealth Share
North America: Canada and U.S. only	6.1%	$190,653	34.3%
Latin America & Caribbean	8.2%	$18,163	4.4%
Europe	14.9%	$67,232	29.5%
Asia: China	22.8%	$3,885	2.6%
Asia: India	15.4%	$1,989	0.9%
Asia: High Income	4.5%	$172,414	22.9%
Asia: Other	18.0%	$5,952	4.3%
Africa	10.2%	$3,558	1.1%

Source: James B. Davies, Susanna Sandstrom, Anthony Shorrocks, Edward N. Wolff. "The World Distribution of Household Wealth," U.N. University-World Institute for Development Economics Research, December 2006.

Note: "Asia: High Income" includes Austrailia, Japan, New Zealand, South Korea, and Taiwan.

Inequality and Economic Crisis

Is this current economic downturn a recession or a depression? John Miller argues that the term "the repression" best captures the nature of this crisis and its causes, while at the same time pointing us toward possible solutions.

WHAT'S IN A NAME?

Part recession, part depression, today's economic meltdown is very much a product of the large dose of economic repression that preceded it.

BY JOHN MILLER
July/August 2009*

A frightening financial panic, a virulent housing bust, and plummeting economic output have left global capitalism facing its worst crisis since the Great Depression.

Economies across the globe are in trouble. The European and Japanese economies shrank at double-digit rates in the first three months of this year; even China's growth rate is slowing precipitously. U.S. autoworkers, European and U.S. finance workers, Japanese electronics workers, Chinese garment workers, and Indian software workers are losing their jobs as their economies slow and world export markets dry up.

In the United States, where the crisis hit first, the downturn that began in December 2007 is now the longest since World War II, with the greatest job losses and, by some measures, the highest unemployment of the postwar period.

Housing prices, the fountainhead of the crisis, have now fallen more than they did during the housing bust of the Great Depression. Record levels of mortgage defaults and foreclosures have spread panic through a rickety global financial system. In a six-month span, three of the five largest U.S. investment banks disappeared. Leading U.S. mortgage company Countrywide bit the dust. Washington Mutual collapsed, the largest commercial bank failure in U.S. history.

The stock market has crashed as well. Stock prices fell to below one-half of their peak value in most indices, matching the initial declines in 1929.

* Date published in *Dollars & Sense* magazine or elsewhere

In brief, the current contraction is no run-of-the-mill recession. But neither, at least at this point, is it comparable to the decade-long Great Depression, in which output fell by one-quarter and more than one-quarter of the U.S. workforce went without work.

So what is it? A recession or a depression? Truth is, economists make no precise distinction between the two other than that recessions are mild and depressions are more severe.

Even with their imprecision, neither term properly fits our current economic decline at this point, although it may yet become inarguably a depression. What term would fit? "The Great Recession," the name favored by former Fed chair Paul Volcker among others, is one candidate. "The Panic of 2008-2009" is another.

But better yet is "The Repression," a name suggested by University of Massachusetts economist (and *D&S* Dr. Dollar) Arthur MacEwan. Part recession, part depression, today's economic meltdown is very much a product of the large dose of economic repression that preceded it. Deregulatory, pro-rich, anti-labor public policy guaranteed that the benefits of economic growth, at least what we had of it this decade, went almost exclusively to the most well-to-do among us, leaving many vulnerable. The latest business cycle, both its expansion beginning in 2001 and its catastrophic downturn now underway, make those consequences clear for all to see. In a very real way, the Repression of 2008 and 2009 has now pushed many people out of the frying pan and into the fire. And not only does the term "repression" describe the causes of the current crisis; it also points us toward its consequences, and toward prospective cures for today's economic woes.

THE FRYING PAN: THE EXPANSION OF 2001–07

Economic expansions are supposed to improve our life chances, not just swell the economy. For some time now, however, economic upswings have done less to improve the lot of most people than they used to.

During the first two decades after World War II, the U.S. economy grew rapidly, lifted incomes and wages, reduced inequality, and alleviated poverty. With its global dominance, the U.S. economy grew an average of 5.0% a year during the expansions between 1950 and 1969. Strong trade unions and expanding government programs helped to protect workers, fight poverty, and spread the benefits of economic growth widely, at least by today's standards.

No subsequent expansion has met those standards. But in this decade the capacity of economic growth to make most people better off all but evaporated. First off, the U.S. economy has grown more slowly in this decade than in any of the earlier post-war decades, even before accounting for the current crisis. Beginning in November 2001, the economy grew for 73 months or just over six years, reaching a peak in December 2007. That is longer than the 57-month average duration of postwar expansions. But GDP grew at an anemic annual rate of 2.5% in the 2001–07 expansion, far below the 4.3% average for postwar expansions. (See Table 1.)

Along with slower growth that failed to engage the productive capacity of the U.S. economy, successive economic expansions have created fewer and fewer jobs. In the last three business cycles, the economy has continued to lose jobs even after an economic recovery was underway. On top of that, recoveries have taken longer and longer to replace the jobs lost in the downturn. (See Table 2.)

In this decade, "the great American jobs machine" truly met its maker. Shockingly, the economy continued to lose jobs *for the first two and half years* of this last expansion. A full four years passed before the economy had added back the jobs lost during the 2001 recession, more than twice as long as in the average expansion since 1970.

The economic expansion from 2001 to the end of 2007 added jobs more slowly than any other expansion since World War II. The number of jobs in the economy increased by just 0.9% a year, about one-third of the 2.5% rate posted by the average postwar expansion.

Sluggish economic growth left employers with little need for new hires. Another drain on U.S. job creation was the increasing number of jobs lost to global outsourcing. Not only manufacturing jobs went abroad, but so did white collar work from back-room office operations (bookkeeping, customer service, and marketing) to engineering and computer software design.

All told, during the eight years of the Bush administration, job growth averaged a meager 0.28% annually. That's just 378,000 new jobs a year, a total we would expect a growing economy to add in a single month.

EXPANSION AND REPRESSION

The sluggish economic growth of the first six years of this decade not only created fewer jobs than earlier postwar expansions, it also, not surprisingly, did less to lift incomes, alleviate poverty, or improve the economic well-being of all but the best-off. Those lopsided results are easily documented:

- For the first time in the postwar period, median household income (corrected for inflation) at the peak of this expansion was still below its level at the previous peak in 2000.
- By 2007, 5.9 million more people were without health insurance than when the expansion began in 2001.
- For the first time in a postwar expansion, the poverty rate failed to decline. In 2007 at the peak of this expansion, the U.S. poverty rate stood at 12.5%, well above the 11.7% rate when the expansion began.
- After correcting for inflation, wages and salaries grew just 1.8% a year during this expansion, less half the 3.8% rate during the average postwar expansion.

TABLE 1: SIZING UP THE 2001–2007 EXPANSION

	2001–07 Expansion	Average Postwar Expansion
Length of Expansion	73 Months	57 Months
GDP Growth	2.5%	4.3%
Employment Gains	0.9%	2.5%
Wage and Salary Growth	1.8%	3.8%
Corporate Profits	10.8%	7.4%

Notes: GDP, employment, wages and salaries, and corporate profits are all measured as annual rates of change and corrected for inflation. The average for postwar expansions is calculated for the six expansions from 1961 to 2001.

Sources: Bureau of Economic Analysis, Bureau of Labor Statistics, and Federal Reserve Board.

TABLE 2: JOB MARKET DECLINE AND RECOVERY IN SIX POSTWAR RECESSIONS (NUMBERS IN MONTHS)

Recession	Length of Recession	Months of Job Losses	Months until Jobs Recovery
Nov. 1969 – Nov. 1970	12	14	19
Dec. 1973 – March 1975	16	16	25
Jan. 1980 – July 1980	6	6	11
July 1981 – Nov. 1982	16	19	29
July 1990 – March 1991	8	11	30
March 2001 – Nov. 2001	8	32	48

Source: Bureau of Labor Statistics.

- At the same time, real corporate profits skyrocketed, increasing 10.8% a year, after adjusting for inflation, compared to the 8.3% average growth rate in other postwar growth periods.

Not surprisingly, inequality, which by 2001 was already unprecedented by postwar standards, continued to worsen during the decade. But just how much of the population missed out on the benefits of economic growth was astonishing. The average real income of the poorest 20% of households declined, but so did that of the best-off 20% of households. The incomes of the three quintiles in between stagnated;

none grew by more than 1.1% over the entire period. Even the average income of the richest 5% declined during this expansion.

The top one percent of households, on the other hand, continued to make out like bandits. Their real income grew by 10.9% each year from 2002 to 2006, reports economist Emmanuel Saez using the most recent data available. That small sliver of the population monopolized 73% of the income growth during those years. In contrast, the bottom 99% of households saw their real incomes grow just 1.0% in each of those years.

As these figures make clear, the combination of sluggish economic growth, few new jobs, stagnant wages and incomes, and extreme inequality left many people behind long before the economy collapsed in 2008.

BUBBLES BURSTING

The economic collapse, however, began before 2008 with the bursting of the housing bubble. Despite spanning the 2001 recession, that ten-year bubble, from 1996 to 2006, drove up housing prices further and for longer than in any period since 1890. According to Yale economist Robert Shiller's long-term U.S. home price index, real (i.e., inflation-adjusted) housing prices increased an unprecedented 84.5% in that period.

Skyrocketing housing prices allowed homeowners to use their homes as ATMs, as economics journalist Doug Henwood first put it, taking out loans on the rising value of their houses. The volume of these so-called mortgage equity withdrawals more than doubled from 2000 to the peak of the housing bubble in 2005–6 and financed about one-third of the growth in consumption over those years.

U.S. housing prices are now down by more than one-quarter from their peak in late 2005. That is not only the sharpest decline of the postwar period, it is the biggest drop in housing prices since the 32.3% drop from 1914 to 1921—including the housing bust during the Great Depression. The collapse of housing prices put the kibosh on consumer spending, precipitated a crisis of mortgage defaults and foreclosures, and punched a hole in the financial system.

The crash of the stock market is unprecedented by postwar standards as well. By March 2, 2009, the Dow Jones Industrial Average of 30 blue-chip stocks had fallen 53.2% from its October 2007 peak. Broader stock indices, such as the Standard & Poor's 500, had registered even sharper declines. In comparison, the high-tech stock market crash earlier this decade had knocked 35.2% off the price of blue-chip stocks at its low point; the bear market of 1973, 42.2%. Only the Great Depression took more out of stock prices. At their low point in June 1932, stocks had lost a stunning 88.8% of their October 1929 value. While the stock market lately has shown some life, the turnaround in stock prices is unlikely to be rapid even if the stock market has already seen its bottom. It took 6 years, 9 years, and 25 years respectively for the stock market to replace the value lost in the 2001, 1973, and 1929 crashes.

THE FIRE: INCREASED REPRESSION IN 2007–09

Dismal labor market conditions were the cutting edge of the economic downturn proper. The economy began shedding jobs long before economic growth plummeted. Even the National Bureau of Economic Research (NBER), which determines the turning points of U.S. business cycles, took notice. In 2008 the economy lost jobs every month of the year for the first time since the Great Depression. The mounting monthly job losses convinced the NBER to declare the recession's start-date December 2007, even though at that point the economy had not yet suffered two consecutive quarters of negative economic growth—the standard definition of a recession.

In other words, in this downturn job losses are no lagging indicator. But don't expect employment to be a leading indicator of the recovery either. Job losses will almost certainly continue even after economic growth returns. Before things are over, the labor market downturn and the suffering endured by all those looking for work will have persisted far longer than the contraction of economic output.

The U.S. economy is losing jobs as never before in the postwar period. Seventeen months into the downturn, the economy has lost more jobs than in any previous downturn and has lost nearly twice the share of its employment base as in the typical postwar recession. (See Table 3.) Construction, manufacturing of all sorts, and the financial industry, all male-dominated employments, have been especially hard hit. But even software giant Microsoft and major law firms are now laying off workers.

The fact that the 2001–2007 economic expansion created so few jobs heightens the effects of this extreme job loss. With few new jobs, especially full-time ones, workers' connection to the labor force is ever more tenuous. By the first quarter of 2009, marginally attached workers (those who want a job and have looked for work in the last year but not in the last month, hence are not counted as unemployed) formed a larger share of the labor force than in the 2001 recession. (Data are available only from 1994 on.) Also, the proportion of the labor force forced to work part-time because they could not find full-time jobs was higher than in any recession since 1970, including the severe 1974–75 and 1982 recessions. (Data are available from 1968 on.) By April 2009, forced part-time workers made up twice the share of the labor force as in the 2001 recession.

The failure of the 2001 expansion to lift incomes is also intensifying the suffering in this crisis. In the nearly decade-long expansion of the 1960s, the income of the median household, corrected for inflation, rose nearly 4% a year. But the 2001 to 2007 expansion added a measly 0.2% a year to real median incomes.

As income stagnated with increasingly repressive economic growth, households went deeper into debt. In the 1982 recession, 10.7% of U.S. households' disposable income went to service debt payments. In December 2007, at the onset of this downturn, that figure had reached 14.3%. It dipped slightly in 2008 as worried households began to cut back on their borrowing, but it is no longer dropping as mounting unemployment has pushed down households' disposable income.

This downturn has already gone on longer than even the two longest postwar downturns, in 1973–75 and 1981–1982, both of which lasted 16 months. Even if the economy begins to recover in the last quarter of 2009, the downturn would have lasted 22 months, more than twice as long as the 10-month average length of postwar recessions.

To date, the loss of output has not matched that in the worst postwar recessions. Through its first five quarters, inflation-adjusted GDP in the current downturn has fallen 2.4%—more than the average loss of output during all postwar recessions of 2.05% but less than the steeper declines in output during the 1974–75 and 1982 recessions. In the first half of 2008 the economy continued to grow slowly even as it shed jobs. Then the contraction began; output fell at annual rates of over 6% in the last quarter of 2008 and the first quarter of 2009. Even the most optimistic forecasts do not see a return to economic growth until the last quarter of 2009. By that time the loss of output over the last two years will surely have outdistanced that of any postwar downturn.

In specific sectors the current loss of output has already outdistanced all postwar recessions. Industrial production, which includes hard-hit manufacturers of automobiles, home electronics, and construction supplies, has fallen off at double-digit rates—more than three times its decline in the average postwar recession. Today's loss of industrial output has already matched the shredding of industry in the 1982 recession, the worst previous case. (See Table 3.)

TABLE 3: THE DEPTH OF THE CURRENT DOWNTURN

	2007–09 "Repression" to Date	Average Postwar Recession
Length of Downturn	17 Months	10 Months
Economic Output Loss	-2.4% (1st five quarters)	-2.05%
Industrial Production	-13.6%	-4.0%
Retail Sales	-11.8%	-3.5%
Employment Losses	-4.1%	-2.1%

Notes: Economic output loss is the cumulative loss of output over a recession measured as the decline of GDP corrected for inflation. The industrial production index is again the cumulative decline in the index over the recession. Retails sales are measured as the total decline in retail sales corrected for inflation. Employment losses are measured as the drop in total employment over the recession. The averages for industrial production, retail sales, and employment losses are for the six recessions from 1969 to 2001. The GDP average is for 10 recessions from 1948 to 2001.

Sources: Bureau of Economic Analysis, Bureau of Labor Statistics, and Federal Reserve Board.

Retail sales have been decimated as well. In the typical postwar recession, retail sales dropped off by about 3.5%, stabilizing within half a year after the onset of the downturn. But this time, retail sales have dropped 12.9% and are still falling. Circuit City, the electronics giant, closed its doors; Filene's Basement, the venerable department store, laid off workers; and even eBay, the internet retailer, issued pink slips.

FIGHTING REPRESSION

The cure to the Repression is to fight repressive policies. Public policy must make the fight by promoting genuine full employment, legalizing card check union drives by passing the Employee Free Choice Act, enforcing labor laws already on the books by expanding the workplace inspection staff of the Department of Labor, and extending health insurance to all. Reducing payroll taxes, the bulk of most people's federal tax bill, will help, along with letting the Bush tax cuts targeted at the wealthy expire in 2010. Those policies would do much to enhance workers' bargaining power, lessen labor abuse, and arrest today's worsening inequality—or if you will, to undo repression.

Realizing those goals would take active and progressive government intervention into the labor markets and substantial funding for government programs that will put people to work repairing our decaying infrastructure and making it greener, restoring the social services cut out of state budgets in the crisis, and providing relief to those who have lost their homes or their jobs. And that spending would also get the economy going and counteract the Repression.

None of that will happen without massive public pressure. The Obama administration must not succumb to the calls of deficit hawks to slash government spending. Their do-nothing strategy, or worse yet more tax cuts for the wealthy, would saddle the federal government with even larger deficits as the economy and tax revenues fell through the floor. And unlike a program of progressive government spending, which holds the potential to spark a period of economic growth that could pay the public debt, a do-nothing strategy would likely lead us into a depression that would impose costs far more serious than a rise in government debt.

In addition, the Obama administration will need to impose strict controls on a financial industry to which it has close ties: one of its most senior economic advisors played a key role in deregulation. It will also have to convert its stress tests of troubled banks into a lever to take over any distressed bank, mortgage house, or insurer that is too big to fail and then run them as mutual savings banks for the benefit of the public.

Those steps will help to end the Repression by getting the economy going and to disable the drivers that have shaped economic growth so lopsidedly in favor of so few while repressing so many. Without them we will see either a return of the kind of economic growth that creates few jobs and does little to alleviate economic repression, or worst yet a decade-long period of economic stagnation and worsening economic suffering.

Sources: Kelly Evans and Robert Guy Matthews, "Manufacturing Tumbles Globally," *Wall Street Journal*, Jan. 3, 2009; *Left Business Observer* #118, Dec. 22, 2008; Josh L. Bivens and John Irons, "A Feeble Recovery: The Fundamental Economic Weaknesses of the 2001-2007 Expansion," Economic Policy Institute Briefing Paper #214, May 1, 2008; Jon Hilsenrath and Kelly Evans, "Mixed Economic Data Show a Changing Business Cycle," *Wall Street Journal*, September 8, 2008; National Bureau of Economic Research, "Determination of the 2007 Peak in Economic Activity," December 11, 2008; John Schmitt and Dean Baker, "What We're In For: Projected Economic Impact of the Next Recession," Center for Economic and Policy Research, January 2008; Marcus Walker et al., "Global Slump Seen Deepening," *Wall Street Journal*, Jan. 1, 2009; Tom Lauricella and Annelena Lobb, "Stocks Hit '97 Level, Signaling Long Slump," *Wall Street Journal*, March 3, 2009; Sudeep Reedy, "Jobless Rate Hits 8.5%," *Wall Street Journal*, April 4, 2009; Charles Gascon, "The Current Recession: How Bad Is It?" Economic Synopsis No. 4, St. Louis Federal Reserve Bank, 2009; Kevin Klieson, "Recession or Depression," Economic Synopsis No. 15, St. Louis Federal Reserve Bank, 2009; Robert Shiller, "Online Data," at www.econ.yale.edu/~shiller/data.htm.

After a long career in mainstream economic development, teaching at Harvard Business School and working for the Ford Foundation and the U.S. Agency for International Development in Southeast Asia, David Korten came to believe that U.S. policies were creating, not curing, poverty and environmental destruction. Since the early 1990s he has promoted an alternative economic agenda. He cofounded and heads the Positive Futures Network, publishers of YES! Magazine, *and is the author of several books including* When Corporations Rule the World *and* The Great Turning: From Empire to Earth Community. *In this excerpt from his new book,* Agenda for a New Economy: From Phantom Wealth to Real Wealth *(Berrett-Koehler, 2009), Korten discusses the fundamental flaws underlying Wall Street's ascendance to a dominant position in U.S. capitalism.*

FROM PHANTOM WEALTH TO REAL WEALTH

Why Wall Street should be replaced, not fixed

BY DAVID C. KORTEN
May/June 2009

Our economic system has failed in every dimension: financial, environmental, and social. And the current financial collapse provides an incontestable demonstration that it has failed even on its own terms. Spending trillions of dollars in an effort to restore this system to its previous condition is a reckless waste of time and resources and may be the greatest misuse of federal government credit in history. The more intelligent course is to acknowledge the failure and to set about redesigning our economic system from the bottom up to align with the realities and opportunities of the twenty-first century.

The Bush administration's strategy focused on bailing out the Wall Street institutions that bore primary responsibility for creating the crisis; its hope was that if the government picked up enough of those institutions' losses and toxic assets, they might decide to open the tap and get credit flowing again. The Obama administration has come into office with a strong focus on economic stimulus, and particularly on green jobs—by far a more thoughtful and appropriate approach.

The real need, however, goes far beyond pumping new money into the economy to alleviate the consequences of the credit squeeze.

The recent credit meltdown has resulted in bailout commitments estimated in November 2008 to be $7.4 trillion, roughly half of the total U.S. gross domestic product (GDP). Large as the bailouts were, the failure of the credit system is only one manifestation of a failed economy that is wildly out of balance with, and devastating to, both humans and the natural environment.

Wages are falling in the face of volatile food and energy prices. Consumer debt and housing foreclosures are setting historic records. The middle class is shrinking. The unconscionable and growing worldwide gap between rich and poor, with its related alienation, is eroding the social fabric to the point of fueling terrorism, genocide, and other violent criminal activity.

At the same time, excessive consumption is pushing Earth's ecosystems into collapse. Climate change and the related increase in droughts, floods, and wildfires are now recognized as serious threats. Scientists are in almost universal agreement that human activity bears substantial responsibility. We face severe water shortages, the erosion of topsoil, the loss of species, and the end of the fossil fuel subsidy. In each instance, a failed economic system that takes no account of the social and environmental costs of monetary profits bears major responsibility.

We face a monumental economic challenge that goes far beyond anything being discussed in the U.S. Congress or the corporate press. The hardships imposed by temporarily frozen credit markets pale in comparison to what lies ahead.

Even the significant funds that the Obama administration is committed to spending on economic stimulus will do nothing to address the deeper structural causes of our threefold financial, social, and environmental crisis. On the positive side, the financial crisis has put to rest the myths that our economic institutions are sound and that markets work best when deregulated. This creates an opportune moment to open a national conversation about what we can and must do to create an economic system that can work for all people for all time.

The capitalist ideal is to create money out of nothing, without a need to produce anything of real value in return. Wall Street has turned this ideal into a high-stakes competitive sport. Money is the means of scoring, and *Forbes* magazine is the unofficial scorekeeper issuing periodic reports on the "richest people" ranked in the order of their total financial assets. The player with the most assets wins. Because the scoring is competitive, no player has "enough" money so long as another player in the game has more.

Making money with no effort can be an addictive experience. I recall my excitement back in the mid-'60s, when Fran, my wife, and I first made a modest investment in a mutual fund and watched our savings grow magically by hundreds and then thousands of dollars with no effort whatever on our part. We felt as if we had discovered the philosopher's stone that turned cheap metals into gold. We got a case of Wall Street fever on what by current standards was a tiny scale.

Of course, most of what we call magic is illusion. When the credit collapse pulled back the curtain to expose Wall Street's inner workings, all the world was able to see the extent to which Wall Street is a world of deception, misrepresentation, and insider dealing in the business of creating phantom wealth without a corresponding contribution to the creation of anything of real value. It was such an ugly picture that Wall Street's seriously corrupted institutions stopped lending even to each other for the very good reason they didn't trust anyone's financial statements.

It is easy to confuse money with the real wealth for which it can be exchanged— our labor, ideas, land, gold, health care, food, and all the other things with value in their own right. The market, of course, makes no distinction between the dollars acquired through means that enriched society, those created by means that impoverished society, and those simply created out of thin air. Money is money, and the more you have, the more the market eagerly responds to your every whim. To believe that paper or electronic money is real wealth, rather than simply a coupon that may be redeemed for goods and services of real intrinsic value, confuses illusion with reality.

Those who create phantom wealth, and those who are the beneficiaries of mutual funds or retirement funds invested in phantom wealth, may never realize that they are giving its holder a claim on the real wealth produced by others, and that phantom-wealth dollars created out of nothing dilute the claims of everyone else to the available stock of real wealth.

They may also fail to realize that Wall Street and its international counterparts have created phantom-wealth claims far in excess of the value of all the world's real wealth, creating expectations of future security and comforts that can never be fulfilled.

While doing the research in 1997 for *The Post-Corporate World: Life after Capitalism*, I read an article in *Foreign Policy* by John Edmunds, then a finance professor at Babson College and the Arthur D. Little School of Management, titled "Securities: The New Wealth Machine." Given that *Foreign Policy* is a highly respected professional journal, I was surprised an article based on such obviously flawed logic had made it through its editorial review process. The following is an excerpt:

> Securitization—the issuance of high-quality bonds and stocks—has become the most powerful engine of wealth creation in today's world economy. Financial securities have grown to the point that they are now worth more than a year's worldwide output of goods and services, and soon they will be worth more than two years' output. While politicians concentrate on trade balances and intellectual property rights, these financial instruments are the leading component of wealth today as well as its fastest-growing generator.

Historically, manufacturing, exporting, and direct investment produced prosperity through income-creation. Wealth was created when a portion of income was diverted from consumption into investment in buildings, machinery, and technological change. Societies accumulated wealth slowly over generations. Now many societies, and indeed the entire world, have learned how to create wealth directly. The new approach requires that a state find ways to increase the *market value* of its stock of productive assets. [Emphasis in the original.] . . . Wealth is also created when money, foreign or domestic, flows into the capital market of a country and raises the value of its quoted securities. . . .

Nowadays, wealth is created when the managers of a business enterprise give high priority to rewarding the shareholders and bondholders. The greater the rewards, the more the shares and bonds are likely to be worth in the financial markets. . . . An economic policy that aims to achieve growth by wealth-creation therefore does not attempt to increase the production of goods and services, except as a secondary objective.

Professor Edmunds is telling government policymakers that they should no longer concern themselves with producing real wealth by increasing the national output of goods and services that have real utility. They should put all that aside. They can grow their national economies faster with less exertion by securitizing real assets so that investors can put them into play in financial markets and pump up their value to create gigantic asset bubbles.

Rarely have I come across such a clear example of the widespread belief, seemingly pervasive on Wall Street, that inflating asset bubbles creates real wealth. Apparently, even the editors of *Foreign Policy* and their editorial reviewers failed to recognize what I'll call the "Edmunds fallacy" for the sake of giving it a shorthand name. Asset bubbles create only phantom wealth that increases the claims of the holder to a society's real wealth and thereby dilutes the claims of everyone else. Edmunds did not invent this fallacy, but his *Foreign Policy* article lent it new intellectual respectability and apparently stirred the imagination of Wall Street insiders. In his 2008 book *Bad Money*, the journalist and former Republican Party political strategist Kevin Phillips notes that the Edmunds article was widely discussed on Wall Street and implies that it may have inspired the securitization of housing mortgages. If it did, that would make it one of history's most influential academic papers.

Reading the Edmunds article reminded me of a conversation I'd had some years earlier with Malaysia's minister of forestry. He told me in all seriousness that Malaysia would be better off once all its trees were cut down and the proceeds were deposited in interest-bearing accounts, because interest grows faster than trees. An image flashed into my mind of a barren and lifeless Malaysian landscape populated only by banks, their computers happily whirring away, calculating the interest on those deposits. This is exactly the kind of disaster to which the Edmunds fallacy leads.

While the housing and financial meltdowns detonated the current economic crisis, these immediate causes trace back to an earlier power shift in favor of corporations and the very rich. Arthur MacEwan analyzes the origins of these changes in the 1970s, and argues that a solution requires a major shift in the opposite direction.

INEQUALITY, POWER, AND IDEOLOGY

Getting It Right About the Causes of the Current Economic Crisis

BY ARTHUR MACEWAN
March/April 2009

It is hard to solve a problem without an understanding of what caused it. For example, in medicine, until we gained an understanding of the way bacteria and viruses cause various infectious diseases, it was virtually impossible to develop effective cures. Of course, dealing with many diseases is complicated by the fact that germs, genes, diet and the environment establish a nexus of causes.

The same is true in economics. Without an understanding of the causes of the current crisis, we are unlikely to develop a solution; certainly we are not going to get a solution that has a lasting impact. And determining the causes is complicated because several intertwined factors have been involved.

The current economic crisis was brought about by a nexus of factors that involved: a growing concentration of political and social power in the hands of the wealthy; the ascendance of a perverse leave-it-to-the-market ideology which was an instrument of that power; and rising income inequality, which both resulted from and enhanced that power. These various factors formed a vicious circle, reinforcing one another and together shaping the economic conditions that led us to the present situation. Several other factors were also involved—the growing role of credit, the puffing up of the housing bubble, and the increasing deregulation of financial markets have been very important. However, these are best understood as transmitters of our economic problems, arising from the nexus that formed the vicious circle.

What does this tell us about a solution? Economic stimulus, repair of the housing market, and new regulation are all well and good, but they do not deal with the underlying causes of the crisis. Instead, progressive groups need to work to shift each of the factors I have noted—power, ideology, and income distribution—in the other direction. In doing so, we can create a *virtuous* circle, with each change reinforcing the other changes. If successful, we not only establish a more stable economy, but we lay the foundation for a more democratic, equitable, and sustainable economic order.

A crisis by its very nature creates opportunities for change. One good place to begin change and intervene in this "circle"—and transform it from vicious to virtuous —is through pushing for the expansion and reform of social programs, programs that directly serve social needs of the great majority of the population (for example: single-payer health care, education programs, and environmental protection and repair). By establishing changes in social programs, we will have impacts on income distribution and ideology, and, perhaps most important, we set in motion *a power shift* that improves our position for preserving the changes. While I emphasize social programs as a means to initiate social and economic change, there are other ways to intervene in the circle. Efforts to re-strengthen unions would be especially important; and there are other options as well.

CAUSES OF THE CRISIS: A LONG TIME COMING

Sometime around the early 1970s, there were some dramatic changes in the U.S. economy. The twenty-five years following World War II had been an era of relatively stable economic growth; the benefits of growth had been widely shared, with wages rising along with productivity gains, and income distribution became slightly less unequal (a good deal less unequal as compared to the pre-Great Depression era). There were severe economic problems in the United States, not the least of which were the continued exclusion of African Americans, large gender inequalities, and the woeful inadequacy of social welfare programs. Nonetheless, relatively stable growth, rising wages, and then the advent of the civil rights movement and the War on Poverty gave some important, positive social and economic character to the era—especially in hindsight!

In part, this comparatively favorable experience for the United States had depended on the very dominant position that U.S. firms held in the world economy, a position in which they were relatively unchallenged by international competition. The firms and their owners were not the only beneficiaries of this situation. With less competitive pressure on them from foreign companies, many U.S. firms accepted unionization and did not find it worthwhile to focus on keeping wages down and obstructing the implementation of social supports for the low-income population. Also, having had the recent experience of the Great Depression, many wealthy people and business executives were probably not so averse to a substantial role for government in regulating the economy.

A Power Grab

By about 1970, the situation was changing. Firms in Europe and Japan had long recovered from World War II, OPEC was taking shape, and weaknesses were emerging in the U.S. economy. The weaknesses were in part a consequence of heavy spending for the Vietnam War combined with the government's reluctance to tax for the war because of its unpopularity. The pressures on U.S. firms arising from these changes had two sets of consequences: slower growth and greater instability; and concerted efforts—a power grab, if you will—by firms and the wealthy to shift the costs of economic deterioration onto U.S. workers and the low-income population.

These "concerted efforts" took many forms: greater resistance to unions and unionization, battles to reduce taxes, stronger opposition to social welfare programs, and, above all, a push to reduce or eliminate government regulation of economic activity through a powerful political campaign to gain control of the various branches and levels of government. The 1980s, with Reagan and Bush Sr. in the White House, were the years in which all these efforts were solidified. Unions were greatly weakened, a phenomenon both demonstrated and exacerbated by Reagan's firing of the air traffic controllers in response to their strike in 1981. The tax cuts of the period were also important markers of the change. But the change had begun earlier; the 1978 passage of the tax-cutting Proposition 13 in California was perhaps the first major success of the movement. And the changes continued well after the 1980s, with welfare reform and deregulation of finance during the Clinton era, to say nothing of the tax cuts and other actions during Bush Jr.

Ideology Shift

The changes that began in the 1970s, however, were not simply these sorts of concrete alterations in the structure of power affecting the economy and, especially, government's role in the economy. There was a major shift in ideology, the dominant set of ideas that organize an understanding of our social relations and both guide and rationalize policy decisions.

Following the Great Depression and World War II, there was a wide acceptance of the idea that government had a major role to play in economic life. Less than in many other countries but nonetheless to a substantial degree, at all levels of society, it was generally believed that there should be a substantial government safety net and that government should both regulate the economy in various ways and, through fiscal as well as monetary policy, should maintain aggregate demand. This large economic role for government came to be called Keynesianism, after the British economist John Maynard Keynes, who had set out the arguments for an active fiscal policy in time of economic weakness. In the early 1970s, as economic troubles developed, even Richard Nixon declared: "We are all Keynesians now."

The election of Ronald Reagan, however, marked a sharp change in ideology, at least at the top. Actions of the government were blamed for all economic ills: government spending, Keynesianism, was alleged to be the cause of the inflation of the 1970s; government regulation was supposedly crippling industry; high taxes were, it was argued, undermining incentives for workers to work and for businesses to invest; social welfare spending was blamed for making people dependent on the government and was charged with fraud and corruption (the "welfare queens"); and so on and so on.

On economic matters, Reagan championed supply-side economics, the principal idea of which was that tax cuts yield an increase in government revenue because the cuts lead to more rapid economic growth through encouraging more work and more investment. Thus, so the argument went, tax cuts would reduce the government deficit. Reagan, with the cooperation of Democrats, got the tax cuts—and, as the loss of revenue combined with a large increase in military spending, the federal

ALAN GREENSPAN, SYMBOL OF AN ERA

One significant symbol of the full rise of the conservative ideology that became so dominant in the latter part of the 20th century was Alan Greenspan, who served from 1974 through 1976 as chairman of the President's Council of Economic Advisers under Gerald Ford and in 1987 became chairman of the Federal Reserve Board, a position he held until 2006. While his predecessors had hardly been critics of U.S. capitalism, Greenspan was a close associate of the philosopher Ayn Rand and an adherent of her extreme ideas supporting individualism and *laissez-faire* (keep-the-government-out) capitalism.

When chairman of the Fed, Greenspan was widely credited with maintaining an era of stable economic growth. As things fell apart in 2008, however, Greenspan was seen as having a large share of responsibility for the non-regulation and excessively easy credit (see article) that led into the crisis.

Called before Congress in October of 2008, Greenspan was chastised by Rep. Henry Waxman (D-Calif.), who asked him: "Do you feel that your ideology pushed you to make decisions that you wish you had not made?" To which Greenspan replied: "Yes, I've found a flaw. I don't know how significant or permanent it is. But I've been very distressed by that fact."

And Greenspan told Congress: "Those of us who have looked to the self-interest of lending institutions to protect shareholders' equity, myself included, are in a state of shocked disbelief."

Greenspan's "shock" was reminiscent of the scene in the film "Casablanca," where Captain Renault (Claude Rains) declares: "I'm shocked, shocked to find that gambling is going on in here!" At which point, a croupier hands Renault a pile of money and says, "Your winnings, sir." Renault replies, *sotto voce*, "Thank you very much."

budget deficit grew by leaps and bounds, almost doubling as a share of GDP over the course of the 1980s. It was all summed up in the idea of keeping the government out of the economy; let the free market work its magic.

Growing Inequality

The shifts of power and ideology were very much bound up with a major redistribution upwards of income and wealth. The weakening of unions, the increasing access of firms to low-wage foreign (and immigrant) labor, the refusal of government to maintain the buying power of the minimum wage, favorable tax treatment of the wealthy and their corporations, deregulation in a wide range of industries and lack of enforcement of existing regulation (e.g., the authorities turning a blind eye to off-shore tax shelters) all contributed to these shifts.

Many economists, however, explain the rising income inequality as a result of technological change that favored more highly skilled workers; and changing technology has probably been a factor. Yet the most dramatic aspect of the rising inequality has been the rapidly rising share of income obtained by those at the very top (see figures below), who get their incomes from the ownership and control of business, not from their skilled labor. For these people the role of new technologies was most important through its impact on providing more options (e.g., international options) for the managers of firms, more thorough means to control labor, and more effective ways—in the absence of regulation—to manipulate finance. All of these gains that might be associated with new technology were also gains brought by the way the government handled, or didn't handle (failed to regulate), economic affairs.

FIGURE 1: PERCENTAGE CHANGE IN REAL FAMILY INCOME BY QUINTILE AND TOP 5%, 1949–1979

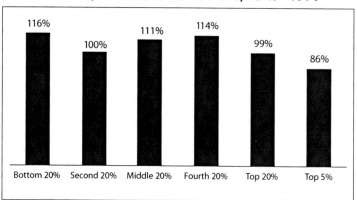

Source: Analysis of U.S. Census Bureau data in Economic Policy Institute, The State of Working America 1994–95 (1994) p. 37.

FIGURE 2: PERCENTAGE CHANGE IN REAL FAMILY INCOME BY QUINTILE AND TOP 5%, 1979–2005

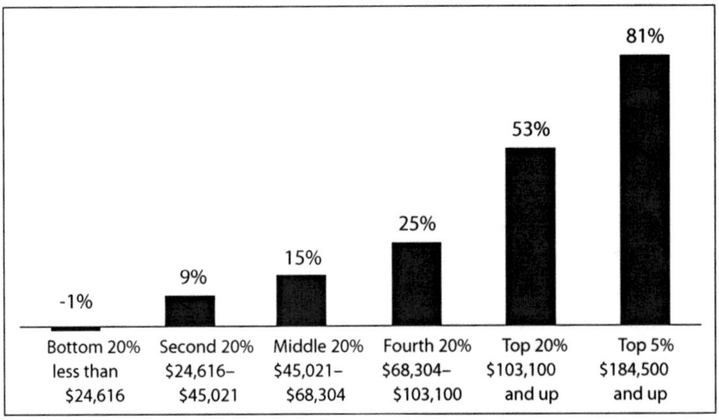

	Bottom 20% less than $24,616	Second 20% $24,616– $45,021	Middle 20% $45,021– $68,304	Fourth 20% $68,304– $103,100	Top 20% $103,100 and up	Top 5% $184,500 and up
	-1%	9%	15%	25%	53%	81%

Source: U.S. Census Bureau, Historical Income Tables, Table F-3.

Several sets of data demonstrate the sharp changes in the distribution of income that have taken place in the last several decades. Most striking is the changing position of the very highest income segment of the population. In the mid-1920s, the share of all pre-tax income going to the top 1% of households peaked at 23.9%. This elite group's share of income fell dramatically during the Great Depression and World War II to about 12% at the end of the war and then slowly fell further during the next thirty years, reaching a low of 8.9% in the mid-1970s. Since then, the top 1% has regained its exalted position of the earlier era, with 21.8% of income in 2005. Since 1993, more than one-half of all income gains have accrued to this highest 1% of the population.

Figures 1 and 2 show the gains (or losses) of various groups in the 1947 to 1979 period and in the 1979 to 2005 period. The difference is dramatic. For example, in the earlier era, the bottom 20% saw its income in real (inflation-adjusted) terms rise by 116%, and real income of the top 5% grew by only 86%. But in the latter era, the bottom 20% saw a 1% decline in its income, while the top 5% obtained a 81% increase.

THE EMERGENCE OF CRISIS

These changes, especially these dramatic shifts in the distribution of income, set the stage for the increasingly large reliance on credit, especially consumer and mortgage credit, that played a major role in the emergence of the current economic crisis. Other factors were involved, but rising inequality was especially important in effecting the increase in both the demand and supply of credit.

Credit Expansion

On the demand side, rising inequality translated into a growing gap between the

JOSEPH STIGLITZ ON THE WAR AND THE ECONOMY

On October 2, 2008, on the Pacifica radio program Democracy Now!, Amy Goodman and Juan Gonzalez interviewed Joseph Stiglitz about the economic situation. Stiglitz was the 2001 winner of the Nobel Prize in Economics, former chief economist at the World Bank, and former chair of President Clinton's Council of Economic Advisers. He is a professor at Columbia University. Following is an excerpt from that interview:

AMY GOODMAN: Joseph Stiglitz, you're co-author of *The Three Trillion Dollar War: The True Cost of the Iraq Conflict.* How does the bailout [of the financial sector] connect to war?

JOSEPH STIGLITZ: Very much. Let me first explain a little bit how the current crisis connects with the war. One of the reasons that we have this crisis is that the Fed flooded the economy with liquidity and had lax regulations. Part of that was this ideology of regulations were bad, but part of the reason was that the economy was weak. And one of the reasons the economy was weak was oil prices were soaring, and part of the reason oil prices were soaring is the Iraq war. When we went to war in 2003, before we went, prices were $23 a barrel. Futures markets thought they would remain at that level. They anticipated the increase in demand, but they thought there would be a concomitant increase in supply from the low-cost providers, mainly in the Middle East. The war changed that equation, and we know what happened to the oil prices.

Well, why is that important? Well, we were spending—Americans were spending hundreds of millions—billions of dollars to buy—more, to buy imported oil. Normally, that would have had a very negative effect on our economy; we would have had a slowdown. Some people have said, you know, it's a mystery why we aren't having that slowdown; we repealed the laws of economics. Whenever anybody says that, you ought to be suspect.

It was actually very simple. The Fed engineered a bubble, a housing bubble to replace the tech bubble that it had engineered in the '90s. The housing bubble facilitated people taking money out of their . . . houses; in one year, there were more than $900 billion of mortgage equity withdrawals. And so, we had a consumption boom that was so strong that even though we were spending so much money abroad, we could keep the economy going. But it was so short-sighted. And it was so clear that we were living on borrowed money and borrowed time. And it was just a matter of time before, you know, the whole thing would start to unravel.

incomes of most members of society and their needs. For the 2000 to 2007 period, average weekly earnings in the private sector were 12% below their average for the 1970s (in inflation-adjusted terms). From 1980 to 2005 the share of income going to the bottom 60% of families fell from 35% to 29%. Under these circumstances, more and more people relied more and more heavily on credit to meet their needs—everything from food to fuel, from education to entertainment, and especially housing.

While the increasing reliance of consumers on credit has been going on for a long time, it has been especially marked in recent decades. Consumer debt as a share of after-tax personal income averaged 20% in the 1990s, and then jumped up to an average of 25% in the first seven years of the new millennium. But the debt expansion was most marked in housing, where mortgage debt as a percent of after-tax personal income rose from 89% to 94% over the 1990s, and then ballooned to 140% by 2006 as housing prices skyrocketed.

On the supply side, especially in the last few years, the government seems to have relied on making credit readily available as a means to bolster aggregate demand and maintain at least a modicum of economic growth. During the 1990s, the federal funds interest rate averaged 5.1%, but fell to an average of 3.4% in the 2000 to 2007 period—and averaged only 1.4% in 2002 to 2004 period. (The federal funds interest rate is the rate that banks charge one another for overnight loans and is a rate directly affected by the Federal Reserve.) Corresponding to the low interest rates, the money supply grew twice as fast in the new millennium as it had in the 1990s.

The increasing reliance of U.S. consumers on credit has often been presented as a moral weakness, as an infatuation with consumerism, and as a failure to look beyond the present. Whatever moral judgments one may make, however, the expansion of the credit economy has been a response to real economic forces—inequality and government policies, in particular.

The Failure to Regulate

The credit expansion by itself, however, did not precipitate the current crisis. Deregulation—or, more generally, the failure to regulate—is also an important part of the story. The government's role in regulation of financial markets has been a central feature in the development of this crisis, but the situation in financial markets has been part of a more general process—affecting airlines and trucking, telecommunications, food processing, broadcasting, and of course international trade and investment. The process has been driven by a combination of power (of large firms and wealthy individuals) and ideology (leave it to the market, get the government out).

The failure to regulate financial markets that transformed the credit expansion into a financial crisis shows up well in three examples:

The 1999 repeal of the Glass-Steagall Act. Glass-Steagall had been enacted in the midst of the Great Depression, as a response to the financial implosion following the stock market crash of 1929. Among other things, it required that different kinds of financial firms—commercial banks, investment banks, insurance companies— be separate. This separation both limited the spread of financial problems and reduced conflicts of interest that could arise were the different functions of these firms combined into a single firm. As perhaps the most important legislation regulating the financial sector, the repeal of Glass-Steagall was not only a substantive change but was an important symbol of the whole process of deregulation.

The failure to regulate mortgage lending. Existing laws and regulations require lending institutions to follow prudent practices in making loans, assuring that borrowers have the capacity to be able to pay back the loans. And of course fraud— lying about the provisions of loans—is prohibited. Yet in an atmosphere where regulation was "out," regulators were simply not doing their jobs. The consequences are illustrated in a December 28, 2008, *New York Times* story on the failed Washington Mutual Bank. The article describes a supervisor at a mortgage processing center as having been "accustomed to seeing baby sitters claiming salaries worthy of college presidents, and schoolteachers with incomes rivaling stockbrokers'. He rarely questioned them. A real estate frenzy was under way and WaMu, as his bank was known, was all about saying yes."

One may wonder why banks—or other lending institutions, mortgage firms, in particular—would make loans to people who were unlikely to be able to pay them back. The reason is that the lending institutions quickly combined such loans into packages (i.e., a security made up of several borrowers' obligations to pay) and sold them to other investors in a practice called "securitization."

Credit-default swaps. Perhaps the most egregious failure to regulate in recent years has been the emergence of credit-default swaps, which are connected to securitization. Because they were made up of obligations by a diverse set of borrowers, the packages of loans were supposedly low-risk investments. Yet those who purchased them still sought insurance against default. Insurance sellers, however, are regulated—required, for example, to keep a certain amount of capital on hand to cover possible claims. So the sellers of these insurance policies on packages of loans called the policies "credit-default swaps" and thus were allowed to avoid regulation. Further, these credit-default swaps, these insurance policies, themselves were bought and sold again and again in unregulated markets in a continuing process of speculation.

The credit-default swaps are a form of derivative, a financial asset the value of which is derived from some other asset—in this case the value of packages of mortgages on which they were the insurance policies. When the housing bubble began to collapse and people started to default on their mortgages, the value of credit-default swaps plummeted and their future value was impossible to determine. No one would buy them, and several banks that had speculated in these derivatives were left holding huge amounts of these "toxic assets."

Bubble and Bust

The combination of easy credit and the failure to regulate together fueled the housing bubble. People could buy expensive houses but make relatively low monthly payments. Without effective regulation of mortgage lending, they could get the loans even when they were unlikely to be able to make payments over the long run. Moreover, as these pressures pushed up housing prices, many people bought houses simply to resell them quickly at a higher price, in a process called "flipping." And such speculation pushed the prices up further. Between 2000 and 2006, housing prices rose by 90% (as consumer prices generally rose by only 17%).

While the housing boom was in full swing, both successful housing speculators and lots of people involved in the shenanigans of credit markets made a lot of money. However, as the housing bubble burst—as all bubbles do—things fell apart. The packages of loans lost value, and the insurance policies on them, the credit-default swaps, lost value. These then became "toxic" assets for those who held them, assets not only with reduced value but with unknown value. Not only did large financial firms—for example, Lehman Brothers and AIG—have billions of dollars in losses, but no one knew the worth of their remaining assets. The assets were called "toxic" because they poisoned the operations of the financial system. Under these circumstances, financial institutions stopped lending to one another—that is, the credit markets "froze up." The financial crisis was here.

The financial crisis, not surprisingly, very quickly shifted to a general economic crisis. Firms in the "real" economy rely heavily on a well-functioning financial system to supply them with the funds they need for their regular operations—loans to car buyers, loans to finance inventory, loans for construction of new facilities, loans for new equipment, and, of course, mortgage loans. Without those loans (or with the loans much more difficult to obtain), there has been a general cut-back in economic activity, what is becoming a serious and probably prolonged recession.

WHAT IS TO BE DONE?

So here we are. The shifts in power, ideology, and income distribution have placed us in a rather nasty situation. There are some steps that will be taken that have a reasonable probability of yielding short-run improvement. In particular, a large increase in government spending—deficit spending—will probably reduce the depth and shorten the length of the recession. And the actions of the Federal Reserve and Treasury to inject funds into the financial system are likely, along with the deficit spending, to "un-freeze" credit markets (the mismanagement and, it seems, outright corruption of the bailout notwithstanding). Also, there is likely to be some re-regulation of the financial industry. These steps, however, at best will restore things to where they were before the crisis. They do not treat the underlying causes of the crisis—the vicious circle of power, ideology, and inequality.

Opportunity for Change

Fortunately, the crisis itself has weakened some aspects of this circle. The cry of "leave it to the market" is still heard, but is now more a basis for derision than a guide to policy. The ideology and, to a degree, the power behind the ideology, have been severely weakened as the role of "keeping the government out" has shown to be a major cause of the financial mess and our current hardships. There is now widespread support among the general populace and some support in Washington for greater regulation of the financial industry.

Whether or not the coming period will see this support translated into effective policy is of course an open question. Also an open question is how much the turn away from "leaving it to the market" can be extended to other sectors of the economy. With regard to the environment, there is already general acceptance of the principle that the government (indeed, many governments) must take an active role in regulating economic activity. Similar principles need to be recognized with regard to health care, education, housing, child care, and other support programs for low-income families.

The discrediting of "keep the government out" ideology provides an opening to develop new programs in these areas and to expand old programs. Furthermore, as the federal government revs up its "stimulus" program in the coming months, opportunities will exist for expanding support for these sorts of programs. This support is important, first of all, because these programs serve real, pressing needs—needs that have long existed and are becoming acute and more extensive in the current crisis.

Breaking the Circle

Support for these social programs, however, may also serve to break into the vicious power-ideology-inequality circle and begin transforming it into a virtuous circle. Social programs are inherently equalizing in two ways: they provide their benefits to low-income people and they provide some options for those people in their efforts to demand better work and higher pay. Also, the further these programs develop, the more they establish the legitimacy of a larger role for social control of—government involvement in—the economy; they tend to bring about an ideological shift. By affecting a positive distributional shift and by shifting ideology, the emergence of stronger social programs can have a wider impact on power. In other words, efforts to promote social programs are one place to start, an entry point to shift the vicious circle to a virtuous circle.

There are other entry points. Perhaps the most obvious ones are actions to strengthen the role of unions. The Employee Free Choice Act may be a useful first step, and it will be helpful to establish a more union-friendly Department of Labor and National Labor Relations Board. Raising the minimum wage—ideally indexing it to inflation—would also be highly desirable. While conditions have changed since the heyday of unions in the middle of the 20th century, and we cannot expect to restore the conditions of that era, a greater role for unions would seem essential in righting the structural conditions at the foundation of the current crisis.

Shifting Class Power

None of this is assured, of course. Simply starting social programs will not necessarily mean that they have the wider impacts that I am suggesting are possible. No one should think that by setting up some new programs and strengthening some existing ones we will be on a smooth road to economic and social change. Likewise, rebuilding the strength of unions will involve extensive struggle and will not be accomplished by a few legislative or executive actions.

Also, all efforts to involve the government in economic activity—whether in finance or environmental affairs, in health care or education, in work support or job training programs—will be met with the worn-out claims that government involvement generates bureaucracy, stifles initiative, and places an excessive burden on private firms and individuals. We are already hearing warnings that in dealing with the financial crisis the government must avoid "over-regulation." Likewise, efforts to strengthen unions will suffer the traditional attacks, as unions are portrayed as corrupt and their members privileged. The unfolding situation with regard to the auto firms' troubles has demonstrated the attack, as conservatives have blamed the United Auto Workers for the industry's woes and have demanded extensive concessions by the union.

Certainly not all regulation is good regulation. Aside from excessive bureaucratic controls, there is the phenomenon by which regulating agencies are often captives of the industries that they are supposed to regulate. And there are corrupt unions. These are real issues, but they should not be allowed to derail change.

The current economic crisis emerged in large part as a shift in the balance of class power in the United States, a shift that began in the early 1970s and continued into the new millennium. Perhaps the present moment offers an opportunity to shift things back in the other direction. Recognition of the complex nexus of causes of the current economic crisis provides some guidance where people might start. Rebuilding and extending social programs, strengthening unions, and other actions that contribute to a more egalitarian power shift will not solve all the problems of U.S. capitalism. They can, however, begin to move us in the right direction.

With the bursting of the housing and stock market bubbles, home and stock prices have plummeted. Arthur MacEwan explains what has happened to the "lost trillions" in home equity and stock values.

WHO GETS THOSE TRILLIONS?

BY ARTHUR MACEWAN
January/February 2009

Dear Dr. Dollar,
As housing prices have fallen, it seems that people have lost a huge amount in terms of the value of their homes. We are told that, over the whole country, trillions of dollars in home equity have been lost. Who gets those trillions? And, likewise, what about the trillions lost in the stock market?

— Carlos Rafael Alicea Negrón, Bronx, N.Y.

Dear Carlos:
The simple answer to your question is that no one gets the lost trillions; they are simply gone. But, like all simple answers, this one doesn't explain very much.

Suppose that seven years ago, you bought your house for $200,000. Housing prices continued to rise, and at the beginning of 2007 you saw that other people in your neighborhood were selling houses similar to yours for $400,000. So you, quite reasonably, figured that your house was worth $400,000.

But now the housing bubble has burst. Similar houses in your neighborhood are selling for "only" $300,000 and thus it is now quite reasonable to figure that the value of your house has dropped by $100,000 as compared to the beginning of 2007. (Multiply this $100,000 by roughly 75 million homes across the country, and you have losses of $7.5 trillion.)

Your house, however, was not involved in any actual transaction at this lower value. So no one has gained the value you lost. If, for example, last year one of your neighbors had sold an equivalent house for $400,000 and now buys your house for $300,000 this neighbor would have gained what you lost. But most houses are not bought and sold in any given year. Their value is determined by those equivalent (or similar) houses that are actually bought and sold.

Moreover, even if someone bought your house at $300,000, that person would gain the value you lost only in the special case of the example above, where the person was lucky enough to have sold an equivalent house at $400,000. If instead that person wasa new entrant to the housing market or a person who had just sold a similar house elsewhere for $300,000, then no one would be gaining what you lost.

Thus in the great majority of cases, the $100,000 value would simply be gone, and no one would have gotten it.

The situation on the stock market is similar. The values of stocks are determined by the sales that actually take place. When we hear that today the value of Mega Corporation's stock fell from $100 a share to $75 dollars a share, this means that the price of shares that were traded today were selling at $75 while those that were traded yesterday were selling for $100. But most shares of Mega Corporation were not actually traded either day. Their value fell—just like the value of your house fell when neighbors sold their houses—but no one gained this lost value. As in the housing market, the values of stocks have declined by trillions, but the trillions are simply gone.

Of course as with the situation in the housing market, some actual gains of value can take place when stock prices fall. If someone sold a share of Mega Corporation yesterday for $100 and bought it today for $75, this person obtained a gain. But with most of the declines in stock values, no one gets a gain.

To understand what has happened recently, it is useful to keep in mind that the high housing values of recent years were the result of a speculative bubble. The values increased not because there was some real change in the houses themselves. The houses were not providing more living services to the degree that their prices rose. The prices of housing rose because people expected them to rise more. The situation was a speculative bubble, and housing prices rose far above their historical trend.

And just as, in general, the loss of value when prices fell was not balanced by a gain, the gains that people saw when the bubbles expanded were not balanced by losses. As the bubble grew and the value of your house rose from $200,000 to $400,000, no one experienced an equivalent loss. Virtually all home buyers and owners were winners.

But speculative bubbles do not last.

The current economic crisis, Rick Wolff argues, is not just a financial crisis and did not even begin with finance. He traces its origins to decades of stagnating wages and rising inequality. Credit took the place of rising real wages as a way for workers to keep up with rising standards of consumption, but now indebtedness has reached unsustainable proportions.

CAPITALISM HITS THE FAN

BY RICK WOLFF
November/December 2008

Let me begin by saying what I think this crisis is not. It is not a *financial* crisis. It is a systemic crisis whose first serious symptom happened to be finance. But this crisis has its economic roots and its effects in manufacturing, services, and, to be sure, finance. It grows out of the relation of wages to profits across the economy. It has profound social roots in America's households and families and political roots in government policies. The current crisis did not start with finance, and it won't end with finance.

From 1820 to around 1970, 150 years, the average productivity of American workers went up each year. Average workers produced more stuff every year than they had the year before. They were trained better, they had more machines, and they had better machines. So productivity went up every year.

And, over this period of time, the wages of American workers rose every decade. Every decade, real wages—the amount of money you get in relation to the prices you pay for the things you use your money for—were higher than the decade before. Profits also went up.

The American working class enjoyed 150 years of rising consumption, so it's not surprising that it would choose to define its own self-worth, measure its own success in life, according to the standard of consumption. Americans began to think of themselves as successful if they lived in the right neighborhood, drove the right car, wore the right outfit, went on the right vacation.

But in the 1970s, the world changed for the American working class in ways that it hasn't come to terms with—at all. Real wages stopped going up. As U.S. corporations moved operations abroad to take advantage of lower wages and higher profits and as they replaced workers with machines (and especially computers), those who lost their jobs were soon willing to work even if their wages stopped rising. So real wages trended down a little bit. The real hourly wage of a worker in the 1970s was higher than what it is today. What you get for an hour of work, in goods and services, is less now that what your parents got.

Meanwhile, productivity kept going up. If what the employer gets from each worker keeps going up, but what you give to each worker does not, then the difference becomes bigger, and bigger, and bigger. Employers' profits have gone wild, and all the people who get their fingers on employers profits—the professionals who sing the songs they like to hear, the shareholders who get a piece of the action on each company's profits—have enjoyed a bonanza over the last thirty years.

The only thing more profitable than simply making the money off the worker is handling this exploding bundle of profits—packaging and repackaging it, lending it and borrowing it, and inventing new mechanisms for doing all that. That's called the finance industry, and they have stumbled all over themselves to get a hold of a piece of this immense pot of profit.

What did the working class do? What happens to a population committed to measuring people's success by the amount of consumption they could afford when the means they had always had to achieve it, rising wages, stop? They can go through a trauma right then and there: "We can't anymore—it's over." Most people didn't do that. They found other ways.

Americans undertook more work. People took a second or third job. The number of hours per year worked by the average American worker has risen by about 20 percent since the 1970s. By comparison, in Germany, France, and Italy, the number of hours worked per year per worker has dropped 20%. American workers began to work to a level of exhaustion. They sent more family members—and especially women—out to work. This enlarged supply of workers meant that employers could find plenty of employees without having to offer higher pay. Yet, with more family members out working, new kinds of costs and problems hit American families. The woman who goes out to work needs new outfits. In our society, she probably needs another car. With women exhausted from jobs outside and continued work demands inside households, with families stressed by exhaustion and mounting bills, interpersonal tensions mounted and brought new costs: child care, psychotherapy, drugs. Such extra costs neutralized the extra income, so it did not solve the problem.

The American working class had to do a second thing to keep its consumption levels rising. It went on the greatest binge of borrowing in the history of any working class in any country at any time. Members of the business community began to realize that they had a fantastic double opportunity. They could get the profits from flat wages and rising productivity, and then they could turn to the working class traumatized by the inability to have rising consumption, and give them the means to consume more. So instead of paying your workers a wage, you're going to lend them the money—so they have to pay it back to you! With interest!

That solved the problem. For a while, employers could pay the workers the same or less, and instead of creating the usual problems for capitalism—workers without enough income to buy all the output their increased productivity yields—rising worker debt seemed magical. Workers could consume ever more; profits exploding in every category. Underneath the magic, however, there were workers who were completely exhausted, whose families were falling apart, and who were now ridden with anxiety because their rising debts were unsustainable. This was a system built to fail, to reach its end when the combination of physical exhaustion and emotional anxiety from the debt made people unable to continue. Those people are, by the millions, walking away from those obligations, and the house of cards comes down.

If you put together (a) the desperation of the American working class and (b) the efforts of the finance industry to scrounge out every conceivable borrower, the idea that the banks would end up lending money to people who couldn't pay it back is not a tough call. The system, however, was premised on the idea that that would not happen, and when it happened nobody was prepared.

The conservatives these days are in a tough spot. The story about how markets and private enterprise interact to produce wonderful outcomes is, even for them these days, a cause for gagging. Of course, ever resourceful, there are conservatives who will rise to the occasion, sort of like dead fish. They rattle off twenty things the government did over the last twenty years, which indeed it did, and draw a line from those things the government did to this disaster now, to reach the conclusion that the reason we have this problem now is too much government intervention. These days they get nowhere. Even the mainstream press has a hard time with this stuff.

What about the liberals and many leftists too? They seem to favor regulation. They think the problem was that the banks weren't regulated, that credit-rating companies weren't regulated, that the Federal Reserve didn't regulate better, or differently, or more, or something. Salaries should be regulated to not be so high. Greed should be regulated. I find this astonishing and depressing.

In the 1930s, the last time we had capitalism hitting the fan in this way, we produced a lot of regulation. Social Security didn't exist before then. Unemployment insurance didn't exist before then. Banks were told: you can do this, but you can't do that. Insurance companies were told: you can do that, but you can't do this. They limited what the board of directors of a corporation could do ten ways to Sunday. They taxed them. They did all sorts of things that annoyed, bothered, and troubled boards of directors because the regulations impeded the boards' efforts to grow their companies and make money for the shareholders who elected them.

You don't need to be a great genius to understand that the boards of directors encumbered by all these regulations would have a very strong incentive to evade them, to undermine them, and, if possible, to get rid of them. Indeed, the boards went to work on that project as soon as the regulations were passed. The crucial fact about the regulations imposed on business in the 1930s is that they did not take away from the boards of directors the freedom or the incentives or the opportunities to undo all the regulations and reforms. The regulations left in place an institution devoted to their undoing. But that wasn't the worst of it. They also left in place boards of directors who, as the first appropriators of all the profits, had the *resources* to undo the regulations. This peculiar system of regulation had a built-in self-destruct button.

Over the last thirty years, the boards of directors of the United States' larger corporations have used their profits to buy the president and the Congress, to buy the public media, and to wage a systematic campaign, from 1945 to 1975, to evade the regulations, and, after 1975, to get rid of them. And it worked. That's why we're here now. And if you impose another set of regulations along the lines liberals propose, not only are you going to have the same history, but you're going to have the same history faster. The right wing in America, the business community, has spent the last fifty years perfecting every technique that is known to turn the population against regulation. And they're going to go right to work to do it again, and they'll do it better, and they'll do it faster.

So what do we do? Let's regulate, by all means. Let's try to make a reasonable economic system that doesn't allow the grotesque abuses we've seen in recent decades. But let's not reproduce the self-destruct button. This time the change has to include the following: The people in every enterprise who do the work of that enterprise, will become collectively their own board of directors. For the first time in American history, the people who depend on the survival of those regulations will be in the position of receiving the profits of their own work and using them to make the regulations succeed rather than sabotaging them.

This proposal for workers to collectively become their own board of directors also democratizes the enterprise. The people who work in an enterprise, the front line of those who have to live with what it does, where it goes, how it uses its wealth, they should be the people who have influence over the decisions it makes. That's democracy.

Maybe we could even extend this argument to democracy in our political life, which leaves a little to be desired—some people call it a "formal" democracy, that isn't real. Maybe the problem all along has been that you can't have a real democracy politically if you don't have a real democracy underpinning it economically. If the workers are not in charge of their work situations, five days a week, 9 to 5, the major time of their adult lives, then how much aptitude and how much appetite are they going to have to control their political life? Maybe we need the democracy of economics, not just to prevent the regulations from being undone, but also to realize the political objectives of democracy.

Homeownership has long been one of the cornerstones of the American Dream. In this prescient article, Howard Karger points out that buying a home can be a much riskier exercise for families with little wealth or low incomes. Karger questions whether homeownership really benefits poorer Americans, especially with all the risky financing options that helped create the subprime mortgage crisis.

THE HOMEOWNERSHIP MYTH

BY HOWARD KARGER
September/October 2007

Anyone who has given the headlines even a passing glance recently knows the subprime mortgage industry is in deep trouble. Since 2006 more than 20 subprime lenders have quit the business or gone bankrupt. Many more are in serious trouble, including the nation's number two subprime lender, New Century Financial. The subprime crisis is also hitting Wall Street brokerages that invested in these loans, with reverberations from Tokyo to London. And the worst may be yet to come. At least $300 billion in subprime adjustable-rate mortgages will reset this year to higher interest rates. CNN reports that one in five subprime mortgages issued in 2005–2006 will end up in foreclosure. If these dire predictions come true, it will be the equivalent of a nuclear meltdown in the mortgage and housing industries.

What's conspicuously absent from the news reports is the effect of the subprime lending debacle on poor and working-class families who bought into the dream of homeownership, regardless of the price. Sold a false bill of goods, many of these families now face foreclosure and the loss of the small savings they invested in their homes. It's critical to examine the housing crisis not only from the perspective of the banks and the stock market, but also from the perspective of the families whose homes are on the line. It is also critical to uncover the systemic reasons for the recent burst of housing-market insanity that saw thousands upon thousands of families getting signed up for mortgage loans that were highly likely to end in failure and foreclosure.

Like most Americans, I grew up believing that buying a home represents a rite of passage in U.S. society. Americans widely view homeownership as the best choice for everyone, everywhere and at all times. The more people who own their own homes, the common wisdom goes, the more robust the economy, the stronger the community, and the greater the collective and individual benefits. Homeownership is the ticket to the middle class through asset accumulation, stability, and civic participation.

For the most part, this is an accurate picture. Homeowners get a foothold in a housing market with an almost infinite price ceiling. They enjoy important tax benefits. Owning a home is often cheaper than renting. Most important, homeownership builds equity and accrues assets for the next generation, in part by promoting forced savings. These savings are reflected in the data showing that, according to the National Housing Institute's Winton Picoff, the median wealth of low-income homeowners is 12 times higher than that of renters with similar incomes. Plus, owning a home is a status symbol: homeowners are seen as winners compared to renters.

Homeownership may have positive effects on family life. Ohio University's Robert Dietz found that owning a home contributes to household stability, social involvement, environmental awareness, local political participation and activism, good health, low crime, and beneficial community characteristics. Homeowners are better citizens, are healthier both physically and mentally, and have children who achieve more and are better behaved than those of renters.

Johns Hopkins University researchers Joe Harkness and Sandra Newman looked at whether homeownership benefits kids even in distressed neighborhoods. Their study concluded that "[h]omeownership in almost any neighborhood is found to benefit children. ... Children of most low-income renters would be better served by programs that help their families become homeowners in their current neighborhoods instead of helping them move to better neighborhoods while remaining renters." (Harkness and Newman also found, however, that the positive effects of homeownership on children are weaker in unstable low-income neighborhoods. Moreover, the study cannot distinguish whether homeownership leads to positive behaviors or whether owners were already predisposed to these behaviors.)

Faith in the benefits of homeownership—along with low interest rates and a range of governmental incentives—have produced a surge in the number of low-income homeowners. In 1994 Bill Clinton set—and ultimately surpassed—a goal to raise the nation's overall homeownership rate to 67.5% by 2000. There are now 71 million U.S. homeowners, representing close to 68% of all households. By 2003, 48% of black households owned their own homes, up from 34.5% in 1950. Much of this gain has been among low-income families.

Government efforts to increase homeownership for low-income families include both demand-side (e.g., homeowner tax credits, housing cost assistance programs) and supply-side (e.g., developer incentives) strategies. Federal housing programs insure more than a million loans a year to help low-income homebuyers. Fannie Mae and Freddie Mac—the large, federally chartered but privately held corporations that buy mortgages from lenders, guarantee the notes, and then resell them to investors—have increasingly turned their attention to low-income homebuyers as the upper-income housing market becomes more saturated. Banking industry regulations such as the Community Reinvestment Act and the Home Mortgage Disclosure Act encourage homeownership by reducing lending discrimination in underserved markets.

The Housing and Urban Development department (HUD) has adapted some of its programs originally designed to help renters to focus on homeownership. For instance, cities and towns can now use the federal dollars they receive through HOME (the Home Investment Partnerships Act) and Community Development Block Grants to provide housing grants, down payment loans, and closing cost assistance. The American Dream Downpayment Initiative, passed by Congress in 2003, authorized up to $200 million a year for down payment assistance to low-income families. Private foundations have followed suit. The Ford Foundation is currently focusing its housing-related grants on homeownership rather than rental housing; the foundation views homeownership as an important form of asset-building and the best option for low-income people.

While homeownership has undeniable benefits, that doesn't mean it is the best option for everyone. For many low-income families, buying a home imposes burdens that end up outweighing the benefits. It is time to reassess the policy emphasis on homeownership, which has been driven by an honest belief in the advantages of homeownership, but also by a wide range of business interests who stand to gain when a new cohort of buyers is brought into the housing market.

THE DOWNSIDES OF HOMEOWNERSHIP

Low-income families can run into a range of pitfalls when they buy homes. These pitfalls may stem from the kinds of houses they can afford to buy (often in poor condition, with high maintenance costs); the neighborhoods they can afford to buy in (often economically distressed); the financing they can get (often carrying high interest rates, high fees, and risky gimmicks); and the jobs they work at (often unstable). Taken together, these factors can make buying a home a far riskier proposition for low-income families than it is for middle- and upper-income households.

Most low-income families only have the financial resources to buy rundown houses in distressed neighborhoods marked by few jobs, high crime rates, a dearth of services, and poor schools. Few middle-class homebuyers would hitch themselves to 30-year mortgages in these kinds of communities; poor families, too, have an interest in making the home-buying commitment in safe neighborhoods with good schools.

Homeownership is no automatic hedge against rising housing costs. On the contrary: lower-end affordable housing stock is typically old, in need of repair, and expensive to maintain. Low-income families often end up paying inflated prices for homes that are beset with major structural or mechanical problems masked by cosmetic repairs. A University of North Carolina study sponsored by the national nonprofit organization NeighborWorks found that almost half of low-income homebuyers experienced major unexpected costs due to the age and condition of their homes. If you rent, you can call the landlord; but a homeowner can't take herself to court because the roof leaks, the plumbing is bad, or the furnace or hot water heater quits working.

Besides maintenance and repairs, the expenses of home ownership also include property taxes and homeowners insurance, both of which have skyrocketed in cost in the last decade. Between 1997 and 2002 property tax rates rose nationally by more than 19%. Ten states (including giants Texas and California) saw their property tax rates rise by 30% or more during that period. In the suburbs of New York City, property tax rates grew two to three times faster than personal income from 2000 to 2004.

Nationally, the average homeowner's annual insurance premiums rose a whopping 62% from 1995 to 2005—twice as fast as inflation. Low-income homeowners in distressed neighborhoods are hit especially hard by high insurance costs. According to a Conning and Co. study, 92% of large insurance companies run credit checks on potential customers. These credit checks translate into insurance scores that are used to determine whether the carrier will insure an applicant at all, and if so, what they will cover and how much they will charge. Those with poor or no credit are denied coverage, while those with limited credit pay high premiums. Needless to say, many low-income homeowners do not have stellar credit scores. Credit scoring may also partly explain why, according to HUD, "Recent studies have shown that, compared to homeowners in predominantly white-occupied neighborhoods, homeowners in minority neighborhoods are less likely to have private home insurance, more likely to have policies that provide less coverage in case of a loss, and are likely to pay more for similar policies."

With few cash reserves, low-income families are a heartbeat away from financial disaster if their wages decline, property taxes or insurance rates rise, or expensive repairs are needed. With most—or all—of their savings in their homes, these families often have no cushion for emergencies. HUD data show that between 1999 and 2001, the only group whose housing conditions worsened—meaning, by HUD's definition, the only group in which a larger share of households spent over 30% of gross household income on housing in 2001 than in 1999—were low- and moderate-income homeowners. The National Housing Conference reports that 51% of working families with critical housing needs (i.e., those spending more than 50% of gross household income on housing) are homeowners.

Most people who buy a home imagine they will live there for a long time, benefiting from a secure and stable housing situation. For many low-income families, this is not what happens. Nationwide data from 1976 to 1993 reveal that 36%

of low-income homeowners gave up or lost their homes within two years and 53% exited within five years, according to a 2005 study by Carolina Katz Reid of the University of Washington. Reid found that very few low-income families ever bought another house after returning to renting. A 2004 HUD research study by Donald Haurin and Stuart Rosenthal reached similar conclusions. Following a national sample of African Americans from youth (ages 14 to 21) in 1979 to middle age in 2000, the researchers found that 63% of the sample owned a home at some point, but only 34% still did in 2000.

Low-income homeowners, often employed in unstable jobs with stagnant incomes, few health care benefits, limited or no sick days, and little vacation time, may find it almost impossible to keep their homes if they experience a temporary job loss or a change in family circumstances, such as the loss of a wage earner. Homeownership can also limit financial opportunities. A 1999 study by economists Richard Green (University of Wisconsin) and Patric Hendershott (Ohio State University) found that states with the highest homeownership rates also had the highest unemployment rates. Their report concluded that homeownership may constrain labor mobility since the high costs of selling a house make unemployed homeowners reluctant to relocate to find work.

Special tax breaks have been a key selling point of homeownership. If mortgage interest and other qualifying expenses come to less than the standard deduction ($10,300 for joint filers in 2006), however, there is zero tax advantage to owning. That is one reason why only 34% of taxpayers itemize their mortgage interest, local property taxes, and other deductions. Even for families who do itemize, the effective tax saving is usually only 10 to 35 cents for every dollar paid in mortgage interest. In other words, the mortgage deduction benefits primarily those in high income brackets who have a need to shelter their income; it means little to low-income homeowners.

Finally, homeownership promises growing wealth as home prices rise. But the homes of low-income, especially minority, homeowners generally do not appreciate as much as middle-class housing. Low-income households typically purchase homes in distressed neighborhoods where significant appreciation is unlikely. Among other reasons, if financially-stressed property owners on the block can't afford to maintain their homes, nearby property values fall. For instance, Reid's longitudinal study surveyed low-income minority homeowners from 1976 to 1994 and found that they realized a 30% increase in the value of their homes after owning for 10 years, while middle- and upper-income white homeowners enjoyed a 60% jump.

"FUNNY MONEY" MORTGAGES AND OTHER TRAVESTIES

Buying a home and taking on a mortgage are scary, and people often leave the closing in a stupor, unsure of what they signed or why. My partner and I bought a house a

THE NEW WORLD OF HOME LOANS

The new home loan products, marketed widely in recent years but especially to low- and moderate-income families, are generally adjustable-rate mortgages (ARMS) with some kind of twist. Here are a few of these "creative" (read: confusing and risky) mortgage options.

Option ARMs: With this loan, borrowers choose each month which of three or four different—and fluctuating—payments to make:

- full (principal+interest) payment based on a 30-year or 15-year repayment schedule.
- interest-only payment—does not reduce the loan principal or build homeowner equity. Borrowers who pay only interest for a period of time then face a big jump in the size of monthly payments or else are forced to refinance.
- minimum payment—may be lower than one month's interest; if so, the shortfall is added to the loan balance. The result is "negative amortization": over time, the principal goes up, not down. Eventually the borrower may have an "upside down" mortgage where the debt is greater than the market value of the home.

According to the credit rating firm Fitch Ratings, up to 80% of all option ARM borrowers choose the minimum monthly payment option, so it's no surprise that in 2005, 20% of Option ARMS were "upside down." When a negative amortization limit is reached, the minimum payment jumps up to fully amortize the loan for the remaining loan term. In other words, borrowers suddenly have to start paying the real bill.

Even borrowers who pay more than the monthly minimums can face payment shocks. Option ARMS often start with a temporary super-low teaser interest rate (and correspondingly low monthly payments) that allows borrowers to qualify for "more house." The catch? Since the low initial monthly payment, based on interest rates as low as 1.25%, is not enough to cover the real interest rate, the borrower eventually faces a sudden increase in monthly payments.

Balloon Loan: This loan is written for a short 5- to 7-year term during which the borrower pays either interest and principal each month or, in a more predatory form, interest only. At the end of the loan term, the borrower must pay off the entire loan in a lump sum—the "balloon payment." At that point, buyers must either refinance or lose their homes. Balloon loans are known to real estate pros as "bullet loans," since if the loan comes due—forcing the owner to refinance—during a period of high interest rates, it's like getting a bullet in the heart. According to the national organizing and advocacy group ACORN, about 10% of all subprime loans are balloons.

Balloon loans are sometimes structured with monthly payments that fail to cover the interest, much less pay down the principal. Although the borrower makes regular payments, her loan balance increases each month: negative amortization. Many borrowers are unaware that they have a negative amortization loan until they have to refinance.

Shared Appreciation Mortgage (SAM): These are fixed-rate loans for up to 30 years that have easier credit qualifications and lower monthly payments than conventional mortgages. In exchange for a lower interest rate, the borrower relinquishes part of the future value of the home to the lender. Interest rate reductions are based on how much appreciation the borrower is willing to give up. SAMs discourage "sweat equity" since the homeowner receives only some fraction of the appreciation resulting from any improvements. Not surprisingly, these loans have been likened to sharecropping.

Stated-Income Loan: Aimed at borrowers who do not draw regular wages from an employer but live on tips, casual jobs that pay under the table, commissions, or investments, this loan does not require W-2 forms or other standard wage documentation. The trade-off: higher interest rates.

No-Ratio Loan: The debt-income ratio (the borrower's monthly payments on debt, including the planned mortgage, divided by her monthly income) is a standard benchmark that lenders use to determine how large a mortgage they will write. In return for a higher interest rate, the no-ratio loan abandons this benchmark; it is aimed at borrowers with complex financial lives or those who are experiencing divorce, the death of a spouse, or a career change.

—*Amy Gluckman*

few years ago; like many buyers, we didn't retain an attorney. The title company had set aside one hour for the closing. During that time more than 125 single-spaced pages (much of it in small print) were put in front of us. More than 60 required our signature or initials. It would have been difficult for us to digest these documents in 24 hours, much less one. When we asked to slow down the process, we were met with impatience. After the closing, Anna asked, "What did we sign?" I was clueless.

Yet buying a home is the largest purchase most families will make in their lifetimes, the largest expenditure in a family budget, and the single largest asset for two-thirds of homeowners. It's also the most fraught with danger.

For low-income families in particular, homeownership can turn out to be more a crushing debt than an asset-building opportunity. The primary reason for this is the growing chasm between ever-higher home prices and the stagnant incomes of millions of working-class Americans. The last decade has seen an unprecedented surge in home prices, which have risen 35% nationally. While the housing bubble is largely confined to specific metropolitan areas in the South, the Southwest, and the two coasts (home prices rose 50% in the Pacific states and 60% in New England), there are also bubbles in midwestern cities like Chicago and Minneapolis. And although the housing bubble is most pronounced in high-end properties, the prices of low-end homes have also spiked in many markets.

Current incomes simply do not support these inflated home prices. For example, only 18% of Californians can afford the median house in the state using traditional loan-affordability calculations. Even the fall in mortgage interest rates in the 1990s and early 2000s was largely neutralized by higher property taxes, higher insurance premiums, and rising utility costs.

This disparity might have put a dent in the mortgage finance business. But no: in 2005, Americans owed $5.7 trillion in mortgages, a 50% increase in just four years. Over the past decade the mortgage finance industry has developed creative schemes designed to squeeze potential homebuyers, albeit often temporarily, into houses they cannot afford. It is a sleight of hand that requires imaginative and risky financing for both buyers and financial institutions.

Most of the "creative" new mortgage products fall into the category of subprime mortgages—those offered to people whose problematic credit drops them into a lower lending category. Subprime mortgages carry interest rates ranging from a few points to ten points or more above the prime or market rate, plus onerous loan terms. The subprime mortgage industry is growing: lenders originated $173 billion in subprime loans in 2005, up from only $25 billion in 1993. By 2006 the subprime market was valued at $600 billion, one-fifth of the $3 trillion U.S. mortgage market.

Subprime lending can be risky. In the 37 years since the Mortgage Bankers Association (MBA) began conducting its annual national mortgage delinquency survey, 2006 saw the highest share of home loans entering foreclosure. In early 2007, according to the MBA, 13.5% of subprime mortgages were delinquent (compared to 4.95% of prime-rate mortgages) and 4.5% were in foreclosure. By all accounts, this is just the tip of the iceberg. However, before the current collapse the rate of return for subprime lenders was spectacular. Forbes claimed that subprime lenders could realize returns up to six times greater than the best-run banks. In the past there were two main kinds of home mortgages: fixed-rate loans and adjustable-rate loans (ARMs). In a fixed-rate mortgage, the interest rate stays the same throughout the 15- to 30-year loan term. In a typical ARM the interest rate varies over the course of the loan, although there is usually a cap. Both kinds of loans traditionally required borrowers to provide thorough documentation of their finances and a down payment of at least 10% of the purchase price, and often 20%.

Adjustable-rate loans can be complicated, and a Federal Reserve study found that fully 25% of homeowners with ARMs were confused about their loan terms. Nonetheless, ARMs are attractive because in the short run they promise a home with an artificially low interest rate and affordable payments.

Even so, traditional ARMs proved inadequate to the tasks of ushering more low-income families into the housing market and generally keeping home sales up in the face of skyrocketing home prices. So in recent years the mortgage industry created a whole range of "affordability" products with names like "no-ratio loans," "option ARMs," and "balloon loans" that it doled out like candy to people who were never fully apprised of the intricacies of these complicated loans. (See sidebar for a glossary of the new mortgage products.) These new mortgage options have opened the door for almost anyone to secure a mortgage, whether or not their circumstances auger well for repayment. They also raise both the costs and risks of buying a home— sometimes steeply—for the low- and moderate-income families to whom they're largely marketed.

Beyond the higher interest rates (at some point in the loan term if not at the start) that characterize the new "affordability" mortgages, low-income homebuyers face other costs as well. For instance, predatory and subprime lenders often require borrowers to carry credit life insurance, which pays off a mortgage if the homeowner dies. This insurance is frequently sold either by the lender's subsidiary or else by a company that pays the lender a commission. Despite low payouts, lenders frequently charge high premiums for this insurance.

As many as 80% of subprime loans include prepayment penalties if the borrower pays off or refinances the loan early, a scam that costs low-income borrowers about $2.3 billion a year and increases the risk of foreclosure by 20%. Prepayment penalties lock borrowers into a loan by making it difficult to sell the home or refinance with a different lender. And while some borrowers face penalties for paying off their loans ahead of schedule, others discover that their mortgages have so-called "call provisions" that permit the lender to accelerate the loan term even if payments are current.

And then there are all of the costs outside of the mortgage itself. Newfangled mortgage products are often sold not by banks directly, but by a rapidly growing crew of mortgage brokers who act as finders or "bird dogs" for lenders. There are approximately 53,000 mortgage brokerage companies in the United States employing an estimated 418,700 people, according to the National Association of Mortgage Brokers; *BusinessWeek* notes that brokers now originate up to 80% of all new mortgages.

Largely unregulated, mortgage brokers live off loan fees. Their transactions are primed for conflicts of interest or even downright corruption. For example, borrowers pay brokers a fee to help them secure a loan. Brokers may also receive kickbacks from lenders for referring a borrower, and many brokers steer clients to the lenders that pay them the highest kickbacks rather than those offering the lowest interest rates. Closing documents use arcane language ("yield spread premiums," "service release fees") to hide these kickbacks. And some hungry brokers find less-than-kosher ways to make the sale, including fudging paperwork, arranging for inflated appraisals, or helping buyers find co-signers who have no intention of actually guaranteeing the loan.

Whether or not a broker is involved, lenders can inflate closing costs in a variety of ways: charging outrageous document preparation fees; billing for recording fees in excess of the law; "unbundling," whereby closing costs are padded by duplicating charges already included in other categories.

All in all, housing is highly susceptible to the predations of the fringe economy. Unscrupulous brokers and lenders have considerable latitude to ply their trade, especially with vulnerable low-income borrowers.

TIME TO CHANGE COURSE

Despite the hype, homeownership is not a cure-all for low-income families who earn less than a living wage and have poor prospects for future income growth. In fact, for some low-income families homeownership only leads to more debt and financial misery. With mortgage delinquencies and foreclosures at record levels, especially among low-income households, millions of people would be better off today if they had remained renters. Surprisingly, rents are generally more stable than housing prices. From 1995 to 2001 rents rose slightly faster than inflation, but not as rapidly as home prices. Beginning in 2004 rent increases began to slow —even in hot markets like San Francisco and Seattle—and fell below the rate of inflation.

In the mid-1980s, low- and no-downpayment mortgages led to increased foreclosures when the economy tanked. Today, these mortgages are back, along with a concerted effort to drive economically marginal households into homeownership and high levels of unsustainable debt. To achieve this goal, the federal government spends $100 billion a year for homeownership programs (including the $70-plus billion that the mortgage interest deduction costs the Treasury).

Instead of focusing exclusively on homeownership, a more progressive and balanced housing policy would address the diverse needs of communities for both homes and rental units, and would facilitate new forms of ownership such as community land trusts and cooperatives. A balanced policy would certainly aim to expand the stock of affordable rental units. Unfortunately, just the opposite is occurring: rental housing assistance is being starved to feed low-income homeownership programs. From 2004 to 2006, President Bush and the Congress cut federal funding for public housing alone by 11%. Over the same period, more than 150,000 rental housing vouchers were cut.

And, of course, policymakers must act to protect those consumers who do opt to buy homes: for instance, by requiring mortgage lenders to make certain not only that a borrower is eligible for a particular loan product, but that the loan is suitable for the borrower.

The reason the United States lacks a sound housing policy is obvious if we follow the money. Overheated housing markets and rising home prices produce lots of winners. Real estate agents reap bigger commissions. Mortgage brokers, appraisers, real estate attorneys, title companies, lenders, builders, home remodelers, and everyone else with a hand in the housing pie does well. Cities raise more in property taxes, and insurance companies enroll more clients at higher premiums. Although housing accounts for only 5% of GDP, it has been responsible for up to 75% of all U.S. job growth in the last four years, according to the consulting firm Oxford Analytica. Housing has buffered the economy, and herding more low-income families into homes, regardless of the consequences, helps keep the industry ticking in the short run. The only losers? Renters squeezed by higher rents and accelerating conversion of rental units into condos. Young middle-income families trying to buy their first house. And, especially, the thousands of low-income families for whom buying a home turns into a financial nightmare.

Sources: Carolina Katz Reid, "Studies in Demography and Ecology: Achieving the American Dream? A Longitudinal Analysis of the Homeownership Experiences of Low-Income Households," Univ. of Washington, CSDE Working Paper No. 04-04; Dean Baker, "The Housing Bubble: A Time Bomb in Low-Income Communities?" *Shelterforce Online*, Issue #135, May/June 2004, www.nhi.org/online/issues/135/bubble.html; Howard Karger, *Shortchanged: Life and Debt in the Fringe Economy* (Berrett-Koehler, 2005); National Multi Housing Council (www.nmhc.org).

The rapid concentration of wealth in recent decades has been accelerated and shaped by a trend known as financialization: the shift of the economy's "center of gravity" away from production and toward finance. Here, economist Ramaa Vasudevan describes the trend and discusses who gains and who loses from it.

FINANCIALIZATION: A PRIMER

BY RAMAA VASUDEVAN
November/December 2008

You don't have to be an investor dabbling in the stock market to feel the power of finance. Finance pervades the lives of ordinary people in many ways, from student loans and credit card debt to mortgages and pension plans.

And its size and impact are only getting bigger. Consider a few measures:

- U.S. credit market debt—all debt of private households, businesses, and government combined—rose from about 1.6 times the nation's GDP in 1973 to over 3.5 times GDP by 2007.
- The profits of the financial sector represented 14% of total corporate profits in 1981; by 2001-02 this figure had risen to nearly 50%.

These are only a few of the indicators of what many commentators have labeled the "financialization" of the economy—a process University of Massachusetts economist Gerald Epstein succinctly defines as "the increasing importance of financial markets, financial motives, financial institutions, and financial elites in the operation of the economy and its governing institutions."

In recent years, this phenomenon has drawn increasing attention. In his latest book, pundit Kevin Phillips writes about the growing divergence between the real (productive) and financial economies, describing how the explosion of trading in myriad new financial instruments played a role in polarizing the U.S. economy. On the left, political economists Harry Magdoff and Paul Sweezy had over many years pointed to the growing role of finance in the operations of capitalism; they viewed the trend as a reflection of the rising economic and political power of "rentiers"— those whose earnings come from financial activities and from forms of income arising from ownership claims (such as interest, rent, dividends, or capital gains) rather than from actual production.

FROM FINANCE TO FINANCIALIZATION

The financial system is supposed to serve a range of functions in the broader economy. Banks and other financial institutions mop up savings, then allocate that capital, according to mainstream theory, to where it can most productively be used. For households and corporations, the credit markets facilitate greatly increased borrowing, which should foster investment in capital goods like buildings and machinery, in turn leading to expanded production. Finance, in other words, is supposed to facilitate the growth of the "real" economy—the part that produces useful goods (like bicycles) and services (like medical care).

In recent decades, finance has undergone massive changes in both size and shape. The basic mechanism of financialization is the transformation of future streams of income (from profits, dividends, or interest payments) into a tradable asset like a stock or a bond. For example, the future earnings of corporations are transmuted into equity stocks that are bought and sold in the capital market. Likewise, a loan, which involves certain fixed interest payments over its duration, gets a new life when it is converted into marketable bonds. And multiple loans, bundled together then "sliced and diced" into novel kinds of bonds ("collateralized debt obligations"), take on a new existence as investment vehicles that bear an extremely complex and opaque relationship to the original loans.

The process of financialization has not made finance more effective at fulfilling what conventional economic theory views as its core function. Corporations are not turning to the stock market as a source of finance for their investments, and their borrowing in the bond markets is often not for the purpose of productive investment either. Since the 1980s, corporations have actually spent more money buying back their own stock than they have taken in by selling newly issued stock. The granting of stock options to top executives gives them a direct incentive to have the corporation buy back its own shares—often using borrowed money to do so—in order to hike up the share price and allow them to turn a profit on the sale of their personal shares. More broadly, instead of fostering investment, financialization reorients managerial incentives toward chasing short-term returns through financial trading and speculation so as to generate ballooning earnings, lest their companies face falling stock prices and the threat of hostile takeover.

What is more, the workings of these markets tend to act like an upper during booms, when euphoric investors chase the promise of quick bucks. During downturns these same mechanisms work like downers, turning euphoria into panic as investors flee. Financial innovations like collateralized debt obligations were supposed to "lubricate" the economy by spreading risk, but instead they tend to heighten volatility, leading to amplified cycles of boom and bust. In the current crisis, the innovation of mortgage-backed securities fueled the housing bubble and encouraged enormous risk-taking, creating the conditions for the chain reaction of bank (and other financial institution) failures that may be far from over.

FINANCIALIZATION AND POWER

The arena of finance can at times appear to be merely a casino—albeit a huge one—where everyone gets to place her bets and ride her luck. But the financial system carries a far deeper significance for people's lives. Financial assets and liabilities represent claims on ownership and property; they embody the social relations of an economy at a particular time in history. In this sense, the recent process of financialization implies the increasing political and economic power of a particular segment of the capitalist class: rentiers. Accelerating financial transactions and the profusion of financial techniques have fuelled an extraordinary enrichment of this elite.

This enrichment arises in different ways. Financial transactions facilitate the reallocation of capital to high-return ventures. In the ensuing shake-up, some sectors of capital profit at the expense of other sectors. More important, the capitalist class as a whole is able to force a persistent redistribution in its favor, deploying its newly expanded wealth to bring about changes in the political-economy that channel even more wealth its way.

The structural changes that paved the way for financialization involved the squashing of working-class aspirations during the Reagan-Thatcher years; the defeats of the miners' strike in England and of the air traffic controllers' (PATCO) strike in the United States were perhaps the most symbolic instances of this process. At the same time, these and other governments increasingly embraced the twin policy mantras of fighting inflation and deregulating markets in place of creating full employment and raising wages. Corporations pushed through legislation to dismantle the financial regulations that inhibited their profitmaking strategies.

Financialization has gathered momentum amid greater inequality. In the United States, the top 1% of the population received 14.0% of the national after-tax income in 2004, nearly double its 7.5% share in 1979. In the same period the share of the bottom fifth fell from 6.8% to 4.9%.

And yet U.S. consumption demand has been sustained despite rising inequality and a squeeze on real wages for the majority of households. Here is the other side of the financialization coin: a massive expansion of consumer credit has played an important role in easing the constraints on consumer spending by filling the gap created by stagnant or declining real wages. The credit card debt of the average U.S. family increased by 53% through the 1990s. About 67% of low-income families with incomes less than $10,000 faced credit card debt, and the debt of this group saw the largest increase—a 184% rise, compared to a 28% increase for families with incomes above $100,000. Offered more and more credit as a privatized means of addressing wage stagnation, then, eventually, burdened by debt and on the edge of insolvency, the working poor and the middle class are less likely to organize as a political force to challenge the dominance of finance. In this sense, financialization becomes a means of social coercion that erodes working-class solidarity.

As the structures created by financial engineering unravel, the current economic crisis is revealing the cracks in this edifice. But even as a growing number of U.S. families are losing their homes and jobs in the wake of the subprime meltdown, the financial companies at the heart of the crisis have been handed massive bailouts and their top executives have pocketed huge pay-outs despite their role in abetting the meltdown—a stark sign of the power structures and interests at stake in this era of financialization.

Sources: Robin Blackburn, "Finance and the Fourth Dimension," *New Left Review* 39 May-June 2006; Robert Brenner, "New Boom or Bubble," *New Left Review* 25 Jan-Feb 2004; Tamara Draut and Javier Silva, "Borrowing to make ends meet," *Demos*, Sept 2003; Gerald Epstein, "Introduction" in G. Epstein, ed., *Financialization and the World Economy*, 2006; John Bellamy Foster, "The Financialization of Capitalism," *Monthly Review*, April 2007; Gretta Krippner, "The financialization of the US economy," *Socio-Economic Review* 3, Feb. 2005; Thomas Palley, "Financialization : What it is and why it matters," Political Economy Research Institute Working Paper #153, November 2007; A. Sherman and Arin Dine, "New CBO data shows inequality continues to widen," Center for Budget Priorities, Jan. 23, 2007; Kevin Phillips, *Bad Money: Reckless Finance, Failed Politics, and the Global Crisis of American Capitalism*, 2008.

The prices of agricultural staples have skyrocketed over the last five years. Ben Collins explores the roles of changes in the world supply and demand for food as well as increasing commodity speculation in the price rises, which threaten food access for the world's poor.

HOT COMMODITIES, STUFFED MARKETS, AND EMPTY BELLIES

What's behind higher food prices?

BY BEN COLLINS
July/August 2008

Since 2003, prices of basic agricultural commodities such as corn, wheat, soybeans, and rice have skyrocketed worldwide, threatening to further impoverish hundreds of millions of the world's poor.

Shifts in fundamental supply and demand factors for food grains have undoubtedly contributed to higher food prices. Prominent among these shifts are the increasing diversion of food crops for biofuel production in the United States and Europe; sustained drought and water scarcity in Australia's wheat-growing regions; flooding in the U.S. grain belt; rising prices for oil and fertilizer worldwide; and the adoption of European and American meat-rich diets by the growing middle classes throughout Asia.

On top of these recent developments, long-term threats to worldwide agricultural output have eroded the world food system's resilience in the face of changing supply and demand. Although decades in the making, a loss of agricultural capacity worldwide caused by soil depletion, climate change, water scarcity, and urbanization has begun to take its toll on food production. Moreover, half a century of import restrictions and cheap agricultural exports by wealthy countries has devastated domestic food production capacity in poorer countries, forcing many countries that were once self-sufficient to rely on imported food from the world market.

At the same time, however, the growing presence of buy-and-hold investors in commodity markets has prompted heated debate among commodity traders, economists, and politicians over other possible causes of higher commodity prices apart from supply and demand shifts.

Since 2001, the declining value of the U.S. dollar, low U.S. interest rates, weak stock market returns, and accelerating inflation have drawn investment dollars away from stocks and into non-traditional investments such as commodities. This flight to perceived safety in commodity markets turned into a stampede in 2007 and early 2008, as a credit-induced financial crisis in the United States compounded these existing stresses on global financial markets.

Rising commodity prices and financial speculation on food are not new phenomena. The 1970s saw a similar rise in commodity prices in the United States, and in the 1920s, U.S. investors formed commodity pools to bet on commodity price movements. But the quantity and liquidity of money flowing through today's global markets is unprecedented in human history. The current commodities boom could be a sign of looming agricultural scarcity, or it may prove to be a short-lived speculative bubble that will deflate over the next few months or years. But regardless of where agricultural commodity prices are headed, the boom has already begun to transform how food is financed, grown, and sold, and may dramatically change how people around the world eat (or don't).

COMMODITY INVESTMENT GOES RETAIL

Commodity exchanges exist as a mechanism for the producers and consumers of grains, energy, and livestock to transfer risk to financial institutions and other traders. For example, wheat farmers might seek to reduce the risk of price fluctuations by selling a contract for the future delivery of their wheat crop on a commodity exchange. This futures contract will guarantee a price for the farmer selling the contract, enabling them to pay for their planting costs, and avoid the risk that the price of wheat may decrease between the date they sell the contract and the date they agree to deliver the wheat. Food giants such as Kraft and Nabisco, as well as smaller bakers and grain consumers, typically purchase commodity futures contracts to avoid the opposite risk—that the price of their raw materials may increase in the future. (Commodity markets also trade "spot" contracts, which entitle the purchaser to the immediate delivery of a commodity.)

Because producers and consumers seek to reduce risk, they function as so-called hedgers in commodity markets. In contrast, commercial trading firms and other speculators bet on the price of a commodity rising or falling, buying and selling futures contracts frequently in order to profit from short-term changes in their prices.

Since 2001, commodity funds have gained in popularity as a mechanism for institutions and individuals to profit from increases in commodity prices. These funds purchase commodity futures contracts in order to simulate ownership of a commodity. By periodically rolling over commodity futures contracts prior to their maturity date and reinvesting the proceeds in new contracts, the funds allow investors to gain investment returns equivalent to the change in price of a single commodity, or an "index" of several commodities (hence the name "index investor").

Investors in these commodity index funds include public pension funds, university endowments, and even individual investors, through mutual funds, for example. Although these investors are similar to traditional commodity speculators in that both seek to profit from changes in price, traditional speculators zero in on short-term price shifts, while index investors are almost exclusively long-term buyers betting on higher commodity prices in the future.

Some observers have argued that index investors themselves may have pushed already-high prices of commodities even higher. Hedge fund manager Michael Masters testified to the U.S. Senate that the total holdings of commodity index investors on regulated U.S. exchanges have increased from $13 billion in 2003 to nearly $260 billion as of March 2008. And as of April 2008, index investors owned approximately 35% of all corn futures contracts on regulated exchanges in the United States, 42% of all soybean contracts, and 64% of all wheat contracts, compared to minimal holdings in 2001. As Masters emphasized, these are immense commodity holdings. The wheat contracts, for example, are good for the delivery of 1.3 billion bushels of wheat, equivalent to twice the United States' annual wheat consumption.

Index fund managers have defended against charges that commodity index investment contributes to higher prices, arguing that because index funds never take delivery on their futures contracts, they simulate commodity price shifts for their investors without affecting the price of the underlying commodity. Some economists have also expressed skepticism that investment demand has driven commodity prices higher. Paul Krugman of Princeton University has noted that there is no evidence of "the usual telltale signs of a speculative price boom" such as physical hoarding of commodities. Furthermore, Krugman and others have pointed to non-exchange traded commodities such as iron ore that have also experienced rapid price increases during recent years, arguing that fundamental supply and demand factors, not investors, are to blame for higher commodity prices.

Other economists and commodity market observers have argued that despite price increases in non-exchange traded commodities, and an absence of physical hoarding, the recent flood of money into commodity markets has altered the balance between speculators and hedgers, leading to higher prices and greater price volatility. Mack Frankfurter, a commodities trading advisor at Cervino Capital Management, suggests that the influx of commodity index investors has transformed commodity futures from tools for risk management to long-term investments, "causing a self-perpetuating feedback loop of ever higher prices."

One reason the precise impact of index investors on commodity prices is difficult to determine is that the U.S. commodity trading regulator, the Commodity Futures

Trading Commission (CFTC), does not collect data on so-called "over-the-counter" commodity trading—that is, trading on unregulated markets—even though the agency estimated that 85% of commodity index investment takes place on these markets. Because Masters's data on the holdings of commodity index investors only include the 15% of index investor contracts that are held on CFTC-regulated exchanges, total commodity index investor holdings may be much higher than his estimates.

In testimony that warned of the influence of these unregulated markets on commodity prices, Michael Greenberger, the former head of the CFTC's Division of Trading and Markets, estimated that if unregulated trading of energy and agricultural commodities were eliminated, the price of oil would drop by 25% to 50% "overnight." If Greenberger is correct, the effect on food commodity prices would likely be similar. However, index investment is just one of many avenues through which money can enter commodity markets, making it difficult to assess the impact of index investors without taking into account the recent deregulation of U.S. commodity markets that has facilitated the current boom in food and energy investments.

A LEXICON OF COMMODITY MARKETS

Hedger—An individual or institution who buys or sells an asset to avoid the risk that the price of the asset may change over time. In agricultural commodity markets, hedgers are typically farmers and end-users of grains.

Speculator—An individual or institution who buys or sells an asset to profit from fluctuations in its price, but takes on the risk of an unfavorable change in the asset's price. In agricultural markets, speculators are typically large financial institutions, but since 2003 a growing number of "index investors" have speculated on the continued rise of commodity prices.

Futures—Tradable financial contracts used to buy or sell an asset at a certain date in the future, at a specified price.

Spot contract/Spot market—A contract for the immediate delivery of the commodity. Also called the "cash market" or "physical market," the spot markets determine the current price of a commodity.

Over-the-counter—Any contract or security traded outside of a regulated exchange. Over-the-counter trading can take place directly between two traders, or on unregulated exchanges or informal dealer networks.

Position Limits—In commodity markets, the maximum number of futures contracts a trader or institution is allowed to hold for a given commodity.

COMMODITY TRADING REGULATION, ENRON-STYLE

Commodity index investment is deeply intertwined with the growth of unregulated commodity trading authorized by the Commodity Futures Modernization Act of 2000. Before 2000, U.S. commodity futures contracts were traded exclusively on regulated exchanges under the oversight of the CFTC. Traders were required to disclose their holdings of each commodity and adhere to strict position limits, which set a maximum number of futures contracts that an individual institution could hold. These regulations were intended to prevent market manipulation by traders who might otherwise attempt to build up concentrated holdings of futures contracts in order to manipulate the price of a commodity.

The 2000 law effectively deregulated commodity trading in the United States by exempting over-the-counter commodity trading outside of regulated exchanges from CFTC oversight. Soon after the bill was passed, several unregulated commodity exchanges opened for trading, allowing investors, hedge funds, and investment banks to trade commodities futures contracts without any position limits, disclosure requirements, or regulatory oversight. Since then, unregulated over-the-counter commodity trading has grown exponentially. The total value of all over-the-counter commodity contracts was estimated to be $9 trillion at the end of 2007, or nearly twice the value of the $4.78 trillion in commodity contracts traded on regulated U.S. exchanges.

Once these unregulated commodity markets were created, energy traders and hedge funds began to use them to place massive bets on commodity prices. Enron famously exploited deregulated electricity markets in 2001, when the firm managed to generate unheard-of profits by using its trading operations to effectively withhold electricity and charge extortionate rates from power grids in California and other western states.

Although Enron went bankrupt later that year, the hedge fund Amaranth later exploited unregulated natural gas markets prior to its 2006 collapse. The fund had been heavily invested in complicated bets on the price of natural gas, borrowing eight times its assets to trade natural gas futures, and lost $6.5 billion when natural gas prices moved in the wrong direction. One month prior to Amaranth's collapse, the New York Mercantile Exchange (NYMEX), which is regulated by the CFTC, asked Amaranth to reduce its huge natural gas position. Amaranth reduced its position at NYMEX's request, but purchased identical positions on the unregulated Inter-Continental Exchange, where its transactions were invisible to regulators until the fund finally collapsed.

Amaranth's implosion demonstrated the ineffectiveness of regulating some commodity exchanges but not others. Thanks to the Commodity Futures Modernization Act, traders could flout position limits and disclosure rules with impunity, simply by re-routing trades to unregulated exchanges. Although index investment in commodities does not typically involve white-knuckle, leveraged bets on a single commodity's short-term performance, index investment was made possible by the same deregulated environment exploited by Amaranth and Enron. Like Amaranth, commodity index investors commonly purchase futures contracts on unregulated markets when they exceed CFTC position limits on futures contracts for a particular commodity. And other financial actors such as investment banks, hedge funds, or even the sovereign wealth funds of other countries may also be heavily invested in these over-the-counter commodity contracts, but since this trading is unregulated and unreported, the holders of these $9 trillion worth of contracts remain anonymous.

This year, the CFTC has faced intense scrutiny from investors, politicians, farmers, and agricultural traders over the unprecedented volatility and price increases of several agricultural and energy commodities traded on U.S. exchanges. A lively CFTC roundtable on commodity markets in April appeared to confirm arguments made by Frankfurter, Greenberger, Masters, and other critics of commodity index invest-ment. Representatives for farmers, grain elevator operators, and commercial bankers at the hearing repeatedly stressed that commodity markets were "broken," while the only pleas for calm came from CFTC economists and representatives for index investors and the financial industry. Unlike index investors, farmers have not ben-efited greatly from higher commodity prices, because extremely high levels of market volatility have made it difficult for some farmers to finance crop planting. National Farmers Union president Tom Buis sounded a particularly dire warning about the consequences of tight commodity supplies and burgeoning index invest-ment demand: "We've got a train wreck coming in agriculture that's bigger than anything else we've seen."

Following these warnings from farmers and food producers about the presence of index investors in commodity markets, the CFTC's acting chair publicly acknowl-edged the ongoing debate over "whether the massive amount of money coming into the markets is overwhelming the system." Despite this admission, Greenberger, the former CFTC official, remains skeptical of the agency's capacity and willingness to regulate commodity markets effectively. He urged Congress and the Federal Trade Commission to circumvent the CFTC's authority and eliminate unregulated over-the-counter commodity trading. Recently, faced with strong criticism from Congress, the CFTC retreated further from its claim that commodity markets are functioning normally. A CFTC commissioner admitted: "We didn't have the data that we needed to make the statements that we made, and the data we did have didn't support our declarative statements. If we were so right, why the heck are we doing a study now?"

THE CONSEQUENCES OF FINANCIALIZING FOOD

Facing political pressure by constituents over high oil and food prices, several members of Congress have sponsored legislation that would bar index investors from com-modity markets. One bill proposed by Sen. Joseph Lieberman (I-Conn.) would prohibit public and private pension funds with more than $500 million in assets from trading in commodity futures, and other bills would limit the maximum number of futures contracts an index investor could hold. These bills may stem the flood of money from index investors into commodities, but comprehensive reform is needed to reverse the Commodity Futures Modernization Act's authorization of over-the-counter commodity trading. Absent an outright repeal of this so-called "Enron loophole," energy and agricultural commodities will continue to be traded outside the reach of government regulation, making future Enron- and Amaranth-style market disruptions inevitable.

Ultimately, eliminating unregulated commodity trading cannot address the fundamental causes of higher agricultural prices. Even if speculative buying is curtailed, supply and demand factors such as falling crop yields, destructive trade policies, and the growing use of biofuels have likely brought the age of cheap food to an end. However, if the critics of commodity index investment are correct, then these investors have amplified recent food price shocks and are needlessly contributing to the impoverishment of the world's poorest citizens. Even though commodity market transparency and regulatory oversight will not solve the global food crisis, eliminating unregulated commodity trading can help resolve the debate over the effects of index investors on commodity prices and restore the accountability of commodity markets to the social interests they were originally established to serve.

Sources: Michael Masters, testimony before the Committee on Homeland Security and Government Affairs, United States Senate, May 20, 2008; Daniel P. Collins, "CFTC to up spec limits," *Futures*, May 1, 2005; Paul Krugman, "Fuels on the Hill," *New York Times*, June 27, 2008; Michael Frankfurter, *The Mysterious Case of the Commodity Conundrum, Securitization of Commodities, and Systemic Concerns*, Parts 1-3, www.marketoracle.co.uk; Michael Frankfurter and Davide Accomazzo, "Is Managed Futures an Asset Class? The Search for the Beta of Commodity Futures," December 31, 2007, *Graziadio Business Report*; "Regulator Admits to Futures Tracking Volatility," Associated Press, June 4, 2008; Commodity Futures Trading Commission, *CFTC Announces Agricultural Market Initiatives.* June 3, 2008; Michael Greenberger, testimony before the Committee on Commerce, Science, and Transportation, United States Senate, June 3, 2008; Sinclair Stewart and Paul Waldie. "Who is responsible for the global food crisis?" *Globe and Mail*, May 30, 2008; Commodity Futures Trading Commission, *Agricultural Markets Roundtable*, April 22, 2008; Ann Davis, "Commodities Regulator Under Fire—CFTC Scrutinized As Congress Looks Into Oil-Price Jump," *Wall Street Journal*, July 7, 2008; Ed Wallace, "ICE, ICE, Baby," *Houston Chronicle*, May 19, 2008; Laura Mandaro, "Lieber-man plans would bar funds from commodities," *Marketwatch*, June 18, 2008; "Our Confusing Economy, Explained," *Fresh Air*, April 3, 2008, www.npr.org.

The economic crisis has hit male employment harder than women. But, Heather Boushey explains, as more women become the sole breadwinners for their families, it is increasingly important for the government to help push for wage equity.

GENDER AND THE RECESSION

Recession Hits Traditionally Male Jobs Hardest

BY HEATHER BOUSHEY
May 2009

A woman is now the primary breadwinner in millions of families across the United States because her husband has lost his job. Three out of four jobs lost during our Great Recession, which began in December 2007, have been men's jobs. This has left women to support their families nationwide— a task made more challenging since women typically earn only 78 cents compared to the male dollar.

Men have lost more jobs than women because the industries with the largest job losses so far during the recession have been ones dominated by men. New Bureau of Labor Statistics Current Establishment Survey data for March 2009 shows that since the recession began men have lost 75.0% of all nonfarm jobs and 72.7% of all private-sector jobs.

Women have become a larger share of payroll employees. As of March 2009, the latest data available, women made up nearly half the labor force: 49.7% of all workers employed in the United States are women, up from 48.7% when the recession began in December 2007.

The recession is playing out differently by gender because men and women tend to work in very different industries and occupations. Women especially predominate in financial activities—mostly because they are the majority of real estate agents, not because they are the majority of bankers—as well as in government, education, and health. (See Figure 1.) Men predominate in transportation, construction, and manufacturing, as well as in certain retail professions, such as the sale of automobiles and electronic appliances.

Larger job losses among men have occurred because the recession is hitting traditionally male working-class jobs. Half of the job losses during this recession so far have occurred in either construction or manufacturing. Another quarter of the total job losses have occurred in professional and business services, mostly among temporary workers. Even though it is the financial sector which is driving the economic crisis, the financial activities industry only accounts for 7.4% of the jobs lost so far in this recession.

Yet, it is not just that men work in industries hardest hit by the recession. Within a number of hard-hit industries, men are also losing a disproportionate share of the jobs. For example, within retail, although men accounted for half (49.8%) of all workers at the beginning of the recession, they held two-thirds (64.5%) of the jobs lost. In finance and insurance, men accounted for over a third (36.7%) of the jobs at the beginning of the recession, but have lost half (50.6%) of the jobs.

It is not unique for blue-collar workers to bear the brunt of job losses in a recession. What is notable in this recession is that while manufacturing and construction accounted for a larger share of total job losses than in prior recessions, the industries that are seeing jobs gains—education, health, and government—are seeing smaller gains than during prior recessions. This does not bode well for women's jobs moving forward, since women are concentrated in these industries.

Notably, during the 1980s recession—when the unemployment rate went above 10%—women actually gained jobs on net because of continued hiring in women-dom-

FIGURE 1: THE RECESSION BY GENDER

Total Change in Employment, December 2007 to April 2009 (000s)

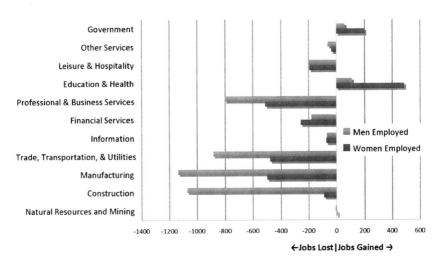

Source: Center for American Progress and the BLS

inated industries. Clearly, that is not the case during the current recession. Women's employment is already 98.5% of its level from December 2007.

As of April 2009 the unemployment rate for adult men was 9.4%—more than double what it was in December 2007. The unemployment rate for adult women was 7.1% in April. The male unemployment rate is now 2.3 percentage points higher than women's—larger than at any other time since 1949.

Women are also less likely than men to be unemployed in married families. The unemployment rate for married men is 6.3%—higher than at any time since 1983. The unemployment rate for married women is 5.5%—the highest since 1986.

That means more and more women in millions of families across the United States will be supporting their families.

Ensuring that those women, and every woman, earn a fair day's pay could not be a more pressing issue for families. A good—and fast—place to start would be for the Obama administration to devote its efforts to simply enforcing the laws already on the books and implementing better monitoring of equal pay. That would be a down payment to help families make ends meet while the labor market is getting back on track.

This article combines two "infographics" written by Heather Boushey, "Gender and The Recession," May 8, 2009, and "The Importance of Women Breadwinners," April 30, 2009. Both are available at the Center for American Progress: http://www.americanprogress. org/issues/2009/05/gender_recession.htm and http://www.americanprogress.org/ issues/2009/04/women_breadwinners.html.

Is a period of already-high unemployment a good time to push for laws increasing pay rates for low-wage workers? Jeannette Wicks-Lim argues that "living-wage" laws, which only cause modest increases in employer costs and have little or no negative effects on employment, are more necessary than ever to protect the most vulnerable workers.

SHOULD WE BE TALKING ABOUT LIVING WAGES *NOW*?

BY JEANNETTE WICKS-LIM
March/April 2009

The Department of Labor announced in January that the U.S. economy shed 2.8 million jobs in 2008, bringing the national unemployment rate to 7.2%— its highest level in 16 years. In today's economic climate, the worst since the Great Depression, are the raises demanded by living-wage campaigns a luxury? Should living-wage campaigns take a back seat to pulling the economy out of recession?

For many, the answer is no. Campaigns across the country continue to build on the widespread success of a movement that has put into place more than 140 living-wage laws since the mid-1990s. Take the Hartford Living Wage Task Force in Connecticut, which is trying to expand the number of workers guaranteed a living wage under its original 1997 law. Or Santa Fe's Living Wage Network, which fought for, and won, a cost-of-living increase to its living wage rate for 2009. Or the Nashville Movement in Tennessee, a group laying the groundwork for a campaign to establish a brand new ordinance.

They are right. Today's economic turmoil challenges us to create practical policies to meet the *heightened* imperative of living wages, not to abandon them.

Why do we need living-wage campaigns? Let's consider first the current legal wage floor. At $7.25 per hour, the federal minimum wage as of July 2009, a full-time year-round worker will bring home $15,080—less than the official poverty threshold of $17,330 for a family of three.

Moreover, poverty experts roundly criticize that official poverty line as too severe. According to the National Survey of American Families, nearly two-thirds of people in households with incomes above the poverty line but below twice that level reported serious economic hardships—failing to pay their rent, having their phone disconnected, worrying about running out of food, or relying on the emergency room for routine medical care.

Consider a more realistic poverty line: the "basic budget" thresholds developed by the Economic Policy Institute as a measure of the income required for "a safe and decent standard of living." These range between two and three times the official poverty line depending on local living costs such as housing. For a family of three, a full-time year-round worker would need to earn between $16 and $24 an hour to reach these basic budget thresholds. Two workers would each need to earn between $8 and $12 per hour. The living-wage ordinances enacted in recent years have typically required rates in this range—on average $10.80, or about 50% above the federal minimum wage.

These basic budgets, however, leave out not only extras such as restaurant meals, but also essential, if not immediate, items such as savings for education, retirement, or even emergencies. Any cut in hours or spell of unemployment can immediately compromise these families' ability to meet their basic needs. Unfortunately, these will be all-too-common occurrences in today's economic climate, which will expose the lowest-paid workers to increasingly severe hardships. This is because businesses tend to let the wages of the lowest-paid workers stagnate or fall unless prodded by a minimum-wage hike or a near-full-employment economy. In the 1980s, for instance, the federal minimum wage remained the same for ten years. Over this period, the lowest-paid workers saw their real (i.e., inflation-adjusted) wages *fall* by 15%.

In other words, to put living-wage campaigns on hold would not simply mean that conditions for low-wage workers and their families would not improve. Instead, these families would face worsening economic hardships.

But perhaps that's inevitable during a recession. Today, with economic indicators falling by the day, can businesses afford to pay a living wage without slashing jobs?

We can learn from the experience of New Jersey's state minimum-wage hikes in the early 1990s: from $3.35 to $3.80 in 1990, then to $4.25 in 1991, and finally to $5.05 in 1992. These three raises, about 10% to 20% each, amounted to a 40% overall rise in the wage floor once adjusted for inflation. The first hike took place in April 1990 when the economy was nearing a business cycle peak. The second and third hikes, however, took place on the heels of the 1990 recession. Economists studied their effects extensively among the businesses likely to be hit hardest—fast-food restaurants—and found no significant negative impact on employment.

One reason businesses can absorb these costs is that for most, minimum-wage hikes require only modest adjustments. For example, in 2003 Santa Fe passed an $8.50 citywide minimum wage. The average low-wage worker, who earned $6.91, received about a 23% raise. The resulting cost increases for restaurants—the most heavily affected businesses—equaled 3% of their sales revenue. In other words, a typical restaurant could offset the entire expense of the minimum-wage hike with a 3% price increase, say, 60¢ on a $20 meal. Unsurprisingly, the city's new wage floor appears to have had no negative impact on jobs.

Even in today's sharp downturn, businesses can likely absorb similar minimum-wage hikes. To see this, consider that U.S. restaurant sales rose by 2.8% between November 2007 and November 2008, almost two percentage points faster than inflation. This is despite a 5% rise in restaurant prices over the same period. In other words, overall sales in this sector grew, albeit sluggishly, even as restaurants raised their prices *and* the recession deepened.

Based on the Santa Fe experience, and using extremely pessimistic assumptions about future sales trends, I estimate that a 20% minimum-wage hike would require, as before, just a 3% price increase to cover these businesses' higher costs.

What can living-wage campaigns draw from these experiences, given that transforming a minimum wage into a living wage requires more dramatic raises on the order of 50%? An obvious possibility is to structure a living-wage ordinance as a series of raises, 10% to 20% each, which gradually achieve an adequate living-wage rate. An added precaution may be in order since we simply do not have extensive data on the impact of minimum-wage hikes during similar economic conditions: each raise could be followed by a year of evaluation, used in turn to adjust future raises up or down. This, by the way, is another lesson Santa Fe's experience offers: the city required exactly such an evaluation before raising its initial $8.50 minimum to $9.50 in 2006.

To turn the economy around we need a significant boost in economic activity—an increase in the demand for businesses' goods and services, not minor adjustments to business costs. This is the logic behind President Obama's stimulus package.

Widespread public support for raising minimum-wage rates (in 2006, more than 60% of voters in six states passed state minimum-wage hikes) suggests, however, that we want not only decent schools, decent medical care, decent roads, and a decent environment, but also decent-paying jobs. To create such jobs, living-wage requirements must be tied to the stimulus plan's funding. Without such mandates, private sector businesses that are the main focus for job creation are unlikely to pass some of that stimulus money along in the form of raises for their lowest-paid workers. Current living-wage laws provide a model: these laws impose living-wage requirements on businesses that contract with, or receive subsidies from, local governments.

Today's economic crisis highlights the vulnerability of the lowest-paid workers and virtually ensures that their living standards will worsen. These facts compel us to pursue living-wage policies with even greater force. Two policy prescriptions are especially important. First, the economic recovery plan, with its extensive government subsidies, provides a tool to impose living-wage requirements. Second, a broader, longer term living-wage policy of multi-step raises guided by interim economic impact studies will allow us to sensibly wean our economy off of poverty wages. Past experience tells us that our economy, even today, can adjust to such a policy.

Both the economic crisis and the policy responses it elicits will shape different groups' access to wealth well beyond the next turn of the business cycle. This op-ed questions a stimulus package focused on repairing highways and building green infrastructure, and calls for equal attention to the "social infrastructure," with its disproportionately female workforce.

BAIL OUT THE SAFETY NET

BY RANDY ALBELDA
January/February 2009

Even before the financial crisis and the recession, a substantial proportion of working families were not making it in America. In 2007, 20% of the population in a family with a breadwinner—that's 41 million people—did not have enough income, including any Food Stamps, Medicaid, housing and child care subsidies, or other public support they received, to pay their basic living expenses.

The good news that the current crisis brings for this bottom 20% is that as their plight of working hard but not making enough to pay the bills is becoming much more generalized, so should the pressure to address it. The bad news, of course, is the recession itself. The hardships these families face are growing by the day. More and more households are falling toward the social safety net.

And what about that safety net? In the 1990s, the Clinton administration ended "welfare as we know it," but at the same time promised work supports as low-wage workers moved up the ladder. Since then, employment rates for poor and low-income mothers have indeed soared, and so has the demand for affordable housing and child care assistance. But funding for them has not, with long waiting lists for both. As a result, by the early 2000s, these government work supports helped only 10% of the population in working families that couldn't meet their basic needs to actually meet them.

Despite expansions in the Earned Income Tax Credit and public health insurance for children in the 1990s, the public support programs for low-income families provide inadequate help, and even that to only a fraction of those who need it. And for workers who lose their jobs: today, only about a third of all unemployed workers receive unemployment benefits.

The safety net is not only tattered; it is nearly obsolete.

Rising unemployment is beginning to take its toll, as are draconian state budget cuts. Congress and President Obama appear ready to enact a large stimulus package to spur the economy and create jobs. Their focus so far is mostly on infrastructure, on "rebuilding our crumbling roads and bridges, modernizing schools..., building wind farms and solar panels," as Obama has said.

But bridge repair and even green jobs are not enough. Our physical infrastructure needs work, but so does our social infrastructure. And it's not just the safety net. Quality care for children and long-term care for disabled and elderly people are in short supply—and unaffordably expensive for many families. Moreover, women are disproportionately employed in these sectors, many at low wages that barely enable them to support their own families. In contrast, the construction and green-energy jobs that often pay decent wages with benefits are overwhelmingly filled by men.

So let's enact a bold recovery plan that promotes employment but also reconstructs the safety net and jump-starts the process of upgrading our social infrastructure. Here are four suggestions:

First, provide federal funding to states to prevent reductions in essential services. Now is not the time to reduce public health investments, stop transportation projects, cut higher education and lay off K–12 and early-education teachers.

Second, recreate our housing infrastructure. In exchange for buying up bad loans, secure foreclosed properties and develop an affordable housing stock.

Third, expand help for families who are struggling to pay for care for children and elders. Doing so will not only help the families struggling to care for their loved ones. It will also provide the job-creation stimulus for women workers that dollars for bridge repair will provide for men.

Fourth, replace our outdated and arbitrary poverty measure with a realistic measure of what it takes to afford basic needs and participate fully in society. This measure should be used to gauge whether the eventual econo-mic recovery is reaching all Americans.

Economic recovery will require bold, public action. Such action isn't limited to reforming our financial system or to traditional stimulus spending. It also means upgrading our social infrastructure in ways that ensure our economy works for all.

The Causes
of Inequality

Capitalist economies are characterized by an almost inexorable tendency toward ever-increasing levels of inequality. Government intervention in the form of regulation, taxation, and redistribution may partially counterbalance that tendency, but in recent decades, the U.S. political system has shifted in the opposite direction, to rig the economic game in favor of corporations and the very rich, at the cost of everyone else. Here are the seven recent government rule changes that have most exacerbated the wealth and income divide.

THE VISIBLE HAND

Seven Government Actions That Have Worsened Inequality

BY CHUCK COLLINS
August 2004

A primary reason that U.S. wealth inequality has accelerated in the last two decades is that power has shifted in our democracy. Corporations, investors, and campaign donors have gained power while main street business, wage earners, and voters have lost power. As political influence has shifted, the rules governing the economy have changed to benefit asset-owners and large corporations at the expense of wage-earners.

These rule changes—the visible hand of government—have worsened the wealth and income divide, putting a heavy thumb on the scale in favor of the rich and powerful. Rules governing taxes, trade, wages, spending priorities, and monetary policy have all changed, and in each case, the government has acted on behalf of corporations and the rich to rig who wins and who loses in the economy.

Of course, the U.S. economy has always been governed by rules that created inequality, from regulations protecting private property, to labor laws stacked against workers, to state taxes that fall disproportionately on the poor. Government actions can either mitigate or exacerbate inequality, and in recent years, hundreds of deliberate public policy choices have made it much worse. Here are seven nominations for the public policy hall of shame.

1. THE PLUMMETING MINIMUM WAGE
Decent wages are a prerequisite for individual wealth accumulation: workers cannot save money when their wages barely pay for basic necessities. Today, even

when they earn a decent wage, most Americans are not able to save much of anything. And it's much worse for those at the bottom. The U.S. minimum wage has plummeted in value over the last 35 years, and today leaves families below the federal poverty line.

Over 2.1 million workers earn today's minimum wage of $5.15 per hour. In 1968, the minimum wage of $1.60—or $7.07 in today's dollars—was 86% of the amount needed to bring a family of four to the federal poverty line. But today the minimum wage is only 61% of that benchmark. A full-time worker earning today's minimum wage has an annual income of just $10,712. And Congress has not raised the minimum wage since 1996.

It didn't have to be this way. While the minimum wage has been falling, worker productivity has skyrocketed, reducing costs for employers and increasing their profits. If worker wages overall had shared in the productivity gains since the late 1970s, they would be 33% higher in real terms than they are today.

2. TAXING WAGES, NOT WEALTH

Over the last 30 years, the federal government has shifted the tax burden off wealth and onto wages. Since 1980, the payroll tax rate—the main tax on work income—has jumped 25%. In the same period, top tax rates on investment income fell by 31% and taxes on large inheritances have been cut by 79%. This shift means that a person who derives millions of dollars solely in dividend income from investments now pays a marginal tax rate of just 15%, down from 28% in 1997. Compare that with a schoolteacher earning an adjusted gross income of $28,400. The teacher pays a payroll tax rate of 15.3% plus a marginal income tax rate of 28% for a total marginal rate of over 43%!

One policy exacerbating this shift was the 1997 Tax Reform Act, signed into law by President Clinton, which reduced capital gains tax rates from 28% to 20%. The 1997 capital gains provision was wrapped in pretty packaging, including expanded child and education credits for the middle class, and it didn't get much attention. But it was a centerpiece of the right-wing tax program. The 2003 Bush tax cut further reduced the capital gains rate to 15% and cut taxes on dividend income, delivering windfalls for the wealthy.

At the same time that the tax burden has been shifted from wealth to wages, the sheer size of recent tax cuts threatens the social programs many wage-earners depend on. The 2001 and 2003 federal tax cuts, which the Bush administration's 2005 budget proposes to make permanent, guarantee further cuts to social spending. The 2001 tax cut was the largest income tax rollback in two decades, and the 2003 cut reduced dividend and capital gains taxes while accelerating the 2001 rate cut for the top income brackets. These tax cuts, which mainly benefit the rich, will cost at least $824.1 billion between 2001 and 2010; if extended, they will cost $5.9 trillion over the next 75 years, according to William G. Gale and Peter R. Orszag of the Brookings Institution. Revenue losses of this magnitude can be sustained only by cutting social programs.

3. STACKING LABOR LAWS AGAINST WORKERS

Collective action is the most effective means that workers have to win a larger share of the economic pie. But U.S. workers face repressive labor laws that make many forms of collective action difficult or even illegal.

Workers who want to organize a union in the United States must overcome obstacles unheard of in Canada and Western Europe. Canadian workers simply need to present signatures showing that a majority of workers wish to form a union. But in the United States, the 1935 National Labor Relations Act, which governs union organizing in most sectors of the economy, requires workers to complete a lengthy election process during which employers can run intimidating anti-union campaigns. Employers force workers to attend meetings, individually and in groups, in which supervisors spread misinformation about unions. They routinely challenge election bids on frivolous grounds, delaying elections and vote-counting for months and years. And employers illegally fire worker organizers in 25% of unionization drives. Workers who seek reinstatement after being illegally fired face years of hearings before the National Labor Relations Board.

Workers who win union representation face other legal obstacles. When protesting their employer, for instance, they cannot conduct "secondary boycotts," or protests targeting firms that do business with their employer. Moreover, U.S. labor law makes it very difficult for workers to strike. Employers can permanently replace workers who strike for "economic" reasons—like wanting higher wages. The 1947 Taft-Hartley Act banned "sympathy strikes" in which workers striking at one employer could be joined by those at other companies and in other sectors of the economy. Taft-Hartley also gave the president the right to end strikes by executive order.

Unions and legal scholars have proposed labor law reforms for decades, but have been thwarted by both Democrats and Republicans in Congress. Union certification procedures have not changed even as employers' anti-union campaigns have grown more virulent. Congress has taken no action on proposals to ban strikebreakers and permanent replacements, or to lift restrictions on secondary boycotts. The legislative record on workers' substantive demands has also been dismal. Congress and state legislatures could have passed laws to raise workplace standards, require minimum benefits, and limit the use of contract or temporary labor. Instead, Congress has passed laws to reclassify jobs in ways that disqualify workers from receiving overtime pay, reducing the paychecks and clout of millions of workers.

4. SHREDDING THE SAFETY NET

The U.S. safety net has historically been much thinner than those in other industrialized nations. Yet, over the last 20 years, state and federal governments have slashed public programs that historically worked to narrow economic inequalities. Cuts in social spending increase Americans' reliance on unequal personal income and savings, and guarantee a growing divide between rich and poor.

In 1996, President Clinton and a Republican Congress ended "welfare as we knew it" by abolishing Aid to Families with Dependent Children (AFDC) and replacing it with Temporary Assistance to Needy Families (TANF). Unlike AFDC, a federal entitlement that provided a guaranteed minimum benefit, TANF includes strict work requirements, a five-year lifetime limit on assistance, and sanctions that can push people off the rolls. TANF is administered by the states with little federal oversight, allowing for inequities in benefit provisions.

Federal Pell grants, created in 1972 to provide aid to working-class college students, are much less generous than they used to be. Whereas the maximum Pell grant in 1975–76 covered 84% of the average cost of attending a four-year public institution, today it covers just 39% of that cost.

In 2004, the Department of Housing and Urban Development (HUD) changed the formulas it uses to finance the Section 8 housing voucher program. Section 8 vouchers help 2 million poor, elderly, and disabled Americans pay their rent and were originally lauded by conservatives as a market-based alternative to public housing. The new HUD formulas mean that the state housing authorities that administer the vouchers received $183 million less than they expected, even though Congress had already appropriated the funds. The new policy wasn't announced until April 23, 2004, but HUD made it effective retroactive to January 1, meaning that local housing authorities have to make up for funds they had already spent. In order to fill the budget gap, housing agencies across the country are being forced to take harmful steps including prohibiting eligible new families from receiving vouchers, reducing the maximum rent that a voucher will cover, and withdrawing newly issued vouchers from families that are still looking for an apartment. The Bush administration's proposed 2005 budget includes $1 billion in cuts for Section 8 housing vouchers, or 5.5% of the program's total funding.

5. LETTING EXECUTIVE PAY SKYROCKET

In 1992, President Clinton was elected calling for reform of executive compensation laws. At the time, corporations deducted the entire value of their bloated CEO pay packages as a tax-reducing business expense. Some salary expense is obviously a business expense, but corporations were using these excessive pay packages to shrink their tax liabilities on paper while bestowing largess on a privileged few. Clinton proposed limiting the "tax deductibility of excessive compensation" to $1 million. This still would have allowed corporations to take tremendous tax deductions, but it would have been a step in the right direction.

However, the final bill that passed was amended to exempt pay packages where compensation was judged to be "performance based." As a result, corporate boards today simply pass resolutions stating that their executive compensation pay packages are "performance based," and circumvent the law's intent. Apparently, it doesn't matter if that performance was abysmal. Safeway CEO Steven Burd cashed out $13 million in stock options in 2003 even as the company lost $169.8 million in net revenue. Imagine if a law with teeth had been in place during the late 1990s, when average executive compensation grew to more than 500 times average worker pay.

6. CHANGING THE RULES ON INVESTMENT AND TRADING

The recent stock market and accounting scandals have had a crushing effect on small stockholders and pension plans but put billions into the pockets of insider investors in America's largest corporations. The scandals were made possible by rule changes and "reforms" that took the few remaining teeth out of the regulatory process. In 1999, Congress repealed the 1933 Glass-Steagall Act, a banking law that prohibited mergers between banks, insurance companies, and securities trading firms. The New Deal-era law was designed to guard against the conflicts of interest that had led to a series of corporate abuses in the 1920s. The finance, insurance, and real estate sectors spent $200 million in campaign contributions, according to the Center for Responsive Politics, to remove this reform. Glass-Steagall was replaced by the Financial Modernization Act, which created a new kind of corporation—the financial holding company—that could bring together any number of these formerly separate financial institutions in a single corporation.

By removing the barriers between banks and securities firms, Congress ushered in a new wave of speculative mega-mergers. Firms such as Citigroup, J.P. Morgan Chase and others took advantage of the new rules by forming mega-conglomerates that financed Enron and other disasters.

Repealing Glass-Steagall also exposed small investors to new risks. Glass-Steagall had required banks to maintain a firewall between investment bankers (who facilitate deals between banks and corporations) and brokers (who buy and sell securities for investors). Eliminating this firewall gave brokers incentives to lie to investors about the quality of securities in order to promote deals that the bankers were pushing. In one case uncovered by New York State Attorney General Eliot Spitzer, Citigroup CEO Sandy Weill was on AT&T's board of directors when he sent an e-mail to Citigroup analyst Jack Grubman asking him to upgrade AT&T's investment rating as a personal favor. Grubman upped the company's rating just before Citigroup secured a deal to manage the AT&T wireless division's initial public offering. Soon after the IPO, Grubman downgraded AT&T's stock, and the price plummeted. Citigroup reaped over $40 million in fees from managing the IPO, while investors were duped out of millions more.

In 2000, Congress passed the Commodity Futures Modernization Act to deregulate derivative investments, which are highly speculative investment vehicles. Sen. Phil

Gramm (R-Texas) attached the act to an omnibus bill immediately after the 2000 Supreme Court decision in favor of Bush's selection. The bill included the infamous "Enron exclusion" that exempted Enron's online energy-trading floor from public oversight, creating the conditions in which Enron was able to manipulate California's electricity market. This law also exempted over-the-counter derivatives from regulation, helping to pave the way for the 2001 Wall Street fiascos. It specifically included an exception for the trading of energy derivatives, a provision strongly supported by Gramm, whose wife Wendy had deregulated energy swaps in 1993 as chairman of the Commodity Futures Trading Commission and then joined Enron's board of directors. These changes helped produce the corporate meltdowns that looted employees and investors alike, fueling wealth inequality.

Finally, thanks to a little-known 1995 rule change, shareholders and pensioners who saw their wealth vanish in the post-1990s corporate debacles found that they had little recourse against corporate malfeasance. This was because the 1995 Private Securities Litigation Reform Act had raised hurdles for investors attempting to file securities-fraud lawsuits in federal court. Investors fleeced by companies like WorldCom have been thwarted in their efforts to recoup their loses.

7. LETTING CORPORATE ACCOUNTING GO WILD

For years, shady corporate accounting left workers' savings and pensions dangerously exposed. The SEC and Congress failed to enact meaningful safeguards, and small investors were left holding the bag when disaster finally struck. Throughout the 1990s, the Financial Accounting Standards Board (FASB) and Securities and Exchange (SEC) Chairman Arthur Leavitt considered a number of reforms to make accounting more transparent and reduce opportunities for corporate manipulation. Leavitt proposed several reforms, including one which would have required companies to treat stock options as expenses. The SEC also proposed a rule requiring auditors to be independent of the companies they audited, as many were not. For instance, a number of accounting firms conducting corporate audits also maintained lucrative consulting contracts with the same firms. Knowing that they might lose consulting revenue if their audits weren't rosy enough, accounting firms had strong incentives to cook the books.

These proposals weathered an onslaught of industry and political attacks during the 1990s. Legislators led by Sen. Joseph Leiberman (D-Conn.), representing Connecticut's insurance industry, intervened to stop the SEC from implementing rules requiring auditor independence. When President Bush came into office, he appointed Harvey Pitt, the former chief lobbyist for the accounting industry, to replace Leavitt—a way of preventing further reforms. Rule changes were thwarted until corporate fraud scandals created a tremendous public backlash. Even then, Congress enacted only modest reforms such as the Sarbanes-Oxley Public Company Accounting and Investor Protection Act of 2002. While this law mandated some restrictions on certain non-auditing services that auditors can provide for their clients, it left in place the cozy auditor-client relationships that encouraged auditors to approve the shady accounting practices of Enron and WorldCom. In the end, even these weak reforms came too late to protect the millions of working Americans who saw their pensions and savings vanish, nor did it insure that similar scandals would be prevented from happening in the future.

Today, economic inequality in the United States is more extreme than at any time since the 1920s. Left to its own devices, the underlying tendency of the U.S. private sector is toward ever-increasing levels of inequality. This tendency must be counteracted by the visible hand of progressive government policies. But the rule changes and policy choices described here have taken the country in exactly the wrong direction. It doesn't have to be that way. We could have public policy that restores the lost purchasing power of the minimum wage; insists that the rich pay their fair share in taxes by blocking the repeal of the estate tax and reinstituting the lost progressivity of the income tax; patches the holes in the social safety net by returning non-defense discretionary spending to its level at the beginning of the Reagan administration (5.2% of GDP); enforces labor laws that oversee an orderly process of helping workers gain a voice in their work life; and reregulates financial markets and large corporations as opposed to celebrating corporate recklessness. These measures would go a long way toward counteracting the two-decade trend of widening inequality of the U.S. economy.

Contrary to the mainstream argument that high tax rates in the United States reduce its competitiveness, John Miller shows that, accounting for loopholes in the law, the effective tax rate for U.S. corporations is at or below the developed country average. He argues for truly boosting U.S. competitiveness by closing these loopholes and redirecting the revenues to infrastructure investments.

ONE-QUARTER OF LARGE U.S. CORPORATIONS DON'T PAY PROFIT TAXES—WHY SHOULD THE REST?

BY JOHN MILLER
September/October 2008

AMERICA THE UNCOMPETITIVE

Our political class has managed to maintain America's rank with the second highest corporate tax rate in the world at 39.3% (average combined federal and state). Only Japan is slightly higher overall.

In Washington, meanwhile, Senator Byron Dorgan of North Dakota waved around a new politically generated study by the Government Accountability Office (GAO) finding that 28% of large U.S. corporations paid no income tax in 2005. "It's time for big corporations to pay their fair share," Mr. Dorgan roared.

Among the large companies that paid no taxes, 85% of them also made no profits that year. American Airlines and General Motors escaped income tax for 2005 through the clever tax dodge of losing $862 million and $10.5 billion, respectively.

The GAO data only add to the case for cutting U.S. corporate rates. America now has the worst of all worlds: high corporate tax rates, but also lots of loopholes passed by Congress at the behest of favored businesses to avoid the confiscatory rate.

> *The average European nation has tax rates on corporate income 10 percent-*
> *age points lower than the U.S., but those countries on average raise 50% more*
> *as a share of GDP in corporate taxes than does the U.S.*
>
> *John McCain has proposed cutting the 35% federal corporate tax rate to*
> *25%. That's a good start, but even that would leave the U.S. with a combined*
> *state and federal rate nearly five percentage points above the global average.*
> *With corporate tax rates falling around the world, and with its damage to*
> *investment increasingly obvious, abolishing the U.S. corporate income tax*
> *should be on the table.*
>
> —*Wall Street Journal* editorial, August 15, 2008

You have to hand it to the *Wall Street Journal* editors: They don't embarrass easily. The Government Accountability Office (GAO) reports that one-quarter of large U.S. corporations paid no income taxes in 2005, and the editors whine that high corporate taxes have rendered the United States uncompetitive and call once again for abolishing the corporate income tax.

Let's start with the title. The editors surely know that U.S. competitiveness has been improving, not worsening, due to the decline in the value of dollar (something they regularly lament). According to KPMG, the international accounting and consulting firm, the cost of doing business in the United States dropped from 2006 to 2008 and is now lower than that in much of Europe, including Germany, Italy, France, and the U.K., as well as in Japan.

Such inaccuracy is a problem. But it pales next to the profound illogic the *Journal* editors are trying to purvey here. The editorial acknowledges that U.S. corporations pay less in corporate income taxes than the average across industrialized countries—despite the higher U.S. "nominal" tax rate. It recognizes that European countries collect *50% more* in corporate income taxes as a share of GDP than does the United States. Nonetheless, the editors still want to argue that high U.S. corporate income taxes are driving investment away to other countries.

But they can't have it both ways. The editors are right that it is myriad tax loopholes that account for the difference between the nominal and effective tax rates on U.S. corporations. If they find loopholes objectionable, then they should propose simplifying the corporate tax code in a revenue-neutral way, with a lower rate and fewer loopholes. But that's entirely different from what they actually propose here: that U.S. corporations should pay less in corporate income taxes altogether. And that is an awfully hard case to make when you have already admitted that U.S. corporations pay less than their counterparts in other industrialized countries.

LOOPHOLES OR LOSSES?

The GAO report does need to be read carefully. It never said that profitable corporations typically avoid federal corporate income taxes, nominally 35% of all taxable income or profits above $10 million. Nonetheless, the report did offer some deservedly headline-grabbing news: 55% of large U.S. corporations reported no tax liability for at least one of the eight years from 1998 to 2005, and 25% paid no corporate income taxes in 2005 alone. That last figure was actually down from its peak of 38% in 2001. But that shift must be viewed in context: corporate profits more than doubled from 2001 to 2005, so it's not surprising that the share of corporations managing to avoid income tax liability entirely declined somewhat over the period.

Why did so many large U.S. corporations pay no corporate income taxes? Was it because they suffered massive losses, as the editors maintain? Or was it because they took advantage of loopholes in the tax code to eliminate *on paper* any taxable income or profits?

The GAO report is silent on that question, but other studies point to the key role that loopholes played in allowing these corporations to escape taxation. For instance, Citizens for Tax Justice (CTJ) conducted a detailed study of the tax liability of 275 of the largest U.S. corporations from 2001 to 2003. Eighty-two of those 275 major corporations, or nearly one-third, paid no corporate income taxes in at least one of those three years. Far from losing money, these 82 corporations made a total of $102 billion in pre-tax U.S. profits in the years for which they paid no taxes. But thanks to tax breaks, these corporations actually *got $12.6 billion back* from the U.S. Treasury. In other words, as a group their effective tax rate—the share of their pre-tax profit they paid in corporate income taxes—was −12.6% (yes, that's a minus sign). Among the rebate recipients were Pepco Holdings, Prudential Financial, ITT Industries, Boeing, Unisys, Fluor, and CSX.

Taken together, all 275 corporations in the CTJ study paid from 21.4% (in 2001) to 17.4% (in 2003) of their pre-tax profits in corporate income taxes, not much more than half the nominal rate of 35%. Other measures also peg the effective tax rate on U.S. corporate profits far below 35%. For instance, using Treasury Department data, tax analyst Martin Sullivan found that the effective tax rate on U.S. corporate profits reached a ten-year low of 22.2% in 2006.

HOW TO AVOID CORPORATE TAXES

What accounts for the stark difference between the effective rates of taxation paid by U.S. corporations and the 35% rate specified in the tax code?

Corporate income taxes are levied against reported corporate profits. Corporations use a variety of mechanisms to inflate their reported costs and thereby reduce their taxable profits, including:

- **Accelerated Depreciation**. This provision allows corporations to write off machinery and equipment or other assets more quickly than those assets actually deteriorate. Enacted in the 1980s and expanded by the Bush administration and Congress, it dramatically lowered the effective tax rate on U.S. corporations. Accelerated depreciation generated $70.9 billion of tax savings from 2001 to 2003 for the 275 corporations in the CTJ study. Fully two-thirds of those savings went to just 25 corporations, including Verizon, Exxon-Mobil, and Wachovia. In fiscal year 2006, accelerated deprecation of machinery and equipment cost the federal government $36.5 billion in lost tax revenues.
- **Stock Options**. Most big corporations give their executives the option to buy the company's stock at a favorable price. Corporations can then take a tax deduction for the difference between what the employee pays for the stock and its market price. Of the 275 corporations in the CTJ study, 269 received stock-option benefits between 2001 and 2003 worth a total of $32 billion in reduced taxes over the period.
- **Debt Financing**. When corporations finance new investment by issuing stock, the dividends they pay to stockholders are not counted as costs, and so do not reduce their taxable profits. But when corporations borrow capital to invest (typically by issuing bonds), the interest payments on that debt do count as costs. This tax advantage that the U.S. tax code grants to debt financing is unusually generous; other countries typically treat debt financing less favorably. Interest deductions accounted for 15% of the total deductions taken by corporations in the GAO study.

The result of these and other corporate tax loopholes is that effective corporate tax rates in the United States are no higher, and in some cases lower, than rates across the Organization for Economic Cooperation and Development (OECD), the group of the world's most industrialized countries. For instance, a Congressional Budget Office study found that effective U.S. corporate income tax rates in 2003 were close to the OECD average for profits derived from equity-financed investments and substantially below the average for profits derived from debt-financed investments.

The U.S. rates, in other words, are hardly prohibitive or non-competitive.

WHAT TO DO WITH $166 BILLION?

Closing loopholes could boost U.S. corporate income tax revenues to the OECD average of 3.4% of GDP. In 2007, that would have added $166 billion to federal government revenues—enough to just restore U.S. infrastructure spending to its level four decades ago, and a large down payment toward the $1.6 trillion of investments over the next five years called for by the American Society of Civil Engineers to repair levees, bridges, schools, and power grids, as well as to build high speed transit and modern sewerage systems and to make many other desperately needed infrastructure investments.

That would do far more to improve U.S. economic competitiveness than the editors' proposal to let the other three-quarters of large U.S. corporations go tax-free. At the same time it would satisfy the demand—not just from Senator Dorgan, but from many Americans—that "big corporations pay their fair share."

Sources: "America the Uncompetitive," *Wall Street Journal*, August 15, 2008; "AP Makes Serious Error in Story on Corporate Income Tax," Tax Foundation, August 12, 2008; "Corporate-Tax Reporting Draws GAO Scrutiny," *WSJ*, August 13, 2008; "Comparison of the Reported Tax Liabilities of Foreign and U.S.-Controlled Corporations, 1998-2005," GAO, July 2008; "Corporate Income Tax Rates: International Comparisons," CBO, Nov. 2005; Joel Friedman, "The Decline of Corporate Income Tax Revenues," Center on Budget and Policy Priorities, October 23, 2003; Robert McIntyre and T.D. Nguyen, "Corporate Income Taxes in the Bush Years," Citizens for Tax Justice, September 2004; "Treasury Conference on Business Taxation and Global Competitiveness: Background Paper," U.S. Treas. Dept., July 23, 2007; "Tax and Economic Growth," OECD, July 11, 2008; Mark Sullivan, "The Effective Corporate Tax Rate is Falling," Tax Analysts, January 22, 2007; Peter Merrill, "The Corporate Tax Conundrum," Tax Analysts, 2007; "U.S. Leaps over Europe as a Cost-Effective Business Cost Location," KPMG in Canada, March 27, 2008; American Society of Civil Engineers, "Report Card for America's Infrastructure," 2005 (updated for 2008).

African Americans and other minorities hold far less wealth than whites. But why should the wealth gap be so large, greater even than the racial income gap? It turns out that government has played a central role. Throughout U.S. history, countless specific laws, policies, rules, and court decisions have made it more difficult for nonwhites to build wealth, and transferred wealth they did own to whites.

DOUBLY DIVIDED

The Racial Wealth Gap

BY MEIZHU LUI
August 2004

Race—constructed from a European vantage point—has always been a basis on which U.S. society metes out access to wealth and power. Both in times when the overall wealth gap has grown and in times when a rising tide has managed to lift both rich and poor boats, a pernicious wealth gap between whites and nonwhite minorities has persisted.

Let's cut the cake by race. If you lined up all African-American families by the amount of assets they owned minus their debts and then looked at the family in the middle, that median family in 2001 had a net worth of $10,700 (excluding the value of automobiles). Line up all whites, and *that* median family had a net worth of $106,400, almost 10 times more. Less than half of African-American families own their own homes, while three out of four white families do. Latinos are even less wealthy: the median Latino family in 2001 had only $3,000 in assets, and less than half own their own homes.

We do not know how much Native Americans have in assets because so little data has been collected, but their poverty rate is 26% compared to 8% for whites, even though more than half own their own homes. Nor is much information collected about Asian Americans. What we do know is that their poverty rate is 13%, and that 60% of Asian Americans own their own homes, compared to 77% of whites.

Almost 40 years after the passage of the 20th century's major civil rights legislation, huge wealth disparities persist. However, the myth that the playing field was leveled by those laws is widespread. For anyone who accepts the myth, it follows that if families of color are not on an economic par with whites today, the problem must lie with *them*.

But the racial wealth gap has nothing to do with individual behaviors or cultural deficits. Throughout U.S. history, deliberate government policies transferred wealth from nonwhites to whites—essentially, affirmative action for whites. The specific mechanisms of the transfer have varied, as have the processes by which people have been put into racial categories in the first place. But a brief review of American history, viewed through the lens of wealth, reveals a consistent pattern of race-based obstacles that have prevented Native Americans, African Americans, Latinos, and Asians from building wealth at all comparable to whites.

NATIVE AMERICANS: IN THE U.S. GOVERNMENT WE "TRUST"?

When European settlers came to what would become the United States, Indian tribes in general did not consider land to be a source of individual wealth. It was a resource to be worshipped, treasured, and used to preserve all forms of life. Unfortunately for them, that concept of common ownership and the way of life they had built around it would clash mightily with the idea that parcels of land should be owned by individuals and used to generate private profit.

After the American Revolution, the official position of the new U.S. government was that Indian tribes had the same status as foreign nations and that good relations with them should be maintained. However, as European immigration increased and westward expansion continued, the settlers increasingly coveted Indian land. The federal government pressured Native Americans to sign one treaty after another giving over land: In the United States' first century, over 400 Indian treaties were signed. Indians were forcibly removed, first from the south and then from the west, sometimes into reservations.

Eventually, the Indians' last large territory, the Great Plains, was essentially handed over to whites. In one of the clearest instances of land expropriation, the 1862 Homestead Act transferred a vast amount of land from Indian tribes to white homesteaders by giving any white family 160 acres of land for free if they would farm it for five years. Of course, this massive land transfer was not accomplished without violence. General William Tecumseh Sherman, of Civil War fame, wrote: "The more [Indians] we can kill this year, the less will have to be killed the next year, for the more I see of these Indians, the more convinced I am that they all have to be killed or be maintained as a species of paupers." (Ironically, the Homestead Act is often cited as a model government program that supported asset-building.)

Out of the many treaties came the legal concept of the U.S. government's "trust responsibility" for the Native nations, similar to the relationship of a legal guardian to a child. In exchange for land, the government was to provide for the needs of the Native peoples. Money from the sale of land or natural resources was to be placed in a trust fund and managed in the best interests of the Indian tribes. The government's mismanagement of Indian assets was pervasive; yet, by law, Indian tribes could not fire the designated manager and hire a better or more honest one.

The Dawes Act of 1887 was designed to pressure Indians to assimilate into white culture: to adopt a sedentary life style and end their tradition of collective land ownership. The law broke up reservation land into individual plots and forced Indians to attempt to farm "western" style; "surplus" land was sold to whites. Under this scheme, millions more acres were transferred from Native Americans to whites.

After 1953, the U.S. government terminated the trust status of the tribes. While the stated purpose was to free Indians from government control, the new policy exacted a price: the loss of tribally held land that was still the basis of some tribes' existence. This blow reduced the remaining self-sufficient tribes to poverty and broke up tribal governments.

Thus, over a 200-year period, U.S. government policies transferred Native Americans' wealth—primarily land and natural resources—into the pockets of white individuals. This expropriation of vast tracts played a foundational role in the creation of the U.S. economy. Only in recent years, through the effective use of lawsuits to resurrect tribal rights assigned under the old treaties, have some tribes succeeded in building substantial pools of wealth, primarily from gaming businesses. This newfound casino wealth, though, cannot make up for the decimation of Native peoples or the destruction of traditional Native economies. Native Americans on average continue to suffer disproportionate poverty.

AFRICAN AMERICANS: SLAVES DON'T OWN, THEY ARE OWNED

From the earliest years of European settlement until the 1860s, African Americans were assets to be tallied in the financial records of their owners. They could be bought and sold, they created more wealth for their owners in the form of children, they had no rights even over their own bodies, and they worked without receiving any wages. Slaves and their labor became the basis of wealth creation for plantation owners, people who owned and operated slave ships, and companies that insured them. This was the most fundamental of wealth divides in American history.

At the end of the Civil War, there was an opportunity to create a new starting line. In the first few years, the Freedmen's Bureau and the occupying Union army actually began to distribute land to newly freed slaves: the famous "40 acres and a mule," a modest enough way to begin. But the Freedmen's Bureau was disbanded after only seven years, and the overwhelming majority of land that freed slaves had been allotted was returned to its former white owners. Unable to get a foothold as self-employed farmers, African Americans were forced to accept sharecropping arrangements. While sharecroppers kept some part of the fruits of their labor as in-kind income, the system kept them perpetually in debt and unable to accumulate any assets.

In 1883, the Supreme Court overturned the Civil Rights Act of 1875, which had given blacks the right to protect themselves and their property. By 1900, the Southern states had passed laws that kept African Americans separate and unequal, at the bottom of the economy. They began migrating to the North and West in search of opportunity.

Amazingly, some African-American families did prosper as farmers and business-people in the early 20th century. Some African-American communities thrived, even establishing their own banks to build savings and investment within the community. However, there was particular resentment against successful African Americans, and they were often targets of the vigilante violence common in this period. State and local governments helped vigilantes destroy their homes, run them out of town, and lynch those "uppity" enough to resist, and the federal government turned a blind eye. Sometimes entire black communities were targeted. For example, the African-American business district in north Tulsa, known as the "Black Wall Street" for its size and success, was torched on the night of June 21, 1921 by white rioters, who destroyed as many as 600 black-owned businesses.

The Depression wiped out black progress, which did not resume at all until the New Deal period. Even then, African Americans were often barred from the new asset-building programs that benefited whites. Under Social Security, workers paid into the system and were guaranteed money in retirement. However, domestic and agricultural work—two of the most significant black occupations—were excluded from the program. Unemployment insurance and the minimum wage didn't apply to domestic workers or farm workers either. Other programs were also tilted toward white people. The Home Owners' Loan Corporation was created in 1933 to help homeowners avoid foreclosure, but not a single loan went to a black homeowner.

Following World War II, a number of new programs provided a ladder into the middle class—for whites. The GI Bill of Rights and low-interest home mortgages provided tax-funded support for higher education and for homeownership, two keys to family wealth building. The GI Bill provided little benefit to black veterans, however, because a recipient had to be accepted into a college—and many colleges did not accept African-American students. Likewise, housing discrimination meant that homeownership opportunities were greater for white families; subsidized mortgages were often simply denied for home purchases in black neighborhoods.

In *The Cost of Being African American*, sociologist Thomas Shapiro shows how, because of this history, even black families whose incomes are equal to whites' generally have unequal economic standing. Whites are more likely to have parents who benefited from the land grants of the Homestead Act, who have Social Security or retirement benefits, or who own their own homes. With their far greater average assets, whites can transfer advantage from parents to children in the form of college tuition payments, down payments on homes, or simply self-sufficient parents who do not need their children to support them in old age.

Thirty-five blocks in Greenwood, a prosperous African-American business district in Tulsa, were destroyed by white rioters on June 1, 1921.

These are the invisible underpinnings of the black-white wealth gap: wealth legally but inhumanely created from the unpaid labor of blacks, the use of violence—often backed up by government power—to stop black wealth-creating activities, tax-funded asset building programs closed to blacks even as they, too, paid taxes. The playing field is not level today. For example, recent studies demonstrate that blatant race discrimination in hiring persists. But even if the playing field were level, the black/white wealth gap would still be with us.

LATINOS: IN THE UNITED STATES' BACK YARD

At the time of the American Revolution, Spain, not England, was the largest colonial landowner on the American continents. Unlike the English, the Spanish intermarried widely with the indigenous populations. In the 20th century, their descendents came to be identified as a distinct, nonwhite group. (In the 1800's, Mexicans were generally considered white.) Today, Latinos come from many countries with varied histories, but the relationship of Mexicans to the United States is the longest, and people of Mexican descent are still the largest Latino group in the United States (67% in 2002).

Mexico won its independence from Spain in 1821. Three years later, the Monroe Doctrine promised the newly independent nations of Latin America "protection" from interference by European powers. However, this doctrine allowed the United States itself to intervene in the affairs of the entire hemisphere. Ever since, this paternalistic relationship (reminiscent of the "trust" relationship with Native tribes) has meant U.S. political and economic dominance in Mexico and Central and South America, causing the "push and pull" of the people of those countries into and out of the United States.

Mexicans and Anglos fought together to free Texas from Mexican rule, creating the Lone Star Republic of Texas, which was then annexed to the United States in 1845. Three years later, the United States went to war against Mexico to gain more territory and continue fulfilling its "manifest destiny"—its God-given right—to expand "from sea to shining sea." Mexico lost the war and was forced to accept the 1848 Treaty of Guadalupe Hidalgo, which gave the United States half of Mexico's land. While individual Mexican landowners were at first assured that they would maintain ownership, the United States did not keep that promise, and the treaty ushered in a huge transfer of land from Mexicans to Anglos. For the first time in these areas, racial categories were used to determine who could obtain land. The English language was also used to establish Anglo dominance; legal papers in English proving land ownership were required, and many Spanish speakers suffered as a result.

In the twentieth century, government policy continued to reinforce a wealth gap between Mexicans and whites. The first U.S.-Mexico border patrol was set up in 1924, and deportations of Mexicans became commonplace. Like African Americans, Latino workers were disproportionately represented in the occupations not covered by the Social Security Act. During World War II, when U.S. farms needed more agricultural workers, the federal government established the Bracero program, under which Mexican workers were brought into the United States to work for subminimum wages and few benefits, then kicked out when their labor was no longer needed. Even today, Mexicans continue to be used as "guest"—or really, reserve—workers to create profits for U.S. agribusiness.

The North American Free Trade Agreement, along with the proposed Central American Free Trade Agreement and Free Trade Agreement of the Americas, is the newest incarnation of the Monroe Doctrine. Trade and immigration policies are still being used to maintain U.S. control over the resources in its "back yard," and at the same time to deny those it is "protecting" the enjoyment of the benefits to be found in papa's "front yard."

ASIAN AMERICANS: PERPETUAL FOREIGNERS

The first Asian immigrants, the Chinese, came to the United States at the same time and for the same reason as the Irish: to escape economic distress at home and take advantage of economic opportunity in America. Like European immigrants, the Chinese came voluntarily, paying their own passage, ready and willing to seize the opportunity to build economic success in a new land. Chinese and Irish immigrants arrived in large numbers in the same decade, but their economic trajectories later diverged.

The major reason is race. While the Irish, caricatured as apes in early cartoons, were soon able to become citizens, the Naturalization Act of 1790 limited eligibility for citizenship to "whites." Asians did not know if they were white or not—but they wanted to be! The rights and benefits of "whiteness" were obvious. Other Americans didn't know whether or not they were white, either. Lawsuits filed first by Chinese, then by Japanese, Indian (South Asian), and Filipino immigrants all claimed that they should be granted "white" status. The outcomes were confusing; for example, South Asians, classified as Caucasian, were at first deemed white. Then, in later cases, courts decided that while they were Caucasian, they were not white.

A series of laws limited the right of Asians to create wealth. Chinese immigrants were drawn into the Gold Rush; the Foreign Miners Tax, however, was designed to push them out of the mining industry. The tax provided 25% of California's annual state budget in the 1860s, but the government jobs and services the tax underwrote went exclusively to whites—one of the first tax-based racial transfers of wealth. And with the passage of the Chinese Exclusion Acts in 1882, the Chinese became the first nationality to be denied the right to join this immigrant nation; the numbers of Chinese-American citizens thus remained small until the 1960s.

The next wave of Asians came from Japan. Excellent farmers, the Japanese bought land and created successful businesses. Resentment led to the passage of the 1924 Alien Land Act, which prohibited noncitizens from owning land. Japanese Americans then found other ways to create wealth, including nurseries and the cut flower business. In 1941, they had $140 million of business wealth.

World War II would change all that. In 1942, the Roosevelt administration forced Japanese Americans, foreign-born and citizen alike, to relocate to internment camps in the inland Western states. They had a week to dispose of their assets. Most had to sell their homes and businesses to whites at fire sale prices—an enormous transfer of wealth. In 1988, a successful suit for reparations gave the survivors of the camps $20,000 each, a mere fraction of the wealth that was lost.

Today, Asians are the group that as a whole has moved closest to economic parity with whites. (There are major variations in status between different Asian nationalities, however, and grouping them masks serious problems facing some groups.) While Asian immigrants have high poverty rates, American-born Asians have moved into professional positions, and the median income of Asians is now higher than that of whites. However, glass ceilings still persist, and as Wen Ho Lee, the Chinese-American nuclear scientist who was falsely accused of espionage in 2002, found out, Asians are still defined by race and branded as perpetual foreigners.

The divergent histories of the Irish and the Chinese in the United States illustrate the powerful role of race in the long-term accumulation of wealth. Irish-Americans faced plenty of discrimination in the labor market: consider the "No Irish Need Apply" signs that were once common in Boston storefronts. But they never faced legal prohibitions on asset ownership and citizenship as Chinese immigrants did, or the expropriation of property as the Japanese did. Today, people of Irish ancestry have attained widespread material prosperity and access to political power, and some of the wealthiest and most powerful men in business and politics are of Irish descent. Meantime, the wealth and power of the Chinese are still marginal.

Throughout history, federal policies—from constructing racial categories, to erecting barriers to asset building by nonwhites, to overseeing transfers of wealth from nonwhites to whites—have created the basis for the current racial wealth divide. If the gap is to be closed, government policies will have to play an important role.

It's long past time to close the gap.

The concept of meritocracy, in which opportunities and wealth are bestowed upon those who most deserve them, seems foundational in a democracy. But according to Harvard law professor Lani Guinier, there are fundamental flaws in how we define and measure "merit." Guinier says the current system undervalues the "merit" of poor people and people of color.

THE MERITOCRACY MYTH

An interview with Lani Guinier

BY REBECCA PARRISH
January/February 2006

Lani Guinier became a household name in 1993 when Bill Clinton appointed her to head the Civil Rights Division of the Justice Department and then, under pressure from conservatives, withdrew her nomination without a confirmation hearing. Guinier is currently the Bennett Boskey Professor of Law at Harvard University where, in 1998, she became the first black woman to be tenured at the law school.

Guinier has authored and co-authored numerous books including, most recently, *The Miner's Canary: Enlisting Race, Resisting Power, Transforming Democracy* (2002, with Gerald Torres); and *Who's Qualified?: A New Democracy Forum on Creating Equal Opportunity in School and Jobs* (2001).

Guinier's forthcoming book is *Meritocracy Inc.: How Wealth Became Merit, Class Became Race, and College Education Became a Gift from the Poor to the Rich* (Harvard University Press*)*; she offered a glimpse of its analysis in this interview with *D&S* intern Rebecca Parrish.

Rebecca Parrish: What is meritocracy? What is the difference between the conventional understanding and the way you are using the term in Meritocracy, Inc.?

Lani Guinier: The conventional understanding of meritocracy is that it is a system for awarding or allocating scarce resources to those who most deserve them. The idea behind meritocracy is that people should achieve status or realize the promise of upward mobility based on their individual talent or individual effort. It is conceived as a repudiation of systems like aristocracy where individuals inherit their social status.

I am arguing that many of the criteria we associate with individual talent and effort do not measure the individual in isolation but rather parallel the phenomena associated with aristocracy; what we're calling individual talent is actually a function of that individual's social position or opportunities gained by virtue of family and ancestry. So, although the system we call "meritocracy" is presumed to be more democratic and egalitarian than aristocracy, it is in fact reproducing that which it was intended to dislodge.

Michael Young, a British sociologist, created the term in 1958 when he wrote a science fiction novel called *The Rise of Meritocracy*. The book was a satire in which he depicted a society where people in power could legitimate their status using "merit" as the justificatory terminology and in which others could be determined not simply to have been poor or left out but to be deservingly disenfranchised.

RP: How did you become interested in studying meritocracy in the first place?

LG: I became interested in the 1990s as a result of looking at the performance of women in law school. A student and I became interested in the disparity between the grades that men and women at an Ivy League law school were receiving. Working with Michelle Fein and Jean Belan, we found that male and female students were coming in with basically the same credentials. The minor difference was that the women tended to have entered with slightly higher undergraduate grades and the men with higher LSATs.

The assumption at that time was that incoming credentials predicted how you would perform. Relying on things like the LSAT allowed law school officials to say they were determining admission based on merit. So several colleagues told me to look at the LSAT scores because they were confident that I might find something to explain the significant differences in performance. But we found that, surprisingly, the LSAT was actually a very poor predictor of performance for both men and women, that this "objective" marker which determined who could even gain access was actually not accomplishing its ostensible mandate.

I then became interested in studying meritocracy because of the attacks poor and working class whites were waging against Affirmative Action. People were arguing that they were rejected from positions because less qualified people of color were taking their spots. I began to question what determines who is qualified. Then, the more research I did, the more I discovered that these so-called markers of merit did not actually correlate with future performance in college but rather correlated more with an applicant's parents' and even grandparents' wealth. Schools were substituting markers of wealth for merit.

RP: As a theorist of democracy, how do you approach issues of educational equity and achievement differently from other scholars? Are current educational institutions democratic?

LG: My approach builds on and borrows from work of many other scholars. It perhaps expands on it or shifts emphasis. For example, many people defend Affirmative Action on grounds that there are multiple measures of merit and that bringing diverse students to the school would benefit the learning environment. The problem with this argument is that it pits diversity as a counterpoint to merit. And, the argument is not strong enough to counter the belief in "merit" as an egalitarian and democratic way to allocate scarce resources. I am arguing that there are fundamental flaws in the over-reliance on these supposedly objective indicators of merit. This approach positions poor people and people of color as the problem rather than problematizing the ways we measure merit in the first place.

RP: Can you talk about the Harvard and Michigan studies?

LG: Harvard University did a study based on thirty Harvard graduates over a thirty-year period. They wanted to know which students were most likely to exemplify the things that Harvard values most: doing well financially, having a satisfying career and contributing to society (especially in the form of donating to Harvard). The two variables that most predicted which students would achieve these criteria were low SAT scores and a blue-collar background.

That study was followed by one at the University of Michigan Law School that found that those most likely to do well financially, maintain a satisfying career, and contribute to society, were black and Latino students who were admitted pursuant to Affirmative Action. Conversely, those with the highest LSAT scores were the least likely to mentor younger attorneys, do pro-bono work, sit on community boards, etc.

So, the use of these so called "measures of merit" like standardized tests is backfiring on our institutions of higher learning and blocking the road to a more democratic society.

RP: You refer to college education as a gift from poor to rich.

LG: Anthony Carnevaly made that statement when he was the vice president of the Educational Testing Service. He did a study of 146 of the most selective colleges and universities and found that 74% of students came from the top 25% of the socio-economic spectrum. Only 3% came from the lowest quartile and 10% (which is 3% plus 7%) came from the bottom half. So that means that 50% of people in the country are providing substantial state and federal taxes to both public and private institutions even though they are among those least well off and are being excluded from the opportunity.

RP: In *Meritocracy Inc.*, you'll be exploring the relationship between class and race in structuring US society. What insights can you offer into their relationship? How can we think about class and race in our efforts to democratize higher education?

LG: The argument I'm making is that in many ways race is being used as a stand in for class. I am not saying that race and class are coterminous but that people look at race and see race because it is highly visible but they don't see class.

RP: Can you give some examples?

LG: In Arkansas in 1957 whites rioted as Central High School in Little Rock was desegregated by nine carefully-chosen middle-class black students. The rage and hate on people's faces was broadcast on national television and President Eisenhower had to send in the National Guard to ensure that blacks could get an education. What most people don't know is that at same time as the leaders of city of Little Rock planned the desegregation of Central High, they built and opened a new high school located in an area where the sons and daughters of the doctors and lawyers lived.

Blacks were coming in at the same time that upper-class whites were exiting and this was part of what provoked the intense backlash; there was the sense among the working-class whites who remained that their chances for upward mobility were lost because they could no longer fraternize with the middle and upper class. Previously, there were only two high schools in Little Rock, one white and one black. So Central High was segregated by race and integrated by class. Now Central was integrated by race and segregated by class.

Beth Roy did interviews with white graduates of Central High thirty years later [for her book *Bitters in the Honey*] and determined that many of them still blame blacks for the failure of themselves and their children to gain a secure toehold in a middle class lifestyle. They think that the American Dream owed them individual opportunity through its promise that if you work hard and play by the rules you will succeed. The problem with the American Dream is that it offers no explanation for failure other than that you deserve your lot in life and that if you fail there must be something wrong with you. Many people are perfectly willing to believe that success is individual but don't want to think about failure as individual and no one wants to believe that they deserve to fail. So they find a scapegoat and blacks were an easy scapegoat in this case. Even thirty years later, the white graduates of Central High claimed that blacks stole the American Dream.

While the integration of Central was hyper-visible, the building of Hall High was kept under wraps—most people still don't know about it. Wealthier whites were able to get away with building Hall High because blacks were used as a scapegoat.

RP: You and Gerald Torres wrote about the Texas Ten Percent Plan in *The Miner's Canary*. How does that relate to this?

LG: Sheryl Hopwood was a white working-class woman who applied to the University of Texas Law School and was denied admission. In 1996, she sued the university for racial discrimination, arguing that less qualified blacks and Latinos had taken her spot. Thirty-nine years after Central, she sued in the district court and then in the Fifth Circuit and won, but the problem with the court's analysis was that they did not look behind the school's claim that all slots, except for those bestowed through Affirmative Action, were distributed based on merit.

It actually turns out that the school's own formula for determining merit disadvantaged Sheryl Hopwood. She went to a community college and the University of Texas Law weighted her LSAT scores with those of other applicants from her school and graduating year. Because her community college drew from a working class population, Hopwood's own LSAT score was negatively weighted. So Hopwood's chance of attending the University of Texas was diminished because of class status not because of her race.

After the ruling in Hopwood's favor, a group of legislators and concerned citizens determined that the University of Texas would not return to its segregationist roots. They started investigating the population of the University of Texas graduate school and found that 75% students admitted according to "merit" were coming from only 10% of high schools in the state. These schools tended to be suburban, white, and middle or upper class. Their logic was that if the University of Texas is supposed to be a flagship school and a place from which the state's leaders would be drawn, then 10% of students from each high school in the state should be automatically eligible for access. So the Texas Ten Percent Plan was passed by the legislature and Governor Bush signed it into law.

It all started with concern about racial diversity but it was discovered that class was also at the core. The law ultimately passed because a conservative republican legislator voted for the law when he learned that not one of his constituents, who were white and poor or working class, had been admitted in the previous cycle. So, "meritocratic" standards were keeping out poor and working class whites, especially the rural poor. Many people worried that if SAT scores were eliminated as marker, then grades would go down. However, those who've come in based on the Ten Percent plan have had higher freshman year grades.

RP: You've said before that race is being used as a decoy.

LG: Race was being used as a decoy for class, leading working-class and poor whites to challenge Affirmative Action, and to challenge the integration of Central High School. In fact, meritocratic standards, which favor the wealthy, have kept them out. Too often, poor and working class whites are willing to throw their lot in with upper class and middle class whites because class is obscured while race is quite visible. People think that if anyone can succeed, if these other whites can succeed, then they can too because merit claims to be about the individual operating without regard to background conditions.

RP: So what are the background conditions of students of color attending elite universities?

LG: Many students admitted through Affirmative Action are not that different from those admitted through conventional standards of merit because schools are so committed to the annual issue of *U.S. News and World Report* that ranks educational institutions according to the their students' standardized test scores.

In Ivy League schools, a large percentage of Latinos and blacks are foreign-born and don't identify with communities of color who are born in the United States. I'm not arguing that international students should not have access to U.S. institutions. It is significant, however, that in the '70s and '80s, blacks and Latinos entering through Affirmative Action were coming in from poor U.S. communities and were passionate about returning to those communities and lifting as they climbed. Currently, schools are more concerned about admitting people that have high SAT scores who will boost their status than recruiting leaders. Education is changing from an opportunity for students to explore and grow to institutions that are consumed with rankings. Education is becoming about providing credentials to obtain high-paying jobs rather than training people for a thriving democracy.

"The feminization of poverty," "the gender gap"—these terms have helped put women's economic status onto the agenda in both rich and poor countries. We know that in the United States, the racial wealth gap outpaces the racial income gap in both magnitude and, very likely, effects. Is the same true for gender? Here, Dollars & Sense *co-editor Amy Gluckman reviews what we know about women and wealth ownership, in the United States and globally.*

WOMEN AND WEALTH: A PRIMER

BY AMY GLUCKMAN
August 2004

Put "wealth" and "women" into the same sentence, and contradictory images jump to mind: from Cleopatra, Marie Antoinette ("let them eat cake"), or Oprah to an anonymous Asian, Latin American, or African woman lugging buckets or bales along a rugged path. Each of these images bears some truth: women's relationship with wealth is not a simple one. Women have, historically, held every possible juxtaposition with wealth and property. They have been property themselves, essentially sold in marriage, and in some instances inherited upon a husband's death by his brother or other male relative. They have almost universally faced restricted rights to own, control, and inherit property compared to men. Yet women have also been fabulously wealthy, and in not insignificant numbers—sometimes benefiting from family-owned wealth, occasionally wealthy in their own right. Today, according to a recent report in Datamonitor, more than half of Britain's millionaires are women.

Furthermore, women's access to wealth is always conditioned by race, ethnicity, class, and all of the other parameters that shape the distribution of wealth in any society. Her gender is never the sole factor that shapes a woman's acquisition or use of property.

Marriage in particular has acted as a double-edged sword for women. On one hand, marriage typically gives a woman access to a man's income and wealth, affording her a higher standard of living than most social orders would have allowed her to achieve on her own. On the other hand, women have widely lost rights to own, control, and inherit wealth when they married. And when divorced or widowed, women have sometimes lost the access that marriage afforded them to their husbands' property without gaining any renewed rights to the property of their natal families.

Discriminatory laws and customs in many parts of the world have broken down, although it's sobering to remember how recent this change has been. In the United States, the first state to enact a comprehensive law removing restrictions on property ownership by married women was New York, in 1848. (Mississippi passed a limited statute in 1839. In a clear illustration of the complicated nexus of race, class, and gender that always shapes wealth ownership, the Mississippi law was primarily focused on giving married women the right to own slaves; the law was likely intended to offer plantation owners a way to avoid having their slaves seized to pay the husband's debts.) Other states were still passing similar laws up to 1900, and discrimination on the basis of sex and marital status in granting credit was made illegal at the federal level only in 1974. And of course, custom and economic institutions continued to discriminate against women in the ownership and control of property, access to credit in their own names, and related matters long after laws had been changed.

Around the world, many countries have only recently granted women—or married women in particular—property rights. A 2000 U.N. report lists Bolivia, the Dominican Republic, Eritrea, Malaysia, Nepal, Uganda, Tanzania, and Zimbabwe among countries that have recently passed laws recognizing women's ownership of land, for example. Many countries still lack statutes giving women an express right to own land or other wealth in their own names.

FREE BUT NOT EQUAL

Even with the right to own wealth, women have not necessarily had the means to accumulate any. Among the factors key to building assets are income, education, and inheritance—and, of course, in each of these, women face obstacles, whether customary or legal.

In the rich countries, women today have largely the same educational attainment as men—up to, but not including, the highest levels. In the United States, for example, more girls than boys graduate from high school, and more women than men are enrolled in bachelor's degree programs. But there are still far more men than women who hold advanced degrees, especially in lucrative fields such as engineering, business, law, and medicine. Women workers remain concentrated in female-dominated occupations that continue to pay less than male-dominated occupations requiring the same degree of skill, preparation, and responsibility. This is a key reason for the persistent gender pay gap. The median income of U.S. men working full-time, year-round was $38,275 in 2001; the equivalent figure for women was $29,215, or only 76% of men's pay.

Women in the global South continue to face far larger education and income gaps, although with great variation among countries. For example, Yemen, Pakistan, and Niger all have female-male adult literacy ratios under 60%, while Jordan, Sri Lanka, and Cameroon all have ratios of 95% or above. Income data disaggregated by sex is not available for many countries, according the most recent U.N. Human Development Report. But the report's rough estimates show a substantial gender gap in income in every country. And in many developing countries, women continue to hold only limited rights to inherit property.

Plenty of factors account for women's lack of wealth accumulation across the globe, but working too little is certainly not one of them. Women work longer hours every day than men in most countries, according to time-use studies assembled by the United Nations. The unequal work burden is most pronounced in rural areas, where women typically work 20% more minutes a day than men. Environmental problems in many countries have exacerbated women's work burden; a Population Reference Bureau report notes that "Given the variety of women's daily interactions with the environment to meet household needs, they are often most keenly affected by its degradation. In the Sudan, deforestation in the last decade has led to a quadrupling of women's time spent gathering fuelwood. Because girls are often responsible for collecting water and fuelwood, water scarcity and deforestation also contribute to higher school dropout rates for girls."

WOMEN'S WEALTH HOLDINGS: WHAT WE KNOW

Today's wealth distribution reflects the accumulation of assets over years, even generations. So it will take time before the uneven but dramatic changes in women's status over the past few decades will show up in the wealth statistics. Given that, what is the distribution of wealth by gender today?

The first thing to note is that we really don't know what it is, for a number of reasons. First, data on personal wealth are scarce. Most countries do not systematically collect data on wealth ownership. Among the few countries that do are the United States, Sweden, Germany, and Britain.

Where data *are* regularly collected, the unit is typically the household, not the individual. Thus the assets of most married couples are assigned to both wife and husband equally in wealth surveys, obscuring any differences in the two spouses' authority to manage or benefit from those assets or to retain them if the marriage ends. This leaves gender comparisons possible only between unmarried men and unmarried women, a minority of the adult population.

In many countries, property ownership is governed by customary or informal rules rather than legal title. The term "ownership" itself is a simplification; ownership is really a bundle of rights that don't necessarily reside in the same person. In statutory systems and particularly in customary systems, women may have limited ownership rights; for example, a woman may have the right to use a piece of property but not to transfer or bequeath it. This limits the value of any simple, quantitative snapshot of wealth distribution by gender. Instead, a complex qualitative portrait is necessary.

Given all of these limitations, what *do* we know?

In the United States, the significant gap is between married and unmarried people. Married-couple households have median net worth far more than two times that of households headed by unmarried adults. However, there is also a gender gap between unmarried men and unmarried women. The median net worth of single female-headed households in 2001 was $28,000; of single male-headed households, $47,000. And this gap has to be viewed in relation to the greater financial responsibilities of single women: a greater portion of single-female headed households include children under 18. There is also a vast wealth gap between white women and women of color: the median net worth of households headed by single white women was $56,590 in 2001; of households headed by single African-American women, $5,700; and of households headed by single Hispanic women, $3,900.

The young baby-boomer cohort, looked at separately, shows nearly no wealth gap between unmarried men and women. This suggests that women are catching up—at least in a rich country like the United States. This is not surprising, as women are moving toward parity with men in several of the factors correlated with higher net worth, such as education and income. However, the income gap has long been smaller between young women and men than between older women and men, at least in part because the workforce participation of women—who typically bear greater parenting responsibilities than men—becomes more uneven over time. As the young boomers age, how much the wealth gap is really shrinking will become more clear.

For the global South, systematic personal wealth data simply do not exist. But it's possible to assess some of the factors that are shaping the distribution of wealth by gender in poor and middle-income nations. The transition to formal systems of property ownership has had complex effects in many poor, predominantly rural countries. In theory, holding legal title to land can benefit small farmers—many of whom around the world are women. With a legal title, a farmer can use the land as collateral and thereby gain access to credit; she can also more confidently invest in improvements. However, in the process of formalizing land titles, governments have often taken land that was customarily under a woman's control and given the title to it to a man. Likewise, land reform programs have often bypassed women. Women were "left out of the agrarian reforms of the 1960s and 1970s" in Latin America, according to a U.N. report, because household heads, to whom land titles were given, were simply assumed to be men. Women do 60% to 80% of the agricultural labor throughout the developing world, but are not nearly as likely to be actual landowners: the percentage of agricultural landowners who are women ranges from 3% in Bangladesh to 57% in Namibia, and their average holdings are smaller than men's.

Lacking formal title to land, women have very limited access to agricultural credit. The same is true outside of agriculture: of the 300 million low-income self-employed women in the global South, hardly any have access to credit (aside from moneylenders, who typically charge exorbitant interest rates that can range up to 100% a month). Microcredit programs have sprung up in many countries and are making a dent in this problem, but just a dent. Although it's now worth some $2.5 billion, the microcredit sector reaches only an estimated 3% of those across the global South (both women and men) who could benefit from it.

Liberalization and structural adjustment policies pressed on third world governments have been hard on women's economic status. Consider the case of Mexico where, following the introduction of economic liberalization in the mid-1980s, growth has been slow for everyone. But women have suffered dispro-portionately. With the opening of lots of export-oriented *maquiladoras*, women's share of industrial jobs grew. But women's industrial wages fell from 80% of men's in 1984 to 57% of men's in 1992. At the same time, the bland term "struc-tural adjustment" means, in practice, often-huge cutbacks in public services such as health care, education, and aid to the poor. Women (and children) are typically more dependent on these programs than men, and so suffer more when they are cut.

WHAT IS WEALTH GOOD FOR?

Does it matter if women have less wealth and less capacity to acquire and control assets than men? Most adult women across the globe are married, and for most married women, these forms of gender-specific discrimination do not prevent them from enjoying a family standard of living underwritten by their husbands' income and wealth. But a woman's ability to own property in her own name turns out to be more important than it might appear. Women with property are less vulnerable to all of life's vicissitudes. Owning property can protect women affected by HIV/AIDS from destitution, for example; the International Center for Research on Women is currently documenting this association.

And asset ownership changes the balance of power between women and men. In a study of 500 urban and rural women in Kerala, India, Pradeep Panda of the Centre for Development Studies, Trivandrum, and Bina Agarwal of the Institute of Economic Growth, Delhi, found that women who are wealthless are considerably more vulnerable to domestic violence than women who own property. The study's remarkable results are worth quoting at length:

> The study's findings did bear out the fact that ownership of immovable property by women is associated with a dramatically lower incidence of both physical and psychological harassment, as well as long-term and current violence. For

example, as many as 49% of the women who owned neither land nor house suffered long-term physical violence, compared with 18% and 10% respectively of those who owned either land or a house, and 7% of those who owned both.

The effect of property ownership on psychological violence is even more dramatic. While 84% of property-less women suffered abuse, the figure was much lower (16%) for women who owned both land and a house.

The ownership of property also offers women the option of leaving an abusive environment—of the 179 women experiencing long-term physical violence, 43 left home. The percentage of women leaving home was much higher among the propertied (71%) than among those without property (19%). Moreover, of the women who left home, although 24 returned, 88% of the returning women were property-less. Few propertied women returned.

So, not only are propertied women less likely to experience marital violence, they are also able to escape further violence. Hence, property ownership serves both as a deterrent and as an exit option for abused women.

Interestingly, while a fair proportion of women (propertied and property-less) faced dowry demands, only 3% of propertied women faced dowry-related beatings by their in-laws and husbands, compared to 44% of property-less women. This suggests another form in which the ownership of personal property lessens the incidence of domestic crimes against women.

The protective impact of house or land ownership on reducing a woman's risk of violence emerged as significant even after such factors as household economic status, a woman's age, duration of marriage, childlessness, educational and employment levels of both husband and wife, spousal gaps in education or employment, the husband's alcohol consumption, childhood exposure to violence and social support from parents and neighbours were controlled.

In contrast to a woman's property ownership status, there seems to be no clear relationship between risk of violence and employment status, except if the woman has a regular job. This reduces the risk only of long-term physical violence. Employment does not offer the same protection to women as does property ownership. ... Land access enhances a woman's livelihood options and gives her a sense of empowerment.

It has long been a shibboleth in the U.S. women's movement that all women can face domestic violence regardless of their economic circumstances. But owning and controlling some wealth surely offers women in rich countries the same kinds of protection the Kerala study revealed: a stronger position in the marital power dynamic, and the ability to exit. And owning some property no doubt underwrites a woman's ability to struggle against patriarchal institutions in other ways too, at least on an individual level, and to achieve her own potential. Virginia Woolf wrote a century ago that a woman who wanted to create needed a modest (unearned) income and a room of her own; Woolf's vision is no less true today.

But today most women around the world still don't have the modest unearned income or the room of their own—and not only because of their gender. What then would a progressive feminist agenda around wealth look like? Of course, it would address all of the remaining customs, statutes, and institutional barriers that limit women's economic rights relative to men's. But it would also seek to reorient all economic institutions toward the provision of social forms of wealth and the deconcentration of private wealth. Only a dual agenda like this can offer any hope—for achieving either gender equity *or* a decent standard of living—to a majority of the world's women.

A society's system of property rights underlies its distribution of wealth. It sets the rules that determine how ownership is defined, what benefits accrue to those defined as owners, and at what cost to the larger social good.

PROPERTY

Who Has a Right to What and Why?

BY ARTHUR MACEWAN
August 2004

I n 1948, siblings Joseph and Agnes Waschak purchased a home in Taylor, Pennsylvania, in the midst of coal mining country. Within a few years, hydrogen sulfide fumes and other gases from the nearby mines and mine waste turned the Waschaks' white house black and stained all the internal fixtures yellowish-brown or black. The Waschaks filed suit for damages. According to evidence presented in the subsequent court case, the Waschaks and other area residents who were forced to breathe the gases "suffered from headaches, throat irritation, inability to sleep, coughing, light-headedness, nausea and stomach ailments."

Eric Freyfogle describes the *Waschak v. Moffat* case in his book *The Land We Share: Private Property and the Common Good* as an illustration of how changing concepts of property relate to the preservation of the natural environment. Eventually, the case worked its way up to the Pennsylvania Supreme Court. *Waschak v. Moffat* was not simply an instance of citizens challenging property owners, but of one set of property owners positioned against another. On one side were the Waschaks and others who claimed that the actions of the coal companies constituted a nuisance that prevented them from fully using their property; on the other side were the coal companies who wanted to use their mines as they saw fit. The court had to decide not *whether* property rights would prevail, but *which* set of property rights had priority.

In 1954, the court ruled that a nuisance existed only when the actions involved were intentional or the result of negligence. The coal companies, the court maintained, intended no harm and were not negligent because they were following standard practices in the mining industry. The Waschaks lost.

Four decades later, concepts of property rights and priorities had changed, as illustrated by a 1998 case in Iowa, *Borman v. Board of Supervisors,* also described by Freyfogle. In this case, the landowning plaintiffs wanted to prevent another landowner from developing a "Confined Animal Feeding Operation" (CAFO) that would involve thousands of animals generating large amounts of waste, odors, and other damage to the surrounding properties. Again, the dispute was between the conflicting rights of two sets of property owners.

The Iowa Supreme Court ruled in favor of the plaintiffs, agreeing that the nuisance that would be created by the CAFO would be an illegitimate interference with their property rights. The court did not deny that its ruling limited the property rights of the CAFO planners, but it gave priority to the rights of the plaintiffs. Moreover, the court ruled that the CAFO planners were not due any compensation by the state, even though it was preventing them from using their land as they chose and thereby reducing the value of that property.

What changed between 1954 and 1998? Many things were different, of course, including the fact that the earlier case was in one state and the later case in another. But the most important difference was that society's views on environmental issues had changed, evolving along with the development of a broad social movement to protect the environment. As a result, concepts regarding property rights changed. What had earlier been seen as legitimate action by a property owner was, by the end of century, viewed as an illegitimate degradation of the environment.

Property rights, it turns out, are not fixed. They change. They are a product of society and of social decisions. As society changes, so too do property rights. And the changes in property rights are contested, subject to political power and social struggle.

WHY DO WE PROTECT PRIVATE PROPERTY?

Although we often take property rights for granted, as though they are based on some absolute standard, in reality they are both changing and ambiguous. Moreover, many widely accepted ideas about property rights start to fall apart when we ask: Why do we protect private property?

For example, suppose a family has a deed on a particular field. Why do we as a society say that another family cannot come along, take part of that field, and sow and reap their own crops? Does it make any difference if the family with the deed has never used the field for any productive purpose, but has simply let it sit idle?

Or, for another example, suppose a pharmaceutical company develops a new antibiotic. Why do we allow that company the right to take out a patent and then prevent other firms or individuals from producing and selling that same antibiotic? Does it make any difference if the antibiotic is one that would save the lives of many people were it more readily available—that is, available at a lower price than the company charges?

Or, for still another example, what if a man owns a large house in the suburbs, an extensive apartment in the city, a ski lodge in the mountains, a beach house at the shore, two or three other homes at convenient sites, three yachts, a jet plane, and seven cars? Why do we prevent a poor man who has nothing—no home, no car, and certainly no yacht or jet plane—from occupying one of these many homes?

Perhaps the most common argument in favor of our protection of private property is the claim: We protect private property because it works to do so. That is, secure property rights are viewed as a basis for a stable and prosperous society. If people do not know that their accumulated wealth—held in the form of cash, land, houses, or factories—will be protected by society, they will see little point in trying to accumulate. According to the argument, if the pharmaceutical company cannot be assured of the profit from its patent, it will have no incentive to finance the research that leads to the drug's development. And if the state did not protect people's wealth, society could be in a continual state of instability and conflict.

As a defense of private property rights, however, this it-works-to-do-so argument is incomplete, as the *Waschak* and *Borman* cases illustrate, because it does not tell us what to do when property rights come into conflict with one another. This defense of property rights is also flawed because it is too vague, failing to provide a sufficiently clear statement of what things can legitimately be held as private property. Can air or water or people be held as private property? Can a patent be held forever?

What's more, the argument puts defenders of property rights in a precarious position because it implicitly concedes that private property rights exist in order to serve the larger good of society. If we determine that the larger good of society dictates a change in property rights—new restrictions on the use of property, for example—then the it-works-to-do-so argument provides no defense.

In many instances, property owners have claimed that environmental regulations infringe on their property rights. Property owners who are prevented from establishing a CAFO as in the Borman case, from filling wetlands, from building along fragile coast lines, or from destroying the habitat of an endangered species argue that government regulation is, in effect, taking away their property because it is reducing the value of that property. And they demand payment for this "taking." Such a claim loses its ideological and legal force, however, in a world where property rights change, where they are a creation of society, and where the larger good of society is the ultimate justification for protecting private property.

While questions about property rights are surrounded by ideology, legal complications, and arguments about the larger good of society, at the core of these questions lie fundamental disputes about the distribution of wealth. Who gets to use a field, the extent of a pharmaceutical company's patent rights, the preservation of a rich man's houses—each of these examples illustrates a conflict over the distribution of wealth as much as it illustrates a complication of how we define and protect property rights. Property rights are the rules of the game by which society's wealth gets divided up, and how we shape those rules is very much connected to how we define the larger good of society.

PATENTS VERSUS LIFE

The relationship between property rights and the larger good of society has come to a head in recent years in the dispute over patent rights and AIDS drugs. It has become increasingly apparent that, when it comes to protecting the property rights of the pharmaceutical companies that hold patents on these life-saving drugs, it-*doesn't*-work-to-do-so.

In low-income countries, multinational pharmaceutical companies have attempted to enforce their patents on life-saving AIDS drugs and prevent the provision of these drugs at affordable prices. The matter has been especially important in several African countries where governments, ignoring the companies' patents, have taken steps to allow local production or importation of low-cost generic forms of the drugs. Large pharmaceutical corporations such as Glaxo, Merck, and Roche have fought back, and their resistance has received extensive support from the U.S. government. In 1998, for example, the South African government of Nelson Mandela passed a law allowing local firms to produce low-cost versions of the AIDS drugs on which U.S. pharmaceutical firms hold patents. The Clinton administration responded on behalf of the firms, accusing the South Africans of "unfair trade practices" and threatening the country with trade sanctions if it implemented the law. The drug companies have since backed off, seeking compromises that would allow access to the drugs in particular cases but that would avoid precedents undermining their property rights in the patents.

The conflict between patent rights and the availability of AIDS drugs, however, has continued and spread. In Thailand, for example, the Government Pharmaceutical Organization (GPO) sought permission from the country's Commerce Department to produce a drug, didanosine, for which Bristol-Myers Squibb holds the patent. In spite of the fact that the locally produced drug would allow treatment of close to a million HIV-positive people in Thailand who would otherwise be unable to afford the didanosine, the permission was rejected because the Thai Commerce Department feared trade retaliation from the United States. Instead, the GPO was only allowed to produce a form of the drug that has greater side effects. Early in 2004, however, Bristol-Myers Squibb ceded the issue. Fearing public outcry and damaging precedents in the courts, the company surrendered in Thailand its exclusive patent rights to manufacture and sell the drug.

These conflicts have not been confined to the particular case of AIDS drugs, but have also been major issues in World Trade Organization (WTO) negotiations on the international extension of patent rights in general. Popular pressure and government actions in several low-income regions of the world have forced compromises from the companies and at the WTO.

But the dispute is far from over, and it is not just about formal issues of property rights and patents. At its core, it is a dispute over whether medical advances will be directed toward the larger good of society or toward greater profits for the pharmaceutical companies and their shareholders. It is a dispute over the distribution of wealth and income.

"FREE THE MOUSE!"

Patents and, similarly, copyrights are a form of property (known as "intellectual property") that is quite clearly a creation of society, and the way society handles patents and copyrights does a great deal to shape the distribution of wealth and income. Acting through the state (the Department of Commerce in the United States), society gives the creator of a new product exclusive rights—in effect, monopoly control —to make, use, or sell the item, based on the general rationale that doing so will encourage the creation of more products (machines, books, music, pharmaceuticals, etc.).

The general rationale for these property rights, however, does not tell us very much about their nature. How long should patents and copyrights last? What can and what cannot be patented? What, exactly, constitutes an infringement of the copyright holder's property rights? And what if the rationale is wrong in the first place? What if patent and copyright protections are not necessary to promote creative activity? The answer to each of these questions is contested terrain, changing time and again as a consequence of larger political and social changes.

Beyond the issue of AIDS drugs, there are several other patent or copyright-related conflicts that illustrate how these rights change through conflict and the exercise of political power. One case is the Napster phenomenon, where people have shared music files over the Internet and generated outcry and lawsuits from music companies. This battle over property rights, inconceivable a generation ago, is now the subject of intense conflict in the courts.

An especially interesting case where rights have been altered by the effective use of political power has been the Mickey Mouse matter. In 1998, Congress passed the Sonny Bono Copyright Term Extension Act, extending copyright protection 20 years beyond what existing regulations provided for. One of the prime beneficiaries of—and one of the strongest lobbyists for—this act was the Disney company; the act assures Disney's control over Mickey Mouse until 2023—and Pluto, Goofy, and Donald Duck until 2025, 2027, and 2029, respectively.

Not surprisingly, the Copyright Extension Act aroused opposition, campaigning under the banner "Free the Mouse!" Along with popular efforts, the act was challenged in the courts. While the challenge had particular legal nuances, it was based on the seemingly reasonable argument that the Copyright Extension Act, which protects creative activity retroactively, could have no impact now on the efforts of authors and composers who created their works in the first half of the 20th century. The Supreme Court, apparently deciding that its view of the law trumped this reasonable argument, upheld the act. Congress and the Court provided a valuable handout to Disney and other firms, but it is hard to see how a 20-year extension of copyright protection will have any significant impact on creative efforts now or in the future.

"COULD YOU PATENT THE SUN?"

Indeed, in a recent paper issued by the Federal Reserve Bank of Minneapolis, economists Michele Boldrin and David K. Levine suggest that the government's granting of protection through patents and copyrights may not be necessary to encourage innovation. When government does grant these protections, it is granting a form of monopoly. Boldrin and Levine argue that when "new ideas are built on old ideas," the monopoly position embodied in patents and copyrights may stifle rather than encourage creativity. Microsoft, a firm that has prospered by building new ideas on old ideas and then protecting itself with patents and copyrights, provides a good example, for it is also a firm that has attempted to control new innovations and limit the options of competitors who might bring further advances. (Microsoft, dependent as it is on microprocessors developed in federal research programs and on the government-sponsored emergence of the Internet, is also a good example of the way property is often brought into being by public, government actions and then appropriated by private interests. But that is another story.)

Boldrin and Levine also point out that historically there have been many periods of thriving innovation in the absence of patents and copyrights. The economic historian David Landes relates how medieval Europe was "one of the most inventive societies that history has known." Landes describes, as examples, the development of the water wheel (by the early 11th century), eyeglasses (by the early 14th century), and the mechanical clock (by the late 13th century). Also, first invented by the Chinese in the ninth century, printing rapidly developed in Europe by the middle of the 15th century with the important addition of movable type. Yet the first patent statute was not enacted until 1474, in Venice, and the system of patents spread widely only with the rise of the Industrial Revolution. (There had been earlier ad hoc patents granted by state authorities, but these had limited force.)

Even in the current era, experience calls into question the necessity of patents and copyrights to spur innovations. The tremendous expansion of creativity on the Internet and the associated advances of open-access software, in spite of Microsoft's best efforts to limit potential competitors, illustrate the point.

The most famous inventor in U.S. history, Benjamin Franklin, declined to obtain patents for his various devices, offering the following principle in his autobiography: "That as we enjoy great Advantages from the Inventions of Others, we should be glad of an Opportunity to serve others by any Invention of ours, and this we should do freely and generously." Probably the most outstanding example of successful research and scientific advance without the motivation of patents and consequent financial rewards is the development of the polio vaccine. Jonas Salk, the principal creator of the polio vaccine, like Franklin, did not seek patents for his invention, one that has saved and improved countless lives around the world. Salk was once asked who would control the new drug. He replied: "Well, the people, I would say. There is no patent. Could you patent the sun?"

It turns out, then, that there is no simple answer to the question: "Why do we protect private property?" because the meaning of private property rights is not fixed but is a continually changing product of social transformation, social conflict, and political power. The courts are often the venue in which property rights are defined, but, as illustrated by the Pennsylvania and Iowa cases, the definitions provided by the courts change along with society.

The scourge of AIDS combined with the advent of the current wave of globalization have established a new arena for conflict over patent laws governing pharmaceuticals, and an international social movement has arisen to contest property laws in this area. The advances of information technology have likewise generated a new round of legal changes, and the interests, demands, and actions of a vast array of music listeners will be a major factor affecting those changes. With the emergence of the environmental movement and widespread concern for the protection of the natural environment, traditional views of how owners can use their land are coming into question. When society begins to question property rights, it is also questioning the distribution of wealth and income, and it is questioning the distribution of power.

Few realms of property rights can be taken for granted for very long. Whether we are talking about property in the most tangible form as land or property in the intangible form of patents and copyrights, the substance of property rights—who has a right to what and why—is continually changing.

The quality of public schools in the U.S. consistently reflects the income levels of the families whose children attend them. Citing examples of four states that have taken alternative approaches to public education funding, Michael Engel argues that there is no excuse for low-income children to be stuck in underfunded schools.

SCHOOL FINANCE: INEQUALITY PERSISTS

BY MICHAEL ENGEL
Spring 2007

The states vary widely among themselves in terms of support for public education, and there are multiple ways of measuring that variation. Accoring to the federal government's National Center for Education Statistics (NCES), median per pupil expenditure in 2003-2004 ranged from $5,862 in Utah to $14,667 in Alaska; the national median was $7,860. A more significant statistic, calculated by the Census Bureau, is the amount spent by each state per $1,000 of personal income. This measures spending against how much the state's population can potentially afford. In 2003–2004, Florida was at the bottom with $34.36, and Alaska was at the top with $62.92. The figure for the nation as a whole was $43.68.

Perhaps more important is the inequality in spending among school districts *within* each state. The "federal range ratio" for school spending, as reported by the NCES, compares per pupil expenditure in districts spending the least and those spending the most. In Montana, for example, districts at the fifth percentile (those that spend less per pupil than 95% of the districts in the state) spend $5,526 per pupil, versus $19,400 per pupil at the 95th percentile; thus Montana's federal range ratio is 2.51, the highest in the country. (A federal range ratio of zero would denote equal spending across all districts; a federal range ratio of one describes a state where districts at the 95th percentile spend twice as much per pupil as districts at the 5th percentile.) States with relatively low range ratios—for instance, Maryland at 0.32 and Florida at 0.38—are the most "egalitarian."

Putting these three sets of figures together offers a detailed picture of educational inequality in the United States (see Table 1). Interestingly, West Virginia, one of the

TABLE 1

Profile of Public School Spending in Selected States, 2004

		MEDIAN PER PUPIL EXPENDITURE	
		Below the National Median	*Above the National Median*
	0.5 or under (Relatively Equal)	Florida Georgia Louisiana	Maryland North Carolina Wisconsin
FEDERAL RANGE RATIO	0.51 – 0.99 (Moderately Unequal)	Michigan Virginia	Kansas New Jersey New York Pennsylvania Vermont
	1.00 and up (Highly Unequal)	Arizona California Colorado Illinois Oregon Texas Washington	Montana New Mexico

Source: National Center for Education Statistics, "Current Expenditures for Public Elementary and Secondary Education: School Year 2003-04," Table 4, July 2006.

poorest states in the union, spends more than the median amounts *and* has the lowest federal range ratio in the country. The state's school districts are county-wide, which may explain its relatively equitable school funding: wealthier suburban towns cannot fund their own schools well without also supporting the schools in nearby cities.

So far, these data reveal the wide spreads between high- and low-budget school districts. But *which* children are getting the short end of the stick? Here we can look to the Education Trust, whose analysts have calculated the state and local dollars per pupil available to the highest- versus the lowest-poverty school districts and to the districts with the highest versus the lowest minority populations in each state (for 2004). They found that in about half of the states, the one-fourth of school districts with the highest share of poor students had less in state and local dollars to spend per pupil than the one-fourth of districts with the lowest share of poor students.

The variation from one state to another is striking. At the more egalitarian end of the spectrum are states such as New Mexico, Massachusetts, Minnesota, and New Jersey, where the highest-poverty districts have between $1,000 and $2,000 *more* to spend per pupil than the lowest-poverty districts. At the other end are Illinois, New Hampshire, New York, and Pennsylvania, where the highest-poverty districts have between $1,000 and $2,000 *less* to spend per pupil than the lowest-poverty districts.

As the Education Trust analysts note, though, it costs more—not the same—to provide an equal education to poor children. So these figures actually understate the disparity. The report offers the same comparisons cost-adjusted by 40% to account for the higher expense of educating poor children. (See Table 2.) Using the cost-adjusted figures, the highest-poverty districts have less to spend per pupil than the lowest-poverty district in two-thirds of the states. The adjusted figures show a funding gap in Illinois and New York that exceeds $2,000 per pupil. (Just imagine how an additional $60,000 a year could transform the educational environment for a class of 30 fourth graders!) In terms of discrimination against both the poor and minorities, the worst offenders are Arizona, Illinois, Montana, New Hampshire, New York, Texas, and Wyoming. States that rank high in shortchanging minority districts include Kansas, Nebraska, North Dakota, South Dakota, and Wisconsin.

In states with large urban centers surrounded by wealthy suburbs, the differences in school funding can be especially dramatic. Among the 69 school districts within 15 miles of downtown Chicago, for instance, the city itself ranks 50th in per-pupil spending, according to NCES data. Chicago spends $8,356 per pupil; compare that to $18,055 for Evanston and $15,421 for Oak Park, both wealthy suburbs. In fact, Illinois has a terrible record in every respect, but the state Supreme Court has twice explicitly rejected any judicial responsibility for reform. Among the 41 school districts in New York state within 20 miles of downtown Manhattan, New York City ranks 37th, with spending of $13,131 per pupil, compared with Great Neck at $20,995, Lawrence at $22,499, and Manhasset at $22,199. Even among suburbs, poorer ones with larger minority populations such as Mount Vernon fall far behind whiter and more prosperous communities. In New York, court battles continue while the legislature stalls, ignoring deadlines for reform already set by the courts.

These inequalities extend even to differences in funding within school districts, mostly in the form of teacher salary differentials. A 2005 report by the Education Trust-West *California's Hidden Teacher Spending Gap* concluded that "the concentration of more experienced and more highly credentialed teachers (along with their corresponding high salaries) in whiter and more affluent schools drives huge funding gaps between schools—even between schools within the very same school district."

Financial inequality in U.S. public schools is not an anomaly, nor is it the result of a lack of possible remedies. States have undertaken countless so-called reforms

TABLE 2

Funding Gaps for School Districts with the Highest Poor and Minority Enrollments (with 40% adjustment for low-income students)

	Gap between Spending per Student in the Highest- and Lowest-Poverty Districts	Gap between Spending per Student in the Highest- and Lowest-Minority Districts
United States	–$1,307	–$1,213
States that Shortchange (Gap of $600 or more in per pupil spending favoring the lowest-poverty or low-est-minority districts)	New York (–$2,927) Illinois (–$2,355) Pennsylvania (–$1,511) New Hampshire (–$1,297) Montana (–$1,148) Michigan (–$1,072) Vermont (–$894) Kansas (–$885) Texas (–$757) Wisconsin (–$742) Arizona (–$736) Alabama (–$656)	New York (–$2,636) New Hampshire (–$2,392) Montana (–$1,838) Kansas (–$1,630) Illinois (–$1,524) Nebraska (–$1,374) North Dakota (–$1,290) Wisconsin (–$1,270) Texas (–$1,167) South Dakota (–$1,140) Wyoming (–$1,041) Colorado (–$1,032) Maine (–$874) Idaho (–$849) Pennsylvania (–$709) Arizona (–$680) Rhode Island (–$639) Vermont (–$613) Connecticut (–$602
States that Help (Gap of $600 or more in per pupil spending favoring the highest-poverty or highest-minority districts)	Alaska ($2,054) New Jersey ($1,069) Minnesota ($950) Massachusetts ($694) New Mexico ($679)	Massachusetts ($1,139) Indiana ($1,096) New Jersey ($1,087) Ohio ($942) Missouri ($662) Minnesota ($623)

Note: Dollar amounts have been adjusted to account for regional cost differences and for the additional cost of educating students with disabilities.

Source: Education Trust, *Funding Gaps 2006*, Tables 3 & 4.

over the past 20 years—to little effect. Only a few states, however, have taken any *serious* steps to guarantee even an adequate, much less an equal, education for all their children.

COURTROOM REMEDIES

As of 2003, cases challenging the constitutionality of education finance systems had been heard in the courts of 44 states; in 18 of those states, the systems were declared unconstitutional. In 12 states the courts refused to act at all. The court decisions are all over the map in terms of setting standards of adequacy, equity, or equality, requiring legislative action, or prescribing specific remedies. Often it has taken a series of decisions over a number of years to force any change at all. The main overall effect of these rulings has been to push reluctant state legislatures, including those in some states where courts had not yet issued decisions, to modify their educational finance systems.

The outcomes, again, are all over the map, but very few have enacted serious and thorough reforms. For the most part, states have merely tinkered with the existing methods of aiding local schools. The most prevalent method—used in forty-one states—is foundation aid, which sets a statewide minimum per- pupil expenditure and appropriates state funds to make up the difference between that amount and the amounts localities are able (or required) to raise from property taxes. Each state uses a different formula, some so complex as to defy comprehension. Most reforms have involved a change in that formula to benefit poor districts, or a higher foundation level financed by increased state appropriations, or separate and additional grant programs.

A less common and even more complex method is known as "district power equalizing", which essentially guarantees a minimum property tax base to each community. In other words, the state determines the amount of revenue that is to be raised by any given local property tax rate and offers aid to communities whose property tax base is too poor to reach that level. Thus if the state determines a 5% rate should raise $10 million, a community that can only raise $7 million at that tax rate will receive $3 million in state aid. A more radical version, such as the one enacted in Vermont, provides for "recapturing" and redistributing the excess revenues raised by wealthier communities.

Some states combine both methods. In any case, although several states, such as New Jersey and Massachusetts, have managed to improve their formulas to the benefit of poorer communities, none of these adjustments address the basic cause of inequality, namely, reliance on local funding. Overall, in that regard there has been no improvement in twenty years. The state share of public school funding across the nation peaked at 49% in 1985; the federal share peaked at 9% in 1980. Federal aid to elementary and secondary education was $41 billion in 2003, a paltry 2% of the entire federal budget. To the extent that communities continue to have to rely on local property taxes to fund their schools, there is no question that serious inequities will persist.

At least four states, however, have gone beyond the norm. It is instructive to examine their experience with devising school funding systems that ostensibly aim for equality, that is, making sure that no district has a significant financial advantage over any other.

Hawaii is unique in the nation in that the whole state is one school district, and the state government is responsible for appropriating funds to the individual schools. On the surface, this appears to be a perfect example of equal education. Unfortunately, it is not. Until quite recently, funds were appropriated on an enrollment basis, without allowing for the extra costs involved in educating students in high-poverty areas or those with special needs. Moreover, Hawaii ranks 50th in terms of the percent of total state and local government revenues allocated for public education. Per pupil expenditure is just slightly above the national median, and the state ranks 35th in spending per $1,000 of personal income. Thus Hawaii resembles a number of southern states in uniformly underfunding all its public schools.

Kansas adopted a new school finance system in 1992, prompted by a lower court decision invalidating the existing one. The School District Finance and Quality Performance Act set a uniform statewide property tax rate, and established a $3,600 foundation funding level per pupil. The pupil count was weighted to take into account factors such as poverty. State aid was to make up the difference between that foundation level and what each community could raise with the property tax. But an escape hatch was provided by allowing a "local option budget" for communities to raise additional monies, up to 25% over the foundation level. The subsequent failure of the state to fully fund this reform led to widespread use of the local option budget. Richer communities were thus able to raise more money, so pre-existing inequalities continued. According to the Education Trust report, Kansas had one of the largest minority funding gaps in the country in 2003, and the poverty gap increased substantially between 1997 and 2003. The Kansas courts are thus still involved in the issue of educational finance.

Michigan's reforms were not inspired by any court actions. Rather, facing widespread anger over high property taxes, in 1993 Republican governor John Engler bit the bullet by getting the legislature to eliminate the property tax as the basis for school funding. He then forced the issue further by slashing the state education budget, creating a financial crisis for the schools. As a result, voters in 1994 approved a 2% sales tax increase to fund education. Reform legislation set a statewide property tax rate, and localities were not allowed to exceed that rate. State aid would be based on a foundation plan. The result was that the state share of school spending more than doubled. But property taxes still accounted for one-third of school budgets, and with the rate frozen by state mandate, communities with low property values still fell behind. Combined with insufficient state funding (per pupil spending is below the national median), this means that although progress was achieved,

Michigan still has a way to go to provide equal and adequate funding to the schools serving its poorest children.

Vermont's Act 60 came closest to bringing schools toward the ideal of educational equality. In 1995, the state's supreme court ruled that the existing finance system violated the state constitution. Two years later the legislature responded with Act 60, the most radical reform in the country. The new law set a statewide property tax rate and foundation spending level. Localities were allowed to levy additional property taxes, but if revenues from a locality exceeded the foundation amount, that excess reverted to the state and was put into a "sharing pool" used to aid poorer communities. This was essentially a district power equalizing program with a socialist twist. Rich communities were hit hard, and their budget process became guesswork since they had no way of knowing in a timely way how much property tax revenue they would be able to keep for the following year. A political uproar ensued; Act 60 was succeeded by Act 68 in 2004, which kept the statewide property tax and increased the state sales tax, but ended the sharing pool. How this will play out is as yet not clear, but as of 2003-2004, Vermont ranked 2nd in per $1000 spending and 8th in per pupil spending with a relatively low poverty gap.

PROSPECTS FOR CHANGE

The complexity and confusion of school finance systems and of all of the efforts to reform them obscure a simple and obvious solution, which no state has chosen: progressive taxation. If public schools were funded entirely by state and local taxes whose effective rates increase with income and wealth, if state aid was weighted sharply in favor of districts with higher educational costs, if federal aid was increased and similarly appropriated, and if strict limits were placed on local supplementation, financial inequality among schools would be history.

To free-market ideologues and neoclassical economists, these alternatives are obviously anathema. But they are rarely mentioned even by liberal or progressive politicians concerned about educational inequality. For they involve confronting two of the most sensitive issues in American politics: taxes and race. All state and local revenue systems in the United States are regressive to one extent or another. And as Jonathan Kozol points out, racial segregation makes it easy for the majority of public officials, and of whites in general, to ignore the disastrous conditions in predominantly-Black schools.

It would thus take enormous public pressure to force the government to choose a new course and pursue financial equality. If that were done, we could build a system of public schools that would offer all students genuinely equal opportunity to learn, and the false promise of the Bush administration—"No Child Left Behind"—could actually become a reality.

Sources: Jonathan Kozol, *Savage Inequalities* (Crown, 1991); *The Shame of the Nation* (Crown, 2005); John Yinger, ed., *Helping Children Left Behind* (MIT Press, 2004); Education Trust, *The Funding Gap 2005, The Funding Gap 2006*; Education Trust—West, *California's Hidden Teacher Spending Gap* (2005); US Census Bureau, *Survey of Local Government Finances* (www.census.gov/govs/www/estimate.html); U.S. Dept. of Education, National Center for Education Statistics, *Education Finance Statistics Center* (www.nced.ed.gov/edfin); National Conference of State Legislatures, *Education Finance Database* (www.ncsl.org/programs/educ/ed_finance); Hawaii Superintendent of Education, *16th Annual Report* (2005); Teachers College, Columbia University, National Access Network (www.schoolfunding.info/).

In the last three decades, the rich have gotten richer—relatively quickly—while wages at the bottom of the income scale have stagnated. John Miller critiques the Wall Street Journal *for claiming that such inequality comes with the territory in an expanding economy. Miller suggests that the* Journal's *editors should go back and read Adam Smith, who feared the corrupting effects of large-scale inequality.*

MIND-BOGGLING INEQUALITY

BY JOHN MILLER
November/December 2005

D o soaring corporate profits (higher as a share of national income than at any time since 1950) and a green Christmas on Wall Street (green as in record-setting multimillion dollar bonuses for investment bankers) have you worried about economic inequality? How about real wages that are lower and poverty rates higher than when the current economic expansion began five years ago? If that is not enough to make you worry, try this. The editors of the *Wall Street Journal* are spilling a whole lot of ink these days to convince their readers that today's inequality is just not a problem. Besides that, there is not much to be done about inequality, say the editors, since taxes are already soaking the rich.

Not even Ben Bernanke, the new head of the Fed, is prepared to swallow the editors' line this time. Inequality in the U.S. economy "is increasing beyond what is healthy," Bernanke told Congress, although like the editors he finds it a "big challenge to think about what to do about it."

There is real reason to worry. By nearly every measure, inequality today is at a level not seen since the Great Depression. And by historical standards, the rich have hardly overpaid in taxes for their decades-long economic banquet.

Once you remove the *Journal* editors' spin, the "actual evidence" from the Congressional Budget Office (CBO) makes clear that the charge of worsening inequality and a declining tax burden on the rich is anything but "trumped up." The CBO's latest numbers document a lopsided economic growth that has done little to improve the lot of most households while it has paid off handsomely for those at the top. From 1979 to 2004, the poorest quintile saw their average real (i.e., inflation-adjusted) income barely budge, increasing just 2.0% over the entire period. The middle-income quintile enjoyed a larger but still modest real-income gain of 14.6% over the 25-year span, while the best-off fifth enjoyed a 63.0% gain. But the 153.9% jump in the real income of the richest 1% far outdistanced even the gains of the near rich. (See figure.)

The *Journal's* editors are right about one thing: a widening income gap is a long-term trend that has persisted regardless of the party in power. The well-to-do made out like bandits during the Clinton years as well as the Bush years. In fact, postwar inequality, after peaking in 2000, did retreat somewhat in the first four Bush years as the stock market bubble burst, cutting into the income share of the most well-off, who hold the vast majority of corporate stock. (In 2004, the wealthiest 1% of U.S. households held 36.9% of common stock by value; the wealthiest 10% held 78.7%.)

The increase in the gulf between the haves and the have-nots during the Bush years, however, has hardly been modest. In 2004, as in 1999 and in 2000, the share of pre-tax income going to the richest 1% is greater than the share they received in any year since 1929, according to the ground-breaking historical study of inequality by economists Thomas Piketty and Emmanuel Saez. *Barron's* magazine, the Dow Jones business and financial weekly, put it succinctly in their recent cover story, "Rich America, Poor America": "never in history have the haves had so much."

FEAST AND FAMINE

The editors' banquet scenario is unconvincing, to say the least. First off, before we examine the bill for the banquet, we ought to look at what the 100 guests were served. Not everyone got the same meal; in fact, the economic banquet of the last two and a half decades was a feast for some and a famine for others. Most people got modest portions indeed. The income, or serving size if you will, of the average guest was just one sixteenth of the economic feast lavished on the richest 1%. Surely even *Wall Street Journal* editors wouldn't expect the average taxpayer to subsidize the culinary indulgences of the rich.

Second, the well-to-do picked up much less of the tab for their banquet than the *Journal*'s editorials suggest. True enough, the richest 1% of taxpayers now pay more than one-third of all income taxes. But the federal tax bill is not confined to income taxes alone. It also includes payroll taxes (like FICA, the Social Security tax) and excise taxes (for example, on cars) that fall more heavily on low-income households than the income tax does, making up much of their tax bill. Taking those taxes into account does make a substantial difference in the share of the total federal tax bill shouldered by the rich. In 2004, the richest 1% paid just over one-quarter (25.3%), not one-third, of all federal taxes. (See table.) No working American ate for free.

Beyond federal tax liabilities, the banquet tab also includes state and local taxes. Those taxes, especially state sales taxes, fall most heavily on those who were served the smallest portions: low-income earners. Once state and local taxes are included,

PERCENT CHANGE IN REAL HOUSEHOLD INCOME 1979–2004 BY INCOME GROUP

[Average household pre-tax cash income*]

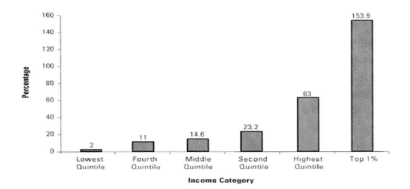

Source: Congressional Budget Office, Historical Effective Tax Rates: 1979 to 2004, Appendix Table 1C.

Pre-tax cash income is the sum of wages, salaries, self-employment income, rents, taxable and non-taxable interest, dividends, realized capital gains, cash transfer payments, and retirement benefits plus employers' share of payroll taxes and employee contributions to 401(k) retirement plans.

the tax share of the richest 1% falls to just over one-fifth, not much more than their share of national income as calculated by the IRS. According to these estimates, provided by the Washington-based think tank Citizens for Tax Justice, the U.S. tax code taken in its entirety does little to redistribute income. By any definition, our tax system is at best mildly progressive, and surely not "highly progressive" as the *Journal* claims.

On top of all that, when the bill for today's economic banquet came due, the Bush administration somehow decided that the guests as a group had overpaid. The purported excess over the amount of the bill should, at least according to the Bush administration's reasoning, go back to each member of the group in tax cuts, in proportion with what they contributed toward paying the bill. Those who contributed the most should get the most back; those who contributed less should get less back. And those whom the rest are treating to dinner, of course, should get nothing back.

But the Bush tax cuts don't manage to conform to even this version of fairness, at least not when it comes to the share of the cuts going to the super-rich. The richest 1% of taxpayers, with average household income well over $1 million, get a whopping 35.9% of the benefits of the Bush tax cuts, or an annual tax cut of $48,311 during this decade, well in excess of their one-quarter (or 25.3% to be exact) share of the federal tax burden.

SHARE OF TOTAL TAX LIABILITIES AND EFFECTIVE TAX RATES PAID BY DIFFERENT INCOME GROUPS, 2004

	Share of Total Tax Liabilities		Effective Tax Rate	
Income Category	Federal	Federal, State, and Local	Federal	Federal, State, and Local
Lowest Quintile	0.9%	2.2%	7.9%	19.7%
Second Quintile	4.5%	5.5%	11.4%	23.3%
Middle Quintile	9.7%	10.5%	15.8%	27.0%
Fourth Quintile	17.6%	19.0%	18.7%	29.8%
Highest Quintile	67.1%	62.6%	21.6%	31.8%
TOP 1%	25.3%	20.8%	24.6%	32.8%

Sources: Congressional Budget Office, *Historical Effective Tax Rates: 1979 to 2004*, Appendix Tables 1b. Citizens for Tax Justice, "Overall Tax Rates Have Flattened Sharply Under Bush," 4/13/04.

All told, the U.S. tax system does not soak the rich, especially after the Bush tax cuts. In 2004, the effective federal tax rate—that is, the share of total income anyone hands over to the government in federal taxes—for the richest 1% was 24.6%, according to Citizens for Tax Justice, far lower than it was in the 1970s. By historical standards, or by any reasonable definition, taxes on the rich have not reached the saturation point.

On top of that, the effective tax rate for all federal, state, and local taxes combined for the poorest fifth of households is 19.7%—well over half the effective tax rate of 32.8% that the richest 1% pay—and that's *after* taking into account the Earned Income Tax Credit that some low-income households receive. With an average income of $1,259,700, as opposed to $15,400, that rate falls far short of exhausting the ability of the superrich to pay. It hardly represents a contribution to the bill for the economic banquet of the last two and a half decades that is in proportion to the large and lavish meal they've enjoyed.

WHAT WOULD ADAM SMITH SAY?

There is no reason to be flummoxed about how to address worsening inequality, even in the short run. *Wall Street Journal* columnist David Wessel, in a November 2006 article on how Democrats might tackle the wealth gap, had no problem enumerating several measures that would lessen inequality. Those included raising the minimum wage, restraining CEO pay, expanding the earned-income tax credit, and rolling back President Bush's upper-income tax cuts.

Just the thought that Congress might actually pass some of these measures was enough for the Journal's editors to minimize the reality of rising inequality and to extol the supposed tax generosity of the rich.

Too bad. Unlike the *Wall Street Journal*'s editors, even Adam Smith, the patron saint of capitalism, recognized the corrupting effect of inequality in a market economy. As Smith put it in *The Theory of Moral Sentiments*, his often overlooked lectures on ethics, the "disposition to admire, and almost to worship, the rich and the powerful, and to despise, or, at least, to neglect persons of poor and mean condition is the great and most universal cause of the corruption of our moral sentiments."

A fitting description of the attitude the *Wall Street Journal*'s editors seem to have toward the rich and the poor. Business executives and policymakers would do well to skip the *Journal* and go back to Smith.

Resources: Congressional Budget Office, "Historical Effective Federal Tax Rates: 1979 to 2004," 12/04; Citizens for Tax Justice, "Overall Tax Rates Have Flattened Sharply Under Bush," 4/13/04; David Wessel, "Fed Chief Warns of Widening Inequality," *Wall Street Journal*, 2/7/07; David Wessel, "Democrats target wealth gap and hope not to hit economy," *Wall Street Journal*, 11/21/06; Adam Smith, *The Theory of Moral Sentiments*, Sec. III, Chap. III, in The Essential Adam Smith ed. Robert Heilbroner (Norton, 1986), p. 86; "Incomes and Politics," *Wall Street Journal* editorial, 9/2/06; "The Top 1% Pay 35%," *Wall Street Journal editorial*, 12/20/06.

Whether economic inequality is rising or falling globally is a matter of intense debate, a key question in the larger dispute over how three decades of intensified economic globalization have affected the world's poor. Bob Sutcliffe is an economist at the University of the Basque Country in Bilbao, Spain, and the author of 100 Ways of Seeing an Unequal World. *He has been analyzing both the statistical details and the broader political-economic import of the debate and shared some of his insights in an interview with* Dollars & Sense.

RICH AND POOR
IN THE GLOBAL ECONOMY

An Interview with Bob Sutcliffe

March/April 2005

Dollars & Sense: If someone asked you whether global inequality has grown over the past 25 years, I assume you'd say, "It depends—on how inequality is defined, on what data is used, on how that data is analyzed." Is that fair?

Bob Sutcliffe: Yes, it's fair, but it's not enough. First, the most basic fact about world inequality is that it is monstrously large; that result is inescapable, whatever the method or definition. As to its direction of change in the last 25 years, to some extent there are different answers. But also there are different questions. Inequality is not a simple one-dimensional concept that can be reduced to a single number. Single overall measures of world inequality (where all incomes are taken into account) give a different result from measures of the relation of the extremes (the richest compared with the poorest). Over the last 25 years, you find that the bottom half of world income earners seems to have gained something in relation to the top half (so, in this sense, there is less inequality), but the bottom 10% have lost seriously in comparison with the top 10% (thus, more inequality), and the bottom 1% have lost enormously in relation to the top 1% (much more inequality). None of these measures is a single true measure of inequality; they are all part of a complex structure of inequalities, some of which can lessen as part of the same overall process in which others increase.

We do have to be clear about one data-related question that has caused huge confusion. To look at the distribution of income in the world, you have to reduce incomes of different countries to one standard. Traditionally it has been done by using exchange rates; this makes inequality appear to change when exchange rates change, which is misleading. But now we have data based on "purchasing power parity" (the comparative buying power, or real equivalence, of currencies). Using PPP values achieves for comparisons over space what inflation-adjusted index numbers have achieved for comparisons over time. Although many problems remain with PPP values, they are the only way to make coherent comparisons of incomes between countries. But they produce estimates that are astonishingly different from exchange rate-based calculations. For instance, U.S. income per head is 34 times Chinese income per head using exchange rates, but only 8 times as great using PPP values. (And, incidentally, on PPP estimates the total size of the U.S. economy is now only 1.7 times that of China, and is likely to be overtaken by it by 2011.) So when you make this apparently technical choice between two methods of converting one currency to another, you come up not only with different figures on income distribution but also with two totally different world economic, and thus political, perspectives.

D&S: So even if some consensus were reached on the choices of definition, data, and method, you're urging a complex, nuanced portrait of what is happening to global inequality, rather than a yes or no answer. Could you give a brief outline of what you think that portrait looks like?

BS: Most integral measures—integral meaning including the entire population rather than comparing the extremes—that use PPP figures suggest that overall income distribution at the global level during the last 25 years has shown a slight decline in inequality, though there is some dissent on this. In any event this conclusion is tremendously affected by China, a country with a fifth of world population which has been growing economically at an unprecedented rate. Second, there seems to me little room for debate over the fact that the relative difference between the very rich and the very poor has gotten worse. And the smaller the extreme proportions you compare, the greater the gap. So the immensely rich have done especially well in the last 25 years, while the extremely poor have done very badly. The top one-tenth of U.S. citizens now receive a total income equal to that of the poorest 2.2 billion people in the rest of the world.

There have also been clear trends within some countries. Some of the fastest growing countries have become considerably more unequal. China is an example, along with some other industrializing countries like Thailand. The most economically liberal of the developed countries have also become much more unequal—for instance, the United States, the United Kingdom, and Australia—and so have the post-communist countries. The most extreme figures for inequality are found in a group of poor countries including Namibia and Botswana in southern Africa and Paraguay and Panama in Latin America.

Finally, the overall index of world inequality (measured by the Gini coefficient, a measure of income distribution) is about the same as that for two infamously unequal countries, South Africa and Brazil. And in the last few years it has shown no signs of improvement whatsoever.

D&S: People use the terms "unimodal" and "bimodal" to describe the global distribution of income. Can you explain what these mean? Also, you have referred elsewhere to a possible trimodal distribution—what does that refer to?

BS: The mode of a distribution is its most common value. In many countries there is one level of income around which a large proportion of the population clusters; at higher or lower levels of income there are progressively fewer people, so the distribution curve rises to a peak and then falls off. That is a unimodal distribution. But in South Africa, for example, due to the continued existence of entrenched ethnic division and economic inequality, the curve of distribution has two peaks—a low one, the most common income received by black citizens, and another, higher one, the the most common received by whites. This is a bimodal distribution because there are two values that are relatively more common than those above or below them. Because of its origins you could call it the "Apartheid distribution." The world distribution is in many respects uncannily like that of South Africa. It could be becoming trimodal in the sense that the frequency distribution of income has three peaks—one including those in very poor countries which have not been growing economically (e.g., parts of Africa), one in those developing countries which really have been developing (e.g., in South and East Asia), and one in the high-income industrialized countries. It's a kind of "apartheid plus" form of distribution.

D&S: In 2002, you wrote that many institutions, like the United Nations and the World Bank, were not being exactly honest in this debate—for example, emphasizing results based on data or methods that they elsewhere acknowledged to be poor. Has this changed over the past few years? Has the quality of the debate over trends in global income inequality improved?

BS: The most egregious pieces of statistical opportunism have declined. But I think there is a strong tendency in general for institutions to seize on optimistic conclusions regarding distribution in order to placate critics of the present world order. This increasingly takes the form of putting too much weight on measures of welfare other than income, for instance, life expectancy, for which there has been more international convergence than in the case of income. But there has been very little discussion of the philosophical basis for using life expectancy instead of or combined with income to measure inequality. If poor people live longer but in income terms remain as relatively poor as ever, has the world become less unequal?

The problem of statistical opportunism is not confined to those who are defending the world economic order; it also exists on the left. So, on the question of inequality, there is a tendency to accept whatever numerical estimate shows greatest inequality on the false assumption that this confirms the wickedness of capitalism. But capitalist inequality is so great that the willful exaggeration of it is not needed as the basis of anti-capitalist propaganda. It is more important for the left to look at the best indicators of the changing state of capitalism, including indicators of inequality, in order to intervene more effectively.

Finally, the quality of the debate, regardless of the intentions of the participants, is still greatly restricted by the shortage of available statistics about inequalities. That has improved somewhat in recent years although there are many things about past and present inequalities which we shall probably never know.

D&S: Do you see any contexts in which it's more important to focus on absolute poverty levels and trends in those levels rather than on inequality?

BS: The short answer is no, I do not. Plans for minimum income guarantees or for reducing the number of people lacking basic necessities can be important. But poverty always has a relative as well as an absolute component. It is a major weakness of the Millenium Development Goals, for example, that they talk about halving the number of people in absolute extreme poverty without a single mention of inequality. [The Millenium Development Goals is a U.N. program aimed at eliminating extreme poverty and achieving certain other development goals worldwide by 2015. —*Eds.*] And there is now a very active campaign on the part of anti-egalitarian, pro-capitalist ideologues in favor of the complete separation of the two. That is wrong not only because inequality is what partly defines poverty but more importantly because inequality and poverty reduction are inseparable. To separate them is to say that redistribution should not form part of the solution to poverty. Everyone is prepared in some sense to regard poverty as undesirable. But egalitarians see riches as pathological too. The objective of reducing poverty is integrally linked to the objective of greater equality and social justice.

D&S: Can you explain the paradox that China's economic liberalization since the late 1970s has increased inequality within China and at the same time reduced global inequality? Some researchers and policymakers interpret China's experience over this period as teaching us that it may be necessary for poor countries to sacrifice some equality in order to fight poverty. Do you agree with this—if not, how would you respond?

BS: When you measure *global* inequality, you are not just totalling the levels of inequality in individual countries. In theory all individual countries could become more unequal and yet the world as a whole become more equal, or vice versa. In China, a very poor country in 1980, average incomes have risen much faster than the world average and this has reduced world inequality. But different sections of the population have done much better than others so that inequality within China has grown. If and when China becomes on average a richer country than it is now, further unequal growth there may contribute to increasing rather than decreasing world inequality.

China's growth has been very inegalitarian, but it has been very fast. And the proportion of the population in poverty seems to have been reduced. But it is possible to envisage a more egalitarian growth path which would have been slower in aggregate but which would have reduced the number of poor people at least as much if not more than China's actual record. So I do not think it is right to say that higher inequality is the cause of reduced poverty, though it may for a time be a feature of the rapid growth which in turn creates employment and reduces poverty.

This does not mean that all increases in inequality are necessarily pathological. The famous Kuznets curve sees inequality first rising and then falling during economic growth as an initially poor population moves by stages from low-income, low-productivity work into high-income, high-productivity work, until at the end of the process 100% of the population is in the second group. If you measure inequality during such a process, it does in fact rise and then fall again to its original level—in this example at the start everyone is equally poor, at the end everyone is equally richer. That might be called transitional inequality; many growth processes may include an element of it. In that case equality is not really being "sacrificed" to reduce poverty—poverty is reduced by a process which increases inequality and then eliminates it again. But at the same time inequality may be growing for many other reasons which are not, like the Kuznets effect, self-eliminating, but rather cumulative. When inequality grows, this malign variety tends to be more important than the self-eliminating variety. But many economists are far too ready to see growing inequality as the more benign, self-eliminating variety.

D&S: Where do you think the question of what is happening to global income inequality fits into the broader debate over neoliberalism and globalization?

BS: Many people say that since some measures of inequality started to improve in about 1980 and that is also when neoliberalism and globalization accelerated, it is those processes which have produced greater equality. There are many problems with this argument, among them the fact that at least on some measures global inequality has grown since 1980. In any case, measures which show global inequality falling in this period are, as we have seen, very strongly influenced by China. China's extraordinary growth has, of course, in part been expressed in and permitted by greater globalization (its internationalization has grown faster than its production), and it is also clear that liberalization of economic policy has played a role, though China hardly has a neoliberal economy. But to permit is not to cause. The real cause is surely to be found not so much in economic policy as in a profound social movement in which a new and highly dynamic capitalist class (combined with a supportive authoritarian state) has once again become an agent of massive capitalist accumulation, as seen before in Japan, the United States, and Western Europe. So, an important part of what we are observing in figures which show declining world inequality is not any growth of egalitarianism, but the dynamic ascent of Chinese and other Asian capitalisms.

This interview also appears on the website of the Political Economy Research Institute at the University of Massachusetts-Amherst, along with Bob Sutcliffe's working paper "A More or Less Unequal World? World Income Distribution in the 20th Century." See <www.umass.edu/peri>.

Illness and medical bills trigger a large fraction of personal bankruptcies—about half in 2001, as this article reports—even though a large majority have health insurance at the time they become ill. As this volume goes to press, a new, larger follow-up study has just been released, finding the share of "medical bankruptcies" rose to over 60% in 2007.

ILL AND INSOLVENT

BY KAYTY HIMMELSTEIN
May/June 2005

In spring 2005, Congress voted overwhelmingly to pass the Bankruptcy Abuse Prevention and Consumer Protection Act, which makes it harder for people to declare bankruptcy. President Bush hurriedly added his signature on April 20, 2005 saying, "America is a nation of personal responsibility where people are expected to meet their obligations." The law, a gift to the banking and credit card industries, imposes new restrictions on bankruptcy filing, including rigid rules for setting repayment schedules, mandatory credit counseling, and a predetermined formula (dubbed a "means test") that takes away judges' discretion in determining whether a person may file for bankruptcy at all.

The means test provision has alarmed legal scholars because it does not allow judges to take individual circumstances into consideration. As Harvard Law School Professor Elizabeth Warren testified to the Senate Judiciary Committee, "The means test as written … treats all families alike. … If Congress is determined to sort the good from the bad, then begin by sorting those who have been laid low by medical debts, those who lost their jobs, those whose breadwinners have been called to active duty and sent to Iraq, those who are caring for elderly parents and sick children from those few who overspend on frivolous purchases."

The new rule is especially worrisome in light of a recent study that found health care costs contributed to about half of America's 1.5 million bankruptcy filings in 2001. The study was coauthored by Elizabeth Warren, David Himmelstein, Deborah Thorne, and Steffie Woolhandler, and published in February 2006 on the website of the journal *Health Affairs*. The authors surveyed 1,771 people who filed for personal bankruptcy, conducting interviews with 931 of them. Nearly half (46.2%) of those surveyed met the authors' criteria for "major medical bankruptcy," and more than half (54.5%) met their broader criteria for "any medical bankruptcy" (see figure). Assuming the data are representative, 1.9 to 2.2 million Americans (filers and dependents) experienced some type of medical bankruptcy in 2001.

CAUSES OF BANKRUPTCY, 2001

Specific reason cited by debtor	Percent of bankruptcies	Number of debtors and dependents in affected U.S. families annually[a]
Illness or injury	28.3	1,039,880
Uncovered medical bills exceeding $1,000 in 2 years before filing	27.0	1,150,302
Debtor or spouse lost at least 2 weeks of work-related income because of illness/injury	21.3	825,113
Mortgaged home to pay medical bills	2.0[b]	
Birth/addition of new family member	7.7	421,256
Death in family	7.6	281,309
Alcohol or drug addiction	2.5	109,180
Uncontrolled gambling	1.2	39,566
Major medical cause (illness or injury listed as specific reason; uncovered medical bills exceeding $1,000; lost at least 2 weeks of work-related income because of illness/injury; or mortgaged home to pay medical bills)	46.2	1,850,098
Any medical cause (any of the above)	54.5	2,227,000

a Extrapolation based on number of bankruptcy filings during 2001 and household size of debtors citing each cause.
b Percentage based on homeowners rather than all debtors.

These are not by and large the uninsured. Three-fourths of medical debtors interviewed had health insurance at the onset of the illness. Many, however, faced lapses in coverage. One-third of those who had private insurance at first lost their coverage during the course of the illness. These gaps in coverage, tied primarily to unaffordable premiums and loss of employment, left debtors with enormous out-of-pocket expenses. Patients who lost private insurance racked up medical costs averaging $18,005 from hospital bills, prescription medicines, and doctor visits. Some who kept their insurance sunk into debt nonetheless, thanks to copayments and deductibles. In sum, private health insurance offers surprisingly little protection from bankruptcy, given involuntary interruptions in coverage and privately borne costs.

Illness triggered financial problems both directly, through medical costs, and indirectly, through lost income. Three-fifths (59.9%) of families bankrupted by medical problems said that bills from medical-care providers contributed to bankruptcy; 47.6% cited drug costs. Thirty-five percent had to curtail employment because of an illness, often to care for someone else. In the interviews, filers described the compounding effects of direct medical costs and indirect employment-related costs— for example, when an illness caused a job loss, which led to the loss of employment-based health coverage, or when parents of chronically ill children had to take time off from work, only to find that the simultaneous costs of the child's medical care and the loss of their income proved catastrophic.

The congressional debate over the bankruptcy bill focused on debtors who cheat the bankruptcy system and pass costs on to more responsible consumers, but the *Health Affairs* study paints a different picture. It shows that about half of those who file for bankruptcy do so because they or their family members have fallen ill or become injured in the context of a shredded health safety net. The new bankruptcy law wrongly treats all debtors as careless spendthrifts. It will make it far more difficult for hundreds of thousands forced by circumstance into overwhelming medical debt to regain their financial footing.

Source: "Illness and Injury as Contributors to Bankruptcy," *Health Affairs Web Exclusive* (2005); authors' analysis of data from the Consumer Bankruptcy Project.

The Consequences of Inequality

When income inequality increases, the rest of the economy suffers too. Since the 1970s, pro-corporate and anti-union economic policies have helped accelerate inequality in the United States. James Cypher explains some of the causes and effects of the growing concentration of income and wealth.

SLICING UP AT THE LONG BARBEQUE

Who Gorges, Who Serves, and Who Gets Roasted?

BY JAMES CYPHER
January/February 2007

Economic inequality has been on the rise in the United States for 30-odd years. Not since the Gilded Age of the late 19th century—during what Mark Twain referred to as "the Great Barbeque"—has the country witnessed such a rapid shift in the distribution of economic resources.

Still, most mainstream economists do not pay too much attention to the distribution of income and wealth—that is, how the value of current production (income) and past accumulated assets (wealth) is divided up among U.S. households. Some economists focus their attention on theory for theory's sake and do not work much with empirical data of any kind. Others who *are* interested in these on-the-ground data simply assume that each individual or group gets what it deserves from a capitalist economy. In their view, if the share of income going to wage earners goes up, that must mean that wage earners are more productive and thus deserve a larger slice of the nation's total income—and vice versa if that share goes down.

Heterodox economists, however, frequently look upon the distribution of income and wealth as among the most important shorthand guides to the overall state of a society and its economy. Some are interested in economic justice; others may or may not be, but nonetheless are convinced that changes in income distribution signal underlying societal trends and perhaps important points of political tension. And the general public appears to be paying increasing attention to income and wealth inequality. Consider the strong support voters have given to recent ballot questions raising state minimum wages and the extensive coverage of economic inequality that has suddenly begun to appear in mainstream news outlets like the *New*

York Times, the *Los Angeles Times*, and the *Wall Street Journal*, all of which published lengthy article series on the topic in the past few years. Just last month, news outlets around the country spotlighted the extravagant bonuses paid out by investment firm Goldman Sachs, including a $53.4 million bonus to the firm's CEO.

By now, economists and others who do pay attention to the issue are aware that income and wealth inequality in the United States rose steadily during the last three decades of the 20th century. But now that we are several years into the 21st, what do we know about income and wealth distribution today? Has the trend toward inequality continued, or are there signs of a reversal? And what can an understanding of the entire post-World War II era tell us about how to move again toward greater economic equality?

The short answers are: (1) Income distribution is even more unequal that we thought; (2) The newest data suggest the trend toward greater inequality continues, with no signs of a reversal; (3) We all do better when we all do better. During the 30 or so years after World War II the economy boomed and every stratum of society did better—pretty much at the same rate. When the era of shared growth ended, so too did much of the growth: the U.S. economy slowed down and recessions were deeper, more frequent, and harder to overcome. Growth spurts that did occur left most people out: the bottom 60% of U.S. households earned only 95 cents in 2004 for every dollar they made in 1979. A quarter century of falling incomes for the vast majority, even though average household income rose by 27% in real terms. Whew!

THE CLASSLESS SOCIETY?

Throughout the 1950s, 1960s, and 1970s, sociologists preached that the United States was an essentially "classless" society in which everyone belonged to the middle class. A new "mass market" society with an essentially affluent, economically homogeneous population, they claimed, had emerged. Exaggerated as these claims were in the 1950s, there was some reason for their popular acceptance. Union membership reached its peak share of the private-sector labor force in the early 1950s; unions were able to force corporations of the day to share the benefits of strong economic growth. The union wage created a target for non-union workers as well, pulling up all but the lowest of wages as workers sought to match the union wage and employers often granted it as a tactic for keeping unions out. Under these circumstances, millions of families entered the lower middle class and saw their standard of living rise markedly. All of this made the distribution of income more equal for decades until the late 1970s. Of course there were outliers—some millions of poor, disproportionately blacks, and the rich family here and there.

Something serious must have happened in the 1970s as the trend toward greater economic equality rapidly reversed. Here are the numbers. The share of income received by the bottom 90% of the population was a modest 67% in 1970, but by

2000 this had shrunk to a mere 52%, according to a detailed study of U.S. income distribution conducted by Thomas Piketty and Emmanuel Saez, published by the prestigious National Bureau of Economic Research in 2002. Put another way, the top 10% increased their overall share of the nation's total income by 15 percentage points from 1970 to 2000. This is a rather astonishing jump—the *gain* of the top 10% in these years was equivalent to more than the *total income received annually* by the bottom 40% of households.

To get on the bottom rung of the top 10% of households in 2000, it would have been necessary to have an adjusted gross income of $104,000 a year. The real money, though, starts on the 99th rung of the income ladder—the top 1% received an unbelievable 21.7% of all income in 2000. To get a handhold on the very bottom of this top rung took more than $384,000.

The Piketty-Saez study (and subsequent updates), which included in its measure of annual household income some data, such as income from capital gains, that generally are not factored in, verified a rising *trend* in income inequality which had been widely noted by others, and a *degree* of inequality which was far beyond most current estimates.

The Internal Revenue Service has essentially duplicated the Piketty-Saez study. They find that in 2003, the share of total income going to the "bottom" four-fifths of households (that's 80% of the population!) was only slightly above 40%. (See Figure 1.) Both of these studies show much higher levels of inequality than were previously thought to exist based on widely referenced Census Bureau studies. The Census studies still attribute 50% of total income to the top fifth for 2003, but this number appears to understate what the top fifth now receives—nearly 60%, according to the IRS.

A BRAVE NEW (GLOBALIZED) WORLD FOR WORKERS

Why the big change from 1970 to 2000? That is too long a story to tell here in full. But briefly, we can say that beginning in the early 1970s, U.S. corporations and the wealthy individuals who largely own them had the means, the motive, and the opportunity to garner a larger share of the nation's income—and they did so.

Let's start with the motive. The 1970s saw a significant slowdown in U.S. economic growth, which made corporations and stockholders anxious to stop sharing the benefits of growth to the degree they had in the immediate postwar era.

Opportunity appeared in the form of an accelerating globalization of economic activity. Beginning in the 1970s, more and more U.S.-based corporations began to set up production operations overseas. The trend has only accelerated since, in part because international communication and transportation costs have fallen dramatically. Until the 1970s, it was very difficult—essentially unprofitable—for giants like General Electric or General Motors to operate plants offshore and then import their

FIGURE 1

Income Share by Quintile: Selected Years 1979–2003

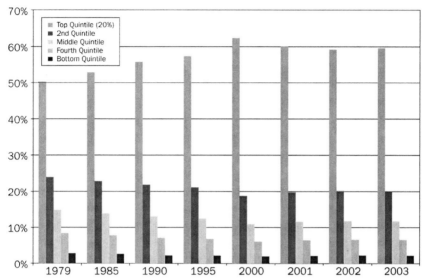

Source: "Further Analysis Of The Distribution Of Income And Taxes, 1979–2002," Michael Strudler and Tom Petska, Statistics of Income Division, Internal Revenue Service, and Ryan Petska, Quantitative Economics and Statistics, Ernst and Young LLP. Accompanying Excel files include data to 2003. Available at www.irs.gov/taxstats/article/0,,id=131260,00.html.

foreign-made products into the United States. So from the 1940s to the 1970s, U.S. workers had a geographic lever, one they have now almost entirely lost. This erosion in workers' bargaining power has undermined the middle class and decimated the unions that once managed to assure the working class a generally comfortable economic existence. And today, of course, the tendency to send jobs offshore is affecting many highly trained professionals such as engineers. So this process of gutting the middle class has not run its course.

Given the opportunity presented by globalization, companies took a two-pronged approach to strengthening their hand vis-à-vis workers: (1) a frontal assault on unions, with decertification elections and get-tough tactics during unionization attempts, and (2) a debilitating war of nerves whereby corporations threatened to move offshore unless workers scaled back their demands or agreed to givebacks of prior gains in wage and benefit levels or working conditions.

A succession of U.S. governments that pursued conservative—or pro-corporate—economic policies provided the means. Since the 1970s, both Republican and Democratic administrations have tailored their economic policies to benefit corporations and shareholders over workers. The laundry list of such policies includes:

- new trade agreements, such as NAFTA, that allow companies to cement favorable deals to move offshore to host nations such as Mexico;
- tax cuts for corporations and for the wealthiest households, along with hikes in the payroll taxes that represent the largest share of the tax burden on the working and middle classes;
- lax enforcement of labor laws that are supposed to protect the right to organize unions and bargain collectively.

EXPLODING MILLIONAIRISM

Given these shifts in the political economy of the United States, it is not surprising that economic inequality in 2000 was higher than in 1970. But at this point, careful readers may well ask whether it is misleading to use data for the year 2000, as the studies reported above do, to demonstrate rising inequality. After all, wasn't 2000 the year the NASDAQ peaked, the year the dot-com bubble reached its maximum volume? So if the wealthiest households received an especially large slice of the nation's total income that year, doesn't that just reflect a bubble about to burst rather than an underlying trend?

To begin to answer this question, we need to look at the trends in income and wealth distribution *since* 2000. And it turns out that after a slight pause in 2000–2001, inequality has continued to rise. Look at household income, for example. According to the standard indicators, the U.S. economy saw a brief recession in 2000–2001 and has been in a recovery ever since. But the median household income has failed to recover. In 2000 the median household had an annual income of $49,133; by 2005, after adjusting for inflation, the figure stood at $46,242. This 6% drop in median household income occurred while the inflation-adjusted Gross Domestic Product *expanded* by 14.4%.

When the Census Bureau released these data, it noted that median household income had gone up slightly between 2004 and 2005. This point was seized upon by Bush administration officials to bolster their claim that times are good for American workers. A closer look at the data, however, revealed a rather astounding fact: Only 23 million households moved ahead in 2005, most headed by someone aged 65 or above. In other words, subtracting out the cost-of-living increase in Social Security benefits and increases in investment income (such as profits, dividends, interest, capital gains, and rents) to the over-65 group, workers again suffered a *decline* in income in 2005.

Another bit of evidence is the number of millionaire households—those with net worth of $1 million or more excluding the value of a primary residence and any IRAs. In 1999, just before the bubbles burst, there were 7.1 million millionaire households in the United States. In 2005, there were 8.9 million, a record number. Ordinary workers may not have recovered from the 2000–2001 rough patch yet, but evidently the wealthiest households have!

FIGURE 2

Real Wages and Productivity of U.S. Production Workers, 1972–2005

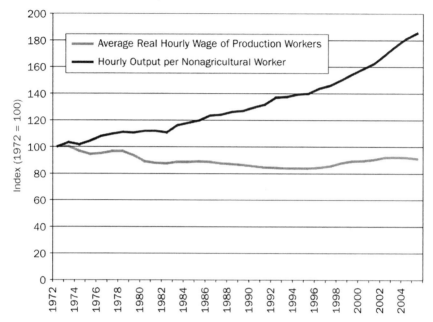

Source: *Economic Report of the President 2006,* Tables B-47 and B-49.

Many economists pay scant attention to income distribution patterns on the assumption that those shifts merely reflect trends in the productivity of labor or the return to risk-taking. But worker productivity *rose* in the 2000-2005 period, by 27.1% (see Figure 2). At the same time, from 2003 to 2005 average hourly pay *fell* by 1.2%. (Total compensation, including all forms of benefits, rose by 7.2% between 2000 and 2005. Most of the higher compensation spending merely reflects rapid increases in the health insurance premiums that employers have to pay just to maintain the same levels of coverage. But even if benefits are counted as part of workers' pay—a common and questionable practice—productivity growth outpaced this elastic definition of "pay" by 50% between 1972 and 2005.)

And at the macro level, recent data released by the Commerce Department demonstrate that the share of the country's GDP going to wages and salaries sank to its lowest postwar level, 45.4%, in the third quarter of 2006 (see Figure 3). And this figure actually overstates how well ordinary workers are doing. The "Wage & Salary" share includes *all* income of this type, not just production workers' pay. Corporate executives' increasingly munificent salaries are included as well. Workers got roughly 65% of total wage and salary income in 2005, according to survey data from the

FIGURE 3

Wages/Salaries vs. Corporate Profits as Shares of U.S. Income, 1972–2006

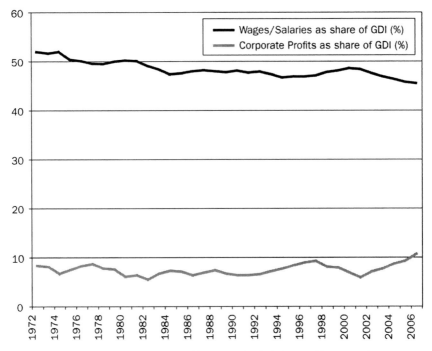

Source: U.S. Dept. of Commerce, Bureau of Economic Analysis, *National Income and Product Accounts 2006*, Table 1.10.

U.S. Department of Labor; the other 35% went to salaried professionals—medical doctors and technicians, managers, and lawyers—who comprised only 15.6% of the sample.

Moreover, the "Wage & Salary" share shown in the National Income and Product Accounts includes bonuses, overtime, and other forms of payment not included in the Labor Department survey. If this income were factored in, the share going to nonprofessional, nonmanagerial workers would be even smaller. Bonuses and other forms of income to top employees can be many times base pay in important areas such as law and banking. Goldman Sachs's notorious 2006 bonuses are a case in point; the typical managing director on Wall Street garnered a bonus ranging between $1 and $3 million.

So, labor's share of the nation's income is falling, as Figure 3 shows, but it is actually falling much faster than these data suggest. Profits, meanwhile, are at their highest level as a share of GDP since the booming 1960s.

These numbers should come as no surprise to anyone who reads the paper: story after story illustrates how corporations are continuing to squeeze workers. For instance, workers at the giant auto parts manufacturer Delphi have been told to prepare for a drop in wages from $27.50 an hour in 2006 to $16.50 an hour in 2007. In order to keep some of Caterpillar's manufacturing work in the United States, the union was cornered into accepting a contract in 2006 that limits new workers to a maximum salary of $27,000 a year—no matter how long they work there—compared to the $38,000 or more that long-time Caterpillar workers make today. More generally, for young women with a high school diploma, average entry-level pay fell to only $9.08 an hour in 2005, down by 4.9% just since 2001. For male college graduates, starter-job pay fell by 7.3% over the same period.

AIDING AND ABETTING

And the federal government is continuing to play its part, facilitating the transfer of an ever-larger share of the nation's income to its wealthiest households. George W. Bush once joked that his constituency was "the haves and the have-mores"—this may have been one of the few instances in which he was actually leveling with his audience. Consider aspects of the four tax cuts for individuals that Bush has implemented since taking office. The first two cut the top *nominal* tax rate from 39.6% to 35%. Then, in 2003, the third cut benefited solely those who hold wealth, reducing taxes on dividends from 39.6% to 15% and on capital gains from 20% to 15%. (Bush's fourth tax cut—in 2006—is expected to drop taxes by 4.8% percent for the top one tenth of one percent of all households, while the median household will luxuriate with an extra nickel per day.)

So, if you make your money by the sweat of your brow and you earned $200,000 in 2003, you paid an *effective* tax rate of 21%. If you earned a bit more, say another $60,500, you paid an effective tax rate of 35% on the additional income. But if, with a flick of the wrist on your laptop, you flipped some stock you had held for six months and cleared $60,500 on the transaction, you paid the IRS an effective tax rate of only 15%. What difference does it make? Well, in 2003 the 6,126 households with incomes over $10 million saw their taxes go down by an average of $521,905 from this one tax cut alone.

These tax cuts represent only one of the many Bush administration policies that have abetted the ongoing shift of income away from most households and toward the wealthiest ones. And what do these top-tier households do with all this newfound money? For one thing, they save. This is in sharp contrast to most households. While the top fifth of households by income has a savings rate of 23%, the bottom 80% as a group dissave—in other words, they go into debt, spending more than they earn. Households headed by a person under 35 currently show a negative savings rate of 16% of income. Today *overall* savings—the savings of the top fifth minus the dis-savings of the bottom four-fifths—are slightly negative, for the first time since the Great Depression.

Here we find the crucial link between income and wealth accumulation. Able to save nearly a quarter of their income, the rich search out financial assets (and sometimes real assets such as houses and businesses) to pour their vast funds into. In many instances, sometimes with inside information, they are able to generate considerable future income from their invested savings. Like a snowball rolling downhill, savings for the rich can have a turbo effect—more savings generates more income, which then accumulates as wealth.

LIFESTYLES OF THE RICH

Make the rich even richer and the creative forces of market capitalism will be unleashed, resulting in more savings and consequently more capital investment, raising productivity and creating abundance for all. At any rate, that's the supply-side/neoliberal theory. However—and reminiscent of the false boom that defined the Japanese economy in the late 1980s—the big money has not gone into productive investments in the United States. Stripping out the money pumped into the residential real estate bubble, inflation-adjusted investment in machinery, equipment, technology, and structures increased only 1.4% from 1999 through 2005—an average of 0.23% per year. Essentially, productive investment has stagnated since the close of the dot-com boom.

Instead, the money has poured into high-risk hedge funds. These are vast pools of unregulated funds that are now generating 40% to 50% of the trades in the New York Stock Exchange and account for very large portions of trading in many U.S. and foreign credit and debt markets.

And where is the income from these investments going? Last fall media mogul David Geffen sold two paintings at record prices, a Jasper Johns ($80 million) and a Willem de Kooning ($63.5 million), to two of "today's crop of hedge-fund billionaires" whose cash is making the art market "red-hot," according to the *New York Times*.

Other forms of conspicuous consumption have their allure as well. Boeing and Lufthansa are expecting brisk business for the newly introduced 787 airplane. The commercial version of the new Boeing jet will seat 330, but the VIP version offered by Lufthansa Technik (for a mere $240 million) will have seating for 35 or fewer, leaving room for master bedrooms, a bar, and the transport of racehorses or Rolls Royces. And if you lose your auto assembly job? It should be easy to find work as a dog walker: High-end pet care services are booming, with sales more than doubling between 2000 and 2004. Opened in 2001, Just Dogs Gourmet expects to have 45 franchises in place by the end of 2006 selling hand-decorated doggie treats. And then there is Camp Bow Wow, which offers piped-in classical music for the dogs (oops, "guests") and a live Camper Cam for their owners. Started only three years ago, the company already has 140 franchises up and running.

According to David Butler, the manager of a premiere auto dealership outside of Detroit, sales of Bentleys, at $180,000 a pop, are brisk. But not many $300,000 Rolls Royces are selling. "It's not that they can't afford it," Butler told the *New York Times*, "it's because of the image it would give." Just what is the image problem in Detroit? Well, maybe it has something to do with those Delphi workers facing a 40% pay cut. Michigan's economy is one of the hardest-hit in the nation. GM, long a symbol of U.S. manu-facturing prowess, is staggering, with rumors of possible bankruptcy rife. The best union in terms of delivering the goods for the U.S. working class, the United Auto Workers, is facing an implosion. Thousands of Michigan workers at Delphi, GM, and Ford will be out on the streets very soon. (The top three domestic car makers are determined to permanently lay off three-quarters of their U.S. assembly-line workers—nearly 200,000 hourly employees. If they do, then the number of autoworkers employed by the Big Three —Ford, Chrysler, and GM—will have shrunk by a staggering 900,000 since 1978.) So, this might not be the time to buy a Rolls. But a mere $180,000 Bentley—why not?

HAD ENOUGH OF THE "HAVES"?

In the era Twain decried as the "great barbeque," the outrageous concentration of income and wealth eventually sparked a reaction and a vast reform movement. But it was not until the onset of the Great Depression, decades later, that massive labor/social unrest and economic collapse forced the country's political elite to check the growing concentration of income and wealth.

Today, it does not appear that there are, as yet, any viable forces at work to put the brakes on the current runaway process of rising inequality. Nor does it appear that this era's power elite is ready to accept any new social compact. In a recent report on the "new king of Wall Street" (a co-founder of the hedge fund/private-equity buyout corporation Blackstone Group) that seemed to typify elite perspectives on today's inequality, the New York Times gushed that "a crashing wave of capital is minting new billionaires each year." Naturally, the Times was too discreet to mention is that those same "crashing waves" have flattened the middle class. And their back-wash has turned the working class every-which-way while pulling it down, down, down.

But perhaps those who decry the trend can find at least symbolic hope in the new boom in yet another luxury good. Private mausoleums, in vogue during that earlier Gilded Age, are back. For $650,000, one was recently constructed at Daytona Memorial Park in Florida—with matching $4,000 Medjool date palms for shade. Another, complete with granite patio, meditation room, and doors of hand cast bronze, went up in the same cemetery. Business is booming, apparently, with 2,000 private mausoleums sold in 2005, up from a single-year peak of 65 in the 1980s. Some cost "well into the millions," according to one the nation's largest makers of cemetery monuments. Who knows: maybe the mausoleum boom portends the ultimate (dead) end for the neo-Gilded Age.

Resources: Jenny Anderson, "As Lenders, Hedge Funds Draw Insider Scrutiny," *NY Times* 10/16/06; Steven Greenhouse, "Many Entry-Level Workers Feel Pinch of Rough Market," *NY Times* 9/4/06; Greenhouse and David Leonhardt, "Real Wages Fail to Match a Rise in Productivity," *NY Times* 8/28/06; Paul Krugman, "Feeling No Pain," *NY Times* 3/6/06; Krugman, "Graduates vs. Oligarchs," *NY Times* 2/27/06; David Cay Johnston, *Perfectly Legal* (Penguin Books, 2003); Johnston, "Big Gain for Rich Seen in Tax Cuts for Investments," *NY Times* 4/5/06; Johnston, "New Rise in Number of Millionaire Families," *NY Times* 3/28/06; Johnston, "'04 Income in US was Below 2000 Level," *NY Times* 11/28/06; Leonhardt, "The Economics of Henry Ford May Be Passé," *NY Times* 4/5/06; Rick Lyman, "Census Reports Slight Increase in '05 Incomes," *NY Times* 8/30/06; Micheline Maynard and Nick Bunkley, "Ford is Offering 75,000 Employees Buyout Packages," *NY Times* 9/15/06; Jeremy W. Peters, "Delphi Is Said to Offer Union a One-Time Sweetener," *NY Times* 3/28/06; Joe Sharky, "For the Super-Rich, It's Time to Upgrade the Old Jumbo Jet," *NY Times* 10/17/06; Guy Trebay, "For a Price, Final Resting Place that Tut Would Find Pleasant" *NY Times* 4/17/06.

Progressives who decry economic inequality just don't know how the economy works—or so say conservative pundits. According to those on the right, inequality fuels economic growth. But as Chris Tilly explains, exactly the opposite is true. In fact, equality boosts economic growth, while inequality puts on the brakes.

GEESE, GOLDEN EGGS, AND TRAPS

Why Inequality Is Bad for the Economy

BY CHRIS TILLY
July/August 2004

Whenever progressives propose ways to redistribute wealth from the rich to those with low and moderate incomes, conservative politicians and economists accuse them of trying to kill the goose that lays the golden egg. The advocates of unfettered capitalism proclaim that inequality is good for the economy because it promotes economic growth. Unequal incomes, they say, provide the incentives necessary to guide productive economic decisions by businesses and individuals. Try to reduce inequality, and you'll sap growth. Furthermore, the conservatives argue, growth actually promotes equality by boosting the have-nots more than the haves. So instead of fiddling with who gets how much, the best way to help those at the bottom is to pump up growth.

But these conservative prescriptions are absolutely, dangerously wrong. Instead of the goose-killer, equality turns out to be the goose. Inequality stifles growth; equality gooses it up. Moreover, economic expansion does *not* necessarily promote equality—instead, it is the types of jobs and the rules of the economic game that matter most.

INEQUALITY: GOOSE OR GOOSE-KILLER?

The conservative argument may be wrong, but it's straightforward. Inequality is good for the economy, conservatives say, because it provides the right incentives for innovation and economic growth. First of all, people will only have the motivation to work hard, innovate, and invest wisely if the economic system rewards them for good economic choices and penalizes bad ones. Robin Hood-style policies that collect from the wealthy and help those who are worse off violate this principle. They reduce the payoff to smart decisions and lessen the sting of dumb ones. The result: people and companies are bound to make less efficient decisions. "We must allow [individuals] to fail, as well as succeed, and we must replace the nanny state with a regime of self-reliance and self-respect," writes conservative lawyer Stephen Kinsella in *The Freeman: Ideas on Liberty* (not clear how the free woman fits in). To prove their point, conservatives point to the former state socialist countries, whose economies had become stagnant and inefficient by the time they fell at the end of the 1980s.

If you don't buy this incentive story, there's always the well-worn trickle-down theory. To grow, the economy needs productive investments: new offices, factories, computers, and machines. To finance such investments takes a pool of savings. The rich save a larger fraction of their incomes than those less well-off. So to spur growth, give more to the well-heeled (or at least take less away from them in the form of taxes), and give less to the down-and-out. The rich will save their money and then invest it, promoting growth that's good for everyone.

Unfortunately for trickle-down, the brilliant economist John Maynard Keynes debunked the theory in his *General Theory of Employment, Interest, and Money* in 1936. Keynes, whose precepts guided liberal U.S. economic policy from the 1940s through the 1970s, agreed that investments must be financed out of savings. But he showed that most often it's changes in investment that drive savings, rather than the other way around. When businesses are optimistic about the future and invest in building and retooling, the economy booms, all of us make more money, and we put some of it in banks, 401(k)s, stocks, and so on. That is, saving grows to match investment. When companies are glum, the process runs in reverse, and savings shrink to equal investment. This leads to the "paradox of thrift": if people try to save too much, businesses will see less consumer spending, will invest less, and total savings will end up diminishing rather than growing as the economy spirals downward. A number of Keynes's followers added the next logical step: shifting money from the high-saving rich to the high-spending rest of us, and not the other way around, will spur investment and growth.

Of the two conservative arguments in favor of inequality, the incentive argument is a little weightier. Keynes himself agreed that people needed financial consequences to steer their actions, but questioned whether the differences in payoffs needed to be so huge. Certainly state socialist countries' attempts to replace material incentives with moral exhortation have often fallen short. In 1970, the Cuban government launched the *Gran Zafra* (Great Harvest), an attempt to reap 10 million tons of sugar cane with (strongly encouraged) volunteer labor. Originally inspired by Che Guevara's ideal of the New Socialist Man (not clear how the New Socialist Woman fit in), the effort ended with Fidel Castro tearfully apologizing to the Cuban people in a nationally broadcast speech for letting wishful thinking guide economic policy.

But before conceding this point to the conservatives, let's look at the evidence about the connection between equality and growth. Economists William Easterly of

New York University and Gary Fields of Cornell University have recently summarized this evidence:

- Countries, and regions within countries, with more equal incomes grow faster. (These growth figures do not include environmental destruction or improvement. If they knocked off points for environmental destruction and added points for environmental improvement, the correlation between equality and growth would be even stronger, since desperation drives poor people to adopt environmentally destructive practices such as rapid deforestation.)
- Countries with more equally distributed land grow faster.
- Somewhat disturbingly, more ethnically homogeneous countries and regions grow faster—presumably because there are fewer ethnically based inequalities.

In addition, more worker rights are associated with higher rates of economic growth, according to Josh Bivens and Christian Weller, economists at two Washington think tanks, the Economic Policy Institute and the Center for American Progress.

These patterns recommend a second look at the incentive question. In fact, more equality can actually *strengthen* incentives and opportunities to produce.

EQUALITY AS THE GOOSE

Equality can boost growth in several ways. Perhaps the simplest is that study after study has shown that farmland is more productive when cultivated in small plots. So organizations promoting more equal distribution of land, like Brazil's Landless Workers' Movement, are not just helping the landless poor—they're contributing to agricultural productivity!

Another reason for the link between equality and growth is what Easterly calls "match effects," which have been highlighted in research by Stanford's Paul Roemer and others in recent years. One example of a match effect is the fact that well-educated people are most productive when working with others who have lots of schooling. Likewise, people working with computers are more productive when many others have computers (so that, for example, e-mail communication is widespread, and know-how about computer repair and software is easy to come by). In very unequal societies, highly educated, computer-using elites are surrounded by majorities with little education and no computer access, dragging down their productivity. This decreases young people's incentive to get more education and businesses' incentive to invest in computers, since the payoff will be smaller.

Match effects can even matter at the level of a metropolitan area. Urban economist Larry Ledebur looked at income and employment growth in 85 U.S. cities and their neighboring suburbs. He found that where the income gap between those in the suburbs and those in the city was largest, income and job growth was slower for everyone.

"Pressure effects" also help explain why equality sparks growth. Policies that close off the low-road strategy of exploiting poor and working people create pressure effects, driving economic elites to search for investment opportunities that pay off by boosting productivity rather than squeezing the have-nots harder. For example, where workers have more rights, they will place greater demands on businesses. Business owners will respond by trying to increase productivity, both to remain profitable even after paying higher wages, and to find ways to produce with fewer workers. The CIO union drives in U.S. mass production industries in the 1930s and 1940s provide much of the explanation for the superb productivity growth of the 1950s and 1960s. (The absence of pressure effects may help explain why many past and present state social-ist countries have seen slow growth, since they tend to offer numerous protections for workers but no right to organize independent unions.) Similarly, if a government buys out large land-holdings in order to break them up, wealthy families who simply kept their fortunes tied up in land for generations will look for new, productive investments. Industrialization in Asian "tigers" South Korea and Taiwan took off in the 1950s on the wings of funds freed up in exactly this way.

INEQUALITY, CONFLICT, AND GROWTH

Inequality hinders growth in another important way: it fuels social conflict. Stark inequality in countries such as Bolivia and Haiti has led to chronic conflict that hob-bles economic growth. Moreover, inequality ties up resources in unproductive uses such as paying for large numbers of police and security guards—attempts to prevent individuals from redistributing resources through theft.

Ethnic variety is connected to slower growth because, on the average, more ethni-cally diverse countries are also more likely to be ethnically divided. In other words, the problem isn't ethnic variety itself, but racism and ethnic conflict that can exist among diverse populations. In nations like Guatemala, Congo, and Nigeria, ethnic strife has crippled growth—a problem alien to ethnically uniform Japan and South Korea. The reasons are similar to some of the reasons that large class divides hurt growth. Where ethnic divisions (which can take tribal, language, religious, racial, or regional forms) loom large, dominant ethnic groups seek to use government power to better themselves at the expense of other groups, rather than making broad-based investments in education and infrastructure. This can involve keeping down the underdogs—slower growth in the U.S. South for much of the country's history was linked to the Southern system of white supremacy. Or it can involve seizing the surplus of ethnic groups perceived as better off—in the extreme, Nazi Germany's expropriation and genocide of the Jews, who often held professional and commercial jobs.

Of course, the solution to such divisions is not "ethnic cleansing" so that each country has only one ethnic group—in addition to being morally abhorrent, this is simply impossible in a world with 191 countries and 5,000 ethnic groups. Rather, the solution is to diminish ethnic inequalities. Once the 1964 Civil Rights Act forced the South to drop racist laws, the New South's economic growth spurt began. Easterly reports that in countries with strong rule of law, professional bureaucracies, protection of contracts, and freedom from expropriation—all rules that make it harder for one ethnic group to economically oppress another—ethnic diversity has *no* negative impact on growth.

If more equality leads to faster growth so everybody benefits, why do the rich typically resist redistribution? Looking at the ways that equity seeds growth helps us understand why. The importance of pressure effects tells us that the wealthy often don't think about more productive ways to invest or reorganize their businesses until they are forced to. But also, if a country becomes very unequal, it can get stuck in an "inequality trap." Any redistribution involves a tradeoff for the rich. They lose by giving up part of their wealth, but they gain a share in increased economic growth. The bigger the disparity between the rich and the rest, the more the rich have to lose, and the less likely that the equal share of boosted growth they'll get will make up for their loss. Once the gap goes beyond a certain point, the wealthy have a strong incentive to restrict democracy, and to block spending on education which might lead the poor to challenge economic injustice—making reform that much harder.

DOES ECONOMIC GROWTH REDUCE INEQUALITY?

If inequality isn't actually good for the economy, what about the second part of the conservatives' argument—that growth itself promotes equality? According to the conservatives, those who care about equality should simply pursue growth and wait for equality to follow.

"A rising tide lifts all boats," President John F. Kennedy famously declared. But he said nothing about which boats will rise fastest when the economic tide comes in. Growth does typically reduce poverty, according to studies reviewed by economist Gary Fields, though some "boats"—especially families with strong barriers to participating in the labor force—stay "stuck in the mud." But inequality can increase at the same time that poverty falls, if the rich gain even faster than the poor do. True, sustained periods of low unemployment, like that in the late 1990s United States, do tend to raise wages at the bottom even faster than salaries at the top. But growth after the recessions of 1991 and 2001 began with years of "jobless recoveries"—growth with inequality.

For decades the prevailing view about growth and inequality within countries was that expressed by Simon Kuznets in his 1955 presidential address to the American Economic Association. Kuznets argued that as countries grew, inequality would first increase, then decrease. The reason is that people will gradually move from the low-income agricultural sector to higher-income industrial jobs—with inequality peaking when the workforce is equally divided between low- and high-income sectors. For mature industrial economies, Kuznets's proposition counsels focusing on growth, assuming that it will bring equity. In developing countries, it calls for enduring current inequality for the sake of future equity and prosperity.

But economic growth doesn't automatically fuel equality. In 1998, economists Klaus Deininger and Lyn Squire traced inequality and growth over time in 48 countries. Five followed the Kuznets pattern, four followed the reverse pattern (decreasing inequality followed by an increase), and the rest showed no systematic pattern. In the United States, for example:

- incomes became more equal during the 1930s through 1940s New Deal period (a time that included economic decline followed by growth)
- from the 1950s through the 1970s, income gaps lessened during booms and expanded during slumps
- from the late 1970s forward, income inequality worsened fairly consistently, whether the economy was stagnating or growing.

The reasons are not hard to guess. The New Deal introduced widespread unionization, a minimum wage, social security, unemployment insurance, and welfare. Since the late 1970s, unions have declined, the inflation-adjusted value of the minimum wage has fallen, and the social safety net has been shredded. In the United States, as elsewhere, growth only promotes equality if policies and institutions to support equity are in place.

TRAPPED?

Let's revisit the idea of an inequality trap. The notion is that as the gap between thrich and everybody else grows wider, the wealthy become more willing to give up overall growth in return for the larger share they're getting for themselves. The "haves" back policies to control the "have-nots," instead of devoting social resources to educating the poor so they'll be more productive.

Sound familiar? It should. After two decades of widening inequality, the last few years have brought us massive tax cuts that primarily benefit the wealthiest, at the expense of investment in infrastructure and the education, child care, and income supports that would help raise less well-off kids to be productive adults. Federal and state governments have cranked up expenditures on prisons, police, and "homeland security," and Republican campaign organizations have devoted major resources to keeping blacks and the poor away from the polls. If the economic patterns of the past are any indication, we're going to pay for these policies in slower growth and stagnation unless we can find our way out of this inequality trap.

D&S *co-editor Amy Gluckman and intern Allison Thuotte spoke with Harvard epidemiologist Ichiro Kawachi in November of 2007 about the impact that growing economic inequality can have on our health.*

INEQUALITY: BAD FOR YOUR HEALTH

AN INTERVIEW WITH ICHIRO KAWACHI
January/February 2008

How do you stay healthy? That's a no brainer, right? Eat the right foods, exercise, quit smoking, get regular medical checkups. Epidemiologist Ichiro Kawachi wants to add a new item to the list: live in a relatively egalitarian society. Kawachi, a professor of social epidemiology at the Harvard School of Public Health, has carried out a wide range of research studies on the social and economic factors that account for average health outcomes in different societies. Among the most novel conclusions of this body of research is that people in societies with high levels of economic inequality are less healthy than those living in more equal societies regardless of their absolute levels of income.

Health policy is at least on the table in this election year. The conversation, however, is almost entirely limited to whether and how to ensure universal health insurance coverage. The work of Kawachi and his colleagues suggests that the public debate about health really needs to be much broader, encompassing a wide range of public policies—in many cases economic policies—that do not explicitly address health but that nonetheless condition how long and how robust our lives will be. Their work traces the multidimensional connection between an individual's health and the qualities of her social world, many of which can shift dramatically when the gap between rich and poor widens.

Dollars & Sense: Your research looks at the relationship between economic factors and health, especially whether living in a more unequal society, in itself, has a negative effect on health outcomes—and you have found evidence that it does. But I want to start by being really clear about what this hypothesis means. There seems to be such a complicated web of possible relationships between income and health.

Ichiro Kawachi: Let's start with how your own income affects your health. Most obviously, income enables people to purchase the goods and services that promote health: purchasing good, healthy food, being able to use the income to live in a safe and healthy neighborhood, being able to purchase sports equipment. Income enables people to carry out the advice of public health experts about how to behave in ways that promote longevity.

But in addition to that, having a secure income has an important psychosocial effect. It provides people with a sense of control and mastery over their lives. And lots of psychologists now say that sense of control, along with the ability to plan for the future, is in itself a very important source of psychological health. Knowing that your future is secure, that you're not going to be too financially stressed, also provides incentives for people to invest in their health Put another way, if my mind is taken up with having to try to make ends meet, I don't have sufficient time to listen to my doctor's advice and invest in my health in various ways.

So there are some obvious ways in which having adequate income is important for health. This is what we call the absolute income effect—that is, the effect of your own income on your own health. If only absolute income matters, then your health is determined by your income alone, and it doesn't matter what anybody else makes. But our hypothesis has been that relative income might also matter: namely, where your income stands in relation to others'. That's where the distribution of income comes in. We have looked at the idea that when the distance between your income and the incomes of the rest of society grows very large, this may pose an additional health hazard.

How could people's relative income have an impact on health, even if their incomes are adequate in absolute terms? There are a couple of possible pathways. One is this ancient theory of relative deprivation: the idea that given a particular level of income, the greater the distance between your income and the incomes of the rest of society, the more miserable you feel. People *are* sensitive to their relative position in society vis-à-vis income. You may have a standard of living above the poverty level; nonetheless, if you live in a community or a society in which everyone else is making so much more, you might feel frustrated or miserable as a result, and this might have deleterious psychological and perhaps behavioral consequences. So that's one idea.

Another hypothesis about why income distribution matters is that when the income or wealth gap between the top and bottom grows, certain things begin to happen within the realm of politics. For example, when the wealthiest segment of society pulls away from the rest of us, they literally begin to segregate themselves in terms of where they live, and they begin to purchase services like health care and education through private means. This translates into a dynamic where wealthy people see that their tax dollars are not being spent for their own benefit, which in turn leads to a reduced basis for cooperation and spending on public goods. So I think there is an entirely separate political mechanism that's distinct from the psychological mechanism involved in notions of relative deprivation.

These are some of the key ways in which income inequality is corrosive for the public's health.

D&S: When you talk about relative deprivation, are you talking primarily about poor people, or does the evidence suggest that inequality affects health outcomes up and down the income ladder? For instance, what about the middle class? I think for the public to understand the inequality effect as something different from just the absolute-income effect, they would have to see that it isn't only poor people who can be hurt by inequality.

IK: Exactly, that's my argument. If you subscribe to the theory that it's only your own income that matters for health, then obviously middle-class people would not have much to worry about—they're able to put food on the table, they have adequate clothing and shelter, they're beyond poverty. What the relative-income theory suggests is that even middle-class people might be less healthy than they would be if they lived in a more egalitarian society.

D&S: That's what I was wondering about. Say we compared a person at the median income level in the United States versus Germany, both of whom certainly have enough income to cover all of the basic building blocks of good health. Would this hypothesis lead you to expect that, other things being equal, the middle-income person in the United States will likely have worse health because economic inequality is greater here?

IK: Yes, that's exactly right. And that's borne out. Americans are much less healthy than Europeans, for example, in spite of having higher average wealth.

D&S: But, unlike most other rich countries, the United States does not have universal health care. Couldn't that explain the poorer health outcomes here?

IK: Not entirely. There was a very interesting paper that came out last year comparing the health of Americans to the health of people in England, using very comparable, nationally representative surveys. They looked at the prevalence of major conditions such as heart attack, obesity, diabetes, hypertension. On virtually every indicator, the *top* third of Americans by income—virtually all of whom had health insurance— were still sicker than the *bottom* third of people in England. The comparison was confined to white Americans and white Britons, so they even abstracted out the contribution of racial disparities.

Health insurance certainly matters—I'm not downgrading its importance—but part of the reason Americans are so sick is because we live in a really unequal society, and it begins to tell on the physiology.

D&S: Has anyone tried to compare countries that have universal health care but have differing levels of inequality?

IK: There have been comparisons across Western European countries, all of which pretty much have universal coverage. If you compare the Scandinavian countries against the U.K. and other European countries, you generally see that the Scandinavians do have a better level of health. The more egalitarian the country, the healthier its citizens tend to be. But that's about as much as we can say. I'm not aware of really careful comparative studies; I'm making a generalization based on broad patterns.

D&S: It sounds like there is still plenty of research to do.

IK: Yes.

D&S: You have already mentioned a couple of possible mechanisms by which an unequal distribution of income could affect health. Are there any other mechanisms that you would point to?

IK: I think those are the two big ones: the political mechanism, which happens at the level of society when the income distribution widens, and then the individual mechanism, which is the relative deprivation that people feel. But I should add that relative deprivation itself can affect health through a variety of mechanisms. For instance, there is evidence that a sense of relative deprivation leads people into a spending race to try to keep up with the Joneses—a pattern of conspicuous, wasteful consumption, working in order to spend, to try to keep up with the lifestyle of the people at the top. This leads to many behaviors with deleterious health consequences, among them overwork, stress, not spending enough time with loved ones, and so forth.

Very interestingly, a couple of economists recently analyzed a study of relative deprivation, which used an index based upon the gap between your income and the incomes of everybody above you within your social comparison group, namely, people with the same occupation, or people in the same age group or living in the same state. What they found was that the greater the gap between a person's own income and the average income of their comparison group, the shorter their lives, the lower their life expectancy, as well as the higher their smoking rates, the higher their utilization of mental health services, and so on. This is suggestive evidence that deprivation relative to average income may actually matter for people's health.

D&S: It's interesting—this part of your analysis almost starts to dovetail with Juliet Schor's work.

IK: Absolutely, that's right. What Juliet Schor writes about in *The Overspent American* is consumerism. It seems to me that in a society with greater income inequality, there's so much more consumerism, that the kind of pathological behavior she describes is so much more acute in unequal societies, driven by people trying to emulate the behavior of those who are pulling away from them.

D&S: Your research no doubt reflects your background as a social epidemiologist. However, it seems as though many mainstream economists view these issues completely differently: many do not accept the existence of *any* causal effect running from income to health, except possibly to the degree that your income affects how much health care you can purchase.

IK: Yes, there is a lot of pushback from economists who, as you say, are even skeptical that absolute income matters for health. What I would say to them is, try to be a little bit open-minded about the empirical evidence. It seems to me that much of the dismissal from economists is not based upon looking at the empirical data. When they do, there is a shift: some economists are now beginning to publish studies that actually agree with what we are saying. For example, the study on relative deprivation and health I mentioned was done by a couple of economists. Another example: some studies by an erstwhile critic of mine, Jeffrey Milyo, and Jennifer Mellor, who in the past have criticized our studies on income distribution and health in the United States as not being robust to different kinds of model specifications— a very technical debate. Anyway, most recently they published an interesting study based on an experiment in which they had participants play a prisoners' dilemma kind of game to see how much they cooperate as opposed to act selfishly. One of the things Mellor and Milyo found was that as they varied the distribution of the honoraria they paid to the participants, the more unequal the distribution of this "income," the more selfishly the players acted. They concluded that their results support what we have been contending, which is that income inequality leads to psychosocial effects where people become less trusting, less cohesive, and less likely to contribute to public spending.

D&S: That's fascinating.

IK: Yes, it's very interesting. So watch this space, because some of the recent evidence from economists themselves has begun to support what we're saying.

D&S: In other parts of the world, and especially in Africa, there are examples of societies whose economies are failing or stagnating *because of* widespread public health issues, for example HIV/AIDS. So it seems as if not only can low income cause poor health, but also that poor health can cause low income. I wonder if your research has anything to say about the complicated web between income and health that those countries are dealing with.

IK: There's no doubt that in sub-Saharan Africa, poor health is the major impediment to economic growth. You have good econometric studies suggesting that the toll of HIV, TB, and malaria alone probably slows economic growth by a measurable amount, maybe 1.5% per year. So there's no question that what those countries need is investment to improve people's health in order for them to even begin thinking about escaping the poverty trap.

The same is true in the United States, by the way. Although I've told the story in which the direction of causation runs from income to health, of course poor health is also a major cause of loss of income. When people become ill, for example, they can lose their jobs and hence their income.

What I'll say about the developing world is that in many ways, the continuing lack of improvement in health in, for example, the African subcontinent is itself an expression of the maldistribution of income in the world. As you know, the rich countries are persistently failing to meet the modest amount of funding that's being asked by the World Health Organization to solve many of these problems, like providing malaria tablets and bed nets and HIV pills for everyone in sub-Saharan Africa. If you look at inequality on a global scale, the world itself could benefit from some more redistribution. Today the top 1% of the world's population owns about a third of the world's wealth. So, although certainly the origins of the HIV epidemic are not directly related to income inequality, I think the solution lies in redistributing wealth and income through overseas development aid, from the 5% of the world who live in the rich countries to everyone else.

D&S: Leaving aside some of the countries with the most devastating public health problems, poor countries in general are often focused just on economic growth, on getting their per capita GDP up, but this often means that inequality increases as well—for example, in China. Do you view the inequality effect as significant enough that a developing country concerned about its health outcomes should aim to limit the growth of inequality even if that meant sacrificing some economic growth?

IK: It depends on the country's objectives. But I'd ask the question: what is the purpose of economic growth if not to assure people's level of well-being, which includes their health? Why do people care about economic growth? In order to lead a satisfying and long life, many people would say. If that's the case, then many people living in developing countries may feel exactly as you suggest: they would prefer policies that attend to egalitarian distribution over policies that are aimed purely at growth.

Amartya Sen has written about this; he has pointed to many countries that are poor but nonetheless enjoy a very good level of health. He cites examples like Costa Rica and the Kerala region in India, which are much, much poorer than the United States but enjoy a high level of health. It really depends on the objectives of the country's politicians. In Kerala and Costa Rica, their health record is very much a reflection of how their governments have invested their income in areas that promote health, like education and basic health services—even if doing so means causing a bit of a drag on economic growth.

China also had this record until perhaps ten years ago. Now they're in this era of maximizing growth, and we're seeing a very steep rise in inequality. Although we don't have good health statistics from China, my guess is that this is probably going to tell on its national health status. Actually, we already know that improvement in their child mortality rates for children under five has begun to slow down in the last 20 years, since the introduction of their economic reforms. In the 1950s and 1960s, the records seemed to suggest quite rapid improvements in health in China. But that's begun to slow down.

D&S: Certainly your research on the health effects of inequality could represent a real challenge in the United States in terms of health care policy. In many ways we have a very advanced health care system, but many people are not well served by it. What effect do you think your work could or should have on U.S. health policy?

IK: Regardless of whether you believe what I'm saying about income inequality, the most basic interpretation of this research is that there are many things that determine people's health besides simply access to good health services. We spend a lot of time discussing how to improve health insurance coverage in this country. In the current presidential debates, when they talk about health policy, they're mostly talking about health insurance. But it's myopic to confine discussions of health policy to what's going to be done about health insurance. There are many social determinants of health and thus many other policy options for improving Americans' health. Investing in education, reducing the disparities in income, attacking problems of poverty, improving housing for poor people, investing in neighborhood services and amenities—these are all actually health policies. The most fundamental point about this whole area of research is that there are many determinants of health besides what the politicians call health policy.

D&S: Besides doctors and medical care.

IK: Yes, that's right. I used to be a physician, and physicians do a lot of good, but much of health is also shaped by what goes on outside the health care system. That's probably the most important thing. The second thing is the implication that income certainly matters for health. So policies that affect peoples' incomes, both absolute and relative income, may have health consequences. For instance, I think the kinds of tax policies we have had in recent years—where most of the benefits have accrued to the top 1% and the resulting budget deficits have led to cutbacks of services to the rest of us, especially those in the bottom half of the income distribution—have been a net negative for public health, through the kind of political mechanism I have described.

D&S: It's almost as though there should be a line for health care in the cost-benefit analysis of any change in tax policies or other economic policies.

IK: Absolutely. There's an idea in public health called the health impact assessment. It's a technique modeled after environmental impact assessments, a set of tools that people are advocating should be used at the Cabinet level. The idea is that when, say, the treasury secretary suggests some new economic measure, then we can formally put the proposal through a modeling exercise to forecast its likely effects on health. Health certainly is very sensitive to decisions that are made elsewhere in the Cabinet besides what goes on in Health and Human Services.

D&S: What about global health policy? Are groups like the World Health Organization paying attention to the kind of research that you do?

IK: Yes, they are. Maybe seven or eight years ago, the WHO had a commission on macroeconomics and health, headed by Jeffrey Sachs. The idea was, by increasing funding to tackle big health problems in the developing world, we can also improve their economic performance and end poverty. That commission posed the direction of causality from health to income. In the last three years, the WHO has had a new commission on the social determinants of health, headed by a social epidemiologist from England, Michael Marmot. That group is looking at the other direction of causality—namely, from poverty to ill health—and considering the ways in which government policies in different areas can improve people's social environment in order to improve their health. I think they are due to report next year with some recommendations as well as case examples from different countries, mostly developing countries whose governments have tried to tackle the economic side of things in order to improve health outcomes.

D&S: Right now the United States is continuing on this path of becoming more and more economically stratified. Your work suggests that that doesn't bode well for us in terms of health. I wonder—this is very speculative—but if we stay on this path of worsening inequality, what do you predict our health as a country is likely to look like in 20 or 30 years?

IK: We're already in the bottom third of the 23 OECD countries, the rich countries, in terms of our average health status. Most people are dimly aware that we spend over half of the medical dollars expended on this planet, so they assume that we should therefore be able to purchase the highest level of health. I teach a course on social determinants of health at Harvard, and many of my students are astonished to discover that America is not number one in life expectancy.

I predict that if we continue on this course of growing income inequality, we will continue to slip further. That gains in life expectancy will continue to slow down. Life expectancy is increasing every year, probably because of medical advances, but I suspect that eventually there will be a limit to how much can be delivered through high-tech care and that our health will slip both in relative terms, compared to the rest of the OECD countries, and maybe even in absolute terms, losing some of the gains we have had over the last half century. For example, some demographers are already forecasting that life expectancy will drop in the coming century because of the obesity academic. Add that to the possible effects of income inequality, and I could easily imagine a scenario in which life expectancy might decline in absolute terms as well as in relative terms. We have not yet seen the full impact of the recent rise in inequality on health status, because it takes a while for the full health effects to become apparent in the population.

Free trade agreements like NAFTA have increased the economic pressures for farmers in poor countries to move to rich ones, a move of desperation that leaves both the migrant workers and their home communities vulnerable. David Bacon discusses how an indigenous community in Mexico is working to reverse the trend by advocating for the right to not migrate.

THE RIGHT TO STAY HOME

Transnational communities are creating new ways of looking at citizenship and residence that correspond to the realities of migration.

BY DAVID BACON
September/October 2008

For almost half a century, migration has been the main fact of social life in hundreds of indigenous towns spread through the hills of Oaxaca, one of Mexico's poorest states. That's made migrants' rights, and the conditions they face, central concerns for communities like Santiago de Juxtlahuaca. Today the right to travel to seek work is a matter of survival. But this June in Juxtlahuaca, in the heart of Oaxaca's Mixteca region, dozens of farmers left their fields, and weavers their looms, to talk about another right—the right to stay home.

In the town's community center two hundred Mixtec, Zapotec, and Triqui farmers, and a handful of their relatives working in the United States, made impassioned speeches asserting this right at the triannual assembly of the Indigenous Front of Binational Organizations (FIOB). Hot debates ended in numerous votes. The voices of mothers and fathers arguing over the future of their children echoed from the cinderblock walls of the cavernous hall. In Spanish, Mixteco, and Triqui, people repeated one phrase over and over: *el derecho de no migrar*—the right to *not* migrate. Asserting this right challenges not just inequality and exploitation facing migrants, but the very reasons why people have to migrate to begin with. Indigenous communities are pointing to the need for social change.

About 500,000 indigenous people from Oaxaca live in the United States, including 300,000 in California alone, according to Rufino Dominguez, one of FIOB's founders. These men and women come from communities whose economies are totally dependent on migration. The ability to send a son or daughter across the border to the north, to work and send back money, makes the difference between eating chicken or eating salt and tortillas. Migration means not having to manhandle a wooden plough behind an ox, cutting furrows in dry soil for a corn crop that can't be sold for what it cost to plant it. It means that dollars arrive in the mail when kids need shoes to go to school, or when a grandparent needs a doctor.

Seventy-five percent of Oaxaca's 3.4 million residents live in extreme poverty, according to EDUCA, an education and development organization. For more than two decades, under pressure from international lenders, the Mexican government has cut spending intended to raise rural incomes. Prices have risen dramatically since price controls and subsidies were eliminated for necessities like gasoline, electricity, bus fares, tortillas, and milk.

Raquel Cruz Manzano, principal of the Formal Primary School in San Pablo Macuiltianguis, a town in the indigenous Zapotec region, says only 900,000 Oaxacans receive organized health care, and the illiteracy rate is 21.8%. "The educational level in Oaxaca is 5.8 years," Cruz notes, "against a national average of 7.3 years. The average monthly wage for non-governmental employees is less than 2,000 pesos [about $200] per family," the lowest in the nation. "Around 75,000 children have to work in order to survive or to help their families." Says Jaime Medina, a reporter for Oaxaca's daily *Noticias*, "A typical teacher earns about 2200 pesos every two weeks [about $220]. From that they have to purchase chalk, pencils and other school supplies for the children." Towns like Juxtlahuaca don't even have waste water treatment. Rural communities rely on the same rivers for drinking water that are also used to carry away sewage.

"There are no jobs here, and NAFTA [the North American Free Trade Agreement] made the price of corn so low that it's not economically possible to plant a crop anymore," Dominguez asserts. "We come to the U.S. to work because we can't get a price for our product at home. There is no alternative." Without large-scale political change, most communities won't have the resources for productive projects and economic development that could provide a decent living.

Because of its indigenous membership, FIOB campaigns for the rights of migrants in the United States who come from those communities. It calls for immigration amnesty and legalization for undocumented migrants. FIOB has also condemned the proposals for guestworker programs. Migrants need the right to work, but "these workers don't have labor rights or benefits," Dominguez charges. "It's like slavery."

At the same time, "we need development that makes migration a choice rather than a necessity—the right to not migrate," explains Gaspar Rivera Salgado, a professor at UCLA. "Both rights are part of the same solution. We have to change the debate from one in which immigration is presented as a problem to a debate over rights. The real problem is exploitation." But the right to stay home, to not migrate,

CITIZENSHIP, POLITICAL RIGHTS, AND LABOR RIGHTS

Citizenship is a complex issue in a world in which transnational migrant communities span borders and exist in more than one place simultaneously. Residents of transnational communities don't see themselves simply as victims of an unfair system, but as actors capable of reproducing culture, of providing economic support to families in their towns of origin, and of seeking social justice in the countries to which they've migrated. A sensible immigration policy would recognize and support migrant communities. It would reinforce indigenous culture and language, rather than treating them as a threat. At the same time, it would seek to integrate immigrants into the broader community around them and give them a voice in it, rather than promoting social exclusion, isolation, and segregation. It would protect the rights of immigrants as part of protecting the rights of all working people.

Transnational communities in Mexico are creating new ways of looking at citizenship and residence that correspond more closely to the reality of migration. In 2005 Jesús Martínez, a professor at California State University in Fresno, was elected by residents of the state of Michoacán in Mexico to their state legislature. His mandate was to represent the interests of the state's citizens living in the United States. "In Michoacán, we're trying to carry out reforms that can do justice to the role migrants play in our lives," Martínez said. In 2006 Pepe Jacques Medina, director of the Comité Pro Uno in Los Angeles' San Fernando Valley, was elected to the Federal Chamber of Deputies on the ticket of the left-leaning Party of the Democratic Revolution (PRD) with the same charge. Transnational migrants insist that they have important political and social rights, both in their communities of origin and in their communities abroad.

The two parties that control the Mexican national congress, the Institutional Revolutionary Party (PRI) and the National Action Party (PAN), have taken steps to provide political rights for migrants. But while Mexico's congress voted over a decade ago to enfranchise Mexicans in the United States, it only set up a system to implement that decision in April 2005. They imposed so many obstacles that in the 2006 presidential elections only 40,000 were able to vote, out of a potential electorate of millions.

While it is difficult for Mexicans in the United States to vote in Mexico, they are barred from voting in the United States altogether. But U.S. electoral politics can't remain forever immune from expectations of representation, and they shouldn't. After all, the slogan of the Boston Tea Party was "No taxation without representation"; those who make economic contributions have political rights. That principle requires recognition of the legitimate social status of everyone living in the United States. Legalization isn't just important to migrants—it is a basic step in the preservation and extension of democratic rights for all people. With and without visas, 34 million migrants living in the United States cannot vote to choose the political representatives who decide basic questions about wages and conditions at work, the education of their children, their health care or lack of it, and even whether they can walk the streets without fear of arrest and deportation.

Migrants' disenfranchisement affects U.S. citizens, especially working people. If all the farm workers and their families in California's San Joaquin Valley were able to vote, a wave of living wage ordinances would undoubtedly sweep the state. California's legislature would pass a single-payer health plan to ensure that every resident receives free and adequate health care. If it failed to pass, San Joaquin Valley legislators, currently among the most conservative, would be swept from office.

When those who most need social change and economic justice are excluded from the electorate, the range of possible reform is restricted, not only on issues of immigration, but on most economic issues that affect working people. Immigration policy, including political and social rights for immigrants, are integral parts of a broad agenda for change that includes better wages and housing, a national healthcare system, a national jobs program, and the right to organize without fear of firing. Without expanding the electorate, it will be politically difficult to achieve any of it. By the same token, it's not possible to win major changes in immigration policy apart from a struggle for these other goals.

Anti-immigrant hysteria has always preached that the interests of immigrants and the native born are in conflict, that one group can only gain at the expense of the other. In fact, the opposite is true. To raise wages generally, the low price of immigrant labor has to rise, which means that immigrant workers have to be able to organize effectively. Given half a chance, they will fight for better jobs, wages, schools, and health care, just like anyone else. When they gain political power, the working class communities around them benefit too. Since it's easier for immigrants to organize if they have permanent legal status, a real legalization program would benefit a broad range of working people, far beyond immigrants themselves. On the other hand, when the government and employers use employer sanctions, enforcement, and raids to stop the push for better conditions, organizing is much more difficult, and unions and workers in general suffer the consequences.

The social exclusion and second-class status imposed by guestworker programs only increases migrants' vulnerability. Delinking immigration status and employment is a necessary step to achieving equal rights for migrant workers, who will never have significant power if they have to leave the country when they lose their jobs. Healthy immigrant communities need employed workers, but they also need students, old and young people, caregivers, artists, the disabled, and those who don't have traditional jobs.

has to mean more than the right to be poor, the right to go hungry and be homeless. Choosing whether to stay home or leave only has meaning if each choice can provide a meaningful future.

In Juxtlahuaca, Rivera Salgado was elected as FIOB's new binational coordinator. His father and mother still live on a ranch half an hour up a dirt road from the main highway, in the tiny town of Santa Cruz Rancho Viejo. There his father Sidronio planted three hundred avocado trees a few years ago, in the hope that someday their fruit would take the place of the corn and beans that were once his staple crops. He's fortunate—his relatives have water, and a pipe from their spring has kept most of his trees, and those hopes, alive. Fernando, Gaspar's brother, has started growing mushrooms in a FIOB-sponsored project, and even put up a greenhouse for tomatoes. Those projects, they hope, will produce enough money that Fernando won't have to go back to Seattle, where he worked for seven years.

This family perhaps has come close to achieving the *derecho de no migrar*. For the millions of farmers throughout the indigenous countryside, not migrating means doing something like what Gaspar's family has done. But finding the necessary resources, even for a small number of families and communities, presents FIOB with its biggest challenge.

Rivera Salgado says, "we will find the answer to migration in our communities of origin. To make the right to not migrate concrete, we need to organize the forces in our communities, and combine them with the resources and experiences we've accumulated in 16 years of cross-border organizing." Over the years FIOB has organized women weavers in Juxtlahuaca, helping them sell their textiles and garments through its chapters in California. It set up a union for rural taxis, both to help farming families get from Juxtlahuaca to the tiny towns in the surrounding hills, and to provide jobs for drivers. Artisan co-ops make traditional products, helped by a cooperative loan fund.

The government does have some money for loans to start similar projects, but it usually goes to officials who often just pocket it, supporters of the ruling PRI, which has ruled Oaxaca since it was formed in the 1940s. "Part of our political culture is the use of *regalos*, or government favors, to buy votes," Rivera Salgado explains. "People want *regalos*, and think an organization is strong because of what it can give. It's critical that our members see organization as the answer to problems, not a gift from the government or a political party. FIOB members need political education."

But for the 16 years of its existence, FIOB has been a crucial part of the political opposition to Oaxaca's PRI government. Juan Romualdo Gutierrez Cortéz, a school teacher in Tecomaxtlahuaca, was FIOB's Oaxaca coordinator until he stepped down at the Juxtlahuaca assembly. He is also a leader of Oaxaca's teachers union, Section 22 of the National Education Workers Union, and of the Popular Association of the People of Oaxaca (APPO).

A June 2006 a strike by Section 22 sparked a months-long uprising, led by APPO, which sought to remove the state's governor, Ulises Ruíz, and make a basic change in development and economic policy. The uprising was crushed by Federal armed intervention, and dozens of activists were arrested. According to Leoncio Vásquez, an FIOB activist in Fresno, "the lack of human rights itself is a factor contributing to migration from Oaxaca and Mexico, since it closes off our ability to call for any change." This spring teachers again occupied the central plaza, or *zócalo*, of the state capital, protesting the same conditions that sparked the uprising two years ago.

In the late 1990s Gutierrez was elected to the Oaxaca Chamber of Deputies, in an alliance between FIOB and Mexico's left-wing Democratic Revolutionary Party (PRD). Following his term in office, he was imprisoned by Ruíz' predecessor, José Murat, until a binational campaign won his release. His crime, and that of many others filling Oaxaca's jails, was insisting on a new path of economic development that would raise rural living standards and make migration just an option, rather than an indispensable means of survival.

Despite the fact that APPO wasn't successful in getting rid of Ruíz and the PRI, Rivera Salgado believes that "in Mexico we're very close to getting power in our communities on a local and state level." FIOB delegates agreed that the organization would continue its alliance with the PRD. "We know the PRD is caught up in an internal crisis, and there's no real alternative vision on the left," Rivera Salgado says. "But there are no other choices if we want to participate in electoral politics. Migration is part of globalization," he emphasizes, "an aspect of state policies that expel people. Creating an alternative to that requires political power. There's no way to avoid that."

Strategies for Change

According to right-wing pundits, taxing wealth is so crazy an idea that no respectable economist could support it. But economist John Miller shows that some of the most influential political economists of the 19th and 20th centuries did just that. So, too, did Andrew Carnegie, the 19th-century robber baron. Today's supporters of the estate tax and other forms of wealth taxation have plenty of intellectual and historical backing.

TAX WEALTH

Great Political Economists and Andrew Carnegie Agree

BY JOHN MILLER
ART BY NICK THORKELSON
August 2004

A few years ago, I appeared regularly on talk radio as part of a campaign to block the repeal of the estate tax. As an economist, my job was to correct the distortions and outright hucksterism that the Heritage Foundation and other right-wing think tanks used to demonize the estate tax. In their hands, this modest tax on the inheritance of the richest 2% of U.S. taxpayers became a "death tax" that double-taxed assets in family estates, destroyed family farms and small businesses, and put a brake on economic growth.

Once that was done, assuming anyone was still listening, I was supposed to make the affirmative case for taxing wealth. But before I got very far, whichever conservative expert I was debating would inevitably interrupt and ask, "Isn't what you advocate straight out of Marx's *Communist Manifesto*?" After my first stammering reply, I got pretty good at saying, "Perhaps, but calls for taxing wealth are also straight out of *The Gospel of Wealth* by Andrew Carnegie. Do you think he was anti-capitalist?" Then it was the conservative's turn to stammer.

In fact, Marx, the philosopher of socialism, and Carnegie, the predatory capitalist turned philanthropist, weren't the only ones to call for heavy taxation of estates. Over the 19th and 20th centuries, they were joined by great political economists who, unlike Marx, were more concerned with saving capitalism from its excesses than replacing it. Let's take a look at what all these writers had to say.

KARL MARX

Sure enough, the manifesto of the Communist League, penned by Karl Marx and Fredrick Engels in 1848, called for the heavy taxation and even confiscation of inherited wealth. In the *Communist Manifesto*, Marx and Engels developed a transitional program intended to lead Europe away from the horrors of industrial capitalism—a system guided by "naked self interest"—and toward a socialist society. The ten-step program that Marx and Engels laid out for the most advanced countries began with these demands:

1. Abolition of property in land and aplication of all rents of land to public purposes.
2. A heavy or progressive graduated income tax.
3. Abolition of all rights of inheritance.

These clauses need to be understood in context of the socialist debate of the day and Marx's other writings. The first clause did not target the capitalist who directed production on the farm or in the mine, but the landowner or rentier who collected a return merely by owning the land or mine. It was their rents, not the capitalist's profits, that Marx and Engels argued should go to the state to be used for public purposes.

A heavy or progressive graduated income tax, the second clause, hardly seems radical. The U.S. federal income tax had a top tax bracket of 90% in the early post-World War II period (prior to 1962), although effective income tax rates were far lower than that.

Abolishing rights of inheritance, on the other hand, would be a radical change. The third clause targeted large estates; despite its wording, it was not intended to apply to small holders of property. "The distinguishing feature of Communism," as Marx and Engels made clear, "is not the abolition of property generally, but the abolition of bourgeois property." Marx and Engels were concerned with the social relation of capital based on the private ownership of the means of production. They saw this as the root of capitalist class power and the basis of class antagonisms that involved "the exploitation of the many by the few." The abolition of capitalist private property was surely the backbone of the *Communist Manifesto*, the most influential economic pamphlet ever written.

JOHN STUART MILL

Writing in the middle of the 19th century as well, the far more respectable John Stuart Mill also called for limitations on inheritance. Mill was a radical, but also a member of the English parliament and the author of the *Principles of Political Economy*, the undisputed bible of economists of his day. Mill regarded the laws of distribution of capitalism (who got paid what) to be a matter of social custom and quite malleable, unlike the inalterable market laws that governed production (how commodities were made). Indeed, he devoted long sections of the later editions of *Principles* to then-novel experiments with workers' cooperatives and utopian communities which he thought could distribute resources more equitably.

Mill openly attacked the institution of inheritance and entered a plea for progressive death duties. Observing the gaping inequalities that the industrial system had produced in England, he wrote that there existed "an immense majority" who were condemned from their birth to a life of "never-ending toil" eking out a "precarious subsistence." At the same time, "a small minority" were born with "all the external advantages of life without earning them by any merit or acquiring them by an any exertion of their own."

To curtail this "unearned advantage," Mill called for the "limitation of the sum which any one person may acquire by gift or inheritance to the amount sufficient to constitute a moderate independence." He argued for a "system of legislation that favors equality of fortunes" to allow individuals to realize "the just claim of the individual to the fruits, whether great or small, of his or her own industry." Otherwise, as he famously observed, all the mechanical inventions of the industrial revolution would only enable "a greater population to live the same life of drudgery and imprisonment and an increased number of manufacturers and others to make fortunes."

HENRY GEORGE

Henry George, a journalist who taught himself economics, burst onto the American scene in 1879 with the publication of *Progress and Poverty*. This instant bestseller launched a crusade for a "single tax" on land that would put an end to the speculation that George saw as the root cause of the country's unjust distribution of wealth. Although rejected by the economics profession, *Progress and Poverty* sold more copies than all the economic texts previously published in the United States. It is easy to see why. In epic prose, George laid out the problem plaguing U.S. society at the close of the 19th century:

"The association of poverty with progress is the greatest enigma of our times. It is the central fact from which spring industrial, social, and political difficulties that perplex the world… It is the riddle which the Sphinx of Fate puts to our civilization and which not to answer is to be destroyed. So long as all the increased wealth which modern progress brings goes but to build up great fortunes, to increase luxury, and make sharper the contrast between the House of Have and the House of Want, progress is not real and cannot be permanent."

George traced the maldistribution of wealth to the institution of private property in land. To end the association of poverty with progress, he argued that "we must make land common property." But, he argued, "it is not necessary to confiscate land; it is only necessary to confiscate rent." Taxation was his means for appropriating rent, and George proposed "to abolish all taxation save that upon land values."

Henry George's single tax on land (excluding improvements) was meant to lift the burden of taxation from labor and all productive effort and place it on the rising of value of land. That rising value, he wrote, was the product of social advancement, and should be socialized. It was unjust for such gains to remain in the hands of an individual land owner—"someone whose grandfather owned a pasture on which two generations later, society saw fit to erect a skyscraper," as Robert Heilbroner, the historian of economic ideas, put it.

Progress and Poverty spawned an impressive grassroots movement dedicated to undoing the wealth gap. Georgist Land and Labor clubs sprang up across the nation, and despite a concerted counter-attack by the economics profession, Georgists exerted considerable influence on U.S. tax policy. Most recently, Alaska adopted a George-like proposition. The state created the Alaska Permanent Fund and in its constitution vested the ownership of the state's oil and natural resources in the people as a whole. The Permanent Fund distributes substantial oil revenues as citizen dividends to state residents.

JOHN MAYNARD KEYNES

During the Great Depression of the 1930s, John Maynard Keynes, the pre-eminent economist of the 20th century, warned that a worsening maldistribution of wealth threatened to bring capitalism to its knees. Keynes was no radical. Instead, he was concerned with rescuing capitalism from its own excesses. Keynes's analysis of the instabilities of capitalist economies, and his prescriptions for taming them, guided U.S. economic policy from the 1940s through the 1970s and are still tremendously influential today.

"The outstanding faults of the economic society in which we live," he wrote in *The General Theory of Employment, Interest, and Money* in 1936, "are its failure to provide for full employment and its arbitrary and inequitable distribution of wealth and incomes." Keynes argued that income inequality and financial instability made for unstable demand among consumers. Without stable demand for goods and services, corporations invested less and cut jobs. Indeed, during the worst years of the Great Depression, this chain of economic events cost more than one-quarter of U.S. workers their jobs.

By 1936, Keynes wrote, British death duties, along with other forms of direct taxation, had made "significant progress toward the removal of very great disparities of wealth and income" of the 19th century. Still, he thought that much more was needed. In the last chapter of the *General Theory*, Keynes went so far as to propose what he called the "euthanasia of the rentier." By this he meant the gradual elimina-

tion of "the functionless investor," who made money not by working but by investing accumulated wealth. Keynes imagined a capitalist economy in which public policy kept interest rates so low that they eroded the income of the functionless investor and at the same time lowered the cost of capital (or borrowing funds) so that it was abundant enough to provide jobs for everyone. This was Keynes's plan to support continuous full employment.

Neither the United States nor Britain ever instituted such a policy, but Keynes provided the theoretical bulwark for the "mixed economy" in which public and private investment complemented one another. He showed how government spending could compensate for the instability of private investment, with government investment rising when private investment fell. The mixed economy, which moderated capitalist instability during the post-war period, remains, in the words of economist Dani Rodrik, "the most valuable heritage the 20th century bequeaths to the 21st century in the realm of economic policy."

Today, just a few years into the 21st century, a conservative movement is trying to rob us of that bequest. The repeal of the estate tax, all but accomplished in 2001, is the sharp end of the axe its adherents are using to cut government down to size. That move is sure to fuel the very excesses that Keynes worried were likely to undo capitalism during the 1930s. It will starve the public sector of revenue, compromising its ability to stabilize the private economy. By showering tax cuts on the richest of our society, it will also exacerbate inequality at a time when the richest 1% already receive their largest share of the nation's income (before taxes) since 1936, the very year that Keynes published the *General Theory*. Finally, repealing the estate tax is unlikely to improve the management of our economic affairs: as Keynes caustically wrote, "the hereditary principle in the transmission of wealth and the control of business is the reason why the leadership of the capitalist cause is weak and stupid."

ANDREW CARNEGIE

It is not easy for me to invoke Andrew Carnegie's defense of the estate tax. For over a decade, I lived in Pittsburgh, where Andrew Carnegie is remembered as the ruthless capitalist who built his public libraries up and down the Monongahela River valley with the money he sweated out of his immigrant workforce, and only after he had busted the union in the local steel mill. Carnegie actually applauded the maldistribution of wealth that Marx, Mill, George, and even Keynes railed against. As he argued, concentrated wealth "is not to be deplored, but welcomed as highly beneficial. Much better this great irregularity than universal squalor."

But despite these apologetics, Carnegie was deeply troubled by large inheritances. "Why should men leave great fortunes to their children?" he asked in his 1889 book, *The Gospel of Wealth*. "If this is done from affection, is it not misguided affection? Observation teaches that, generally speaking, it is not well for the children that they should be so burdened."

Carnegie was also an unabashed supporter of the estate tax. "The growing disposition to tax more and more heavily large estates left at death," Carnegie declared, "is a cheering indication of the growth of a salutary change in public opinion." He added that "of all forms of taxation, this seems the wisest. ... By taxing estates heavily at death, the state marks its condemnation of the selfish millionaire's unworthy life." Finally, Carnegie warned that "the more society is organized around the preservation of wealth for those who already have it, rather than building new wealth, the more impoverished we will all be."

FROM HERE TO THERE

Today, whether one is out to save capitalism from its excesses or to bring capitalist exploitation to a halt, taxing accumulated wealth and especially large estates is essential. On that point, Marx, Mill, George, Keynes, and even Carnegie all agreed. But to subject wealth to fair taxation, we will need to do more than resurrect the ideas of these thinkers. We will need a spate of grassroots organizing—from workers' organizations to organizations of the socially-conscious well-to-do—dedicated to the demand that those who have benefited most from our collective efforts give back the most.

This can be done. A hundred years ago, populists concerned about the concentration of wealth forced Congress to enact the original estate tax. They also pushed through a constitutional amendment allowing a progressive income tax that raised revenue for public services. These kinds of advances can happen again.

It will be no easy task. Politics at the beginning of the 21st century are far less progressive than they were at the beginning of the 20th century. But with the greatest of political economists and even a predatory capitalist on our side, perhaps we have a chance.

Chuck Collins and Dedrick Muhammad propose tying the estate tax to a bold set of asset-building initiatives in order to mobilize support for wealth taxation.

TAX WEALTH TO BROADEN WEALTH

BY CHUCK COLLINS AND DEDRICK MUHAMMAD
January/February 2004

For the past decade, a coalition of business lobbyists and wealthy families has waged a crusade to abolish the nation's only tax on inherited wealth. They've misled the public into believing that the estate tax falls on everyone (when it applies to fewer than the wealthiest 1.5%) and that it destroys small businesses and family farms (it doesn't). In 2001, their multimillion-dollar lobbying effort paid off. Congress voted to phase out the estate tax by gradually raising the exemption level from $1 million in 2002 to $3.5 million in 2009. The tax will disappear in 2010—millionaires and billionaires who die that year will pass on their fortunes tax-free. Its fate after 2010 has yet to be determined. The tax will return to its 2002 levels in 2011 unless Congress revisits the issue.

In a time of state budget crises, a skyrocketing national deficit, and continued cuts to the social safety net, this gift to the richest 1.5% comes at too high a price. Last year, the estate tax added $28 billion to the U.S. Treasury and stimulated an estimated $10 billion in charitable giving. Its abolition is expected to cost the nation $1 trillion over 20 years, and will only deepen the growing wealth divide.

Progressives need to respond to this polarizing economic agenda with a bold economic agenda of their own. One proposal that has real potential to galvanize public support for preserving the tax is a plan to link it to wealth-broadening policies that would directly augment people's personal and household assets. If estate tax revenues were dedicated to a "wealth opportunity fund"—a public trust fund—and used to underwrite wealth-expanding programs, the benefits of taxing inherited fortunes would be made clear: the wealth tax would directly reduce asset disparities, including longstanding racial inequities. In the process, the proposal would reassert a positive role for redistributive government spending.

DIVERGING FORTUNES
The concentration and polarization of wealth have reached levels that would have

been unfathomable just 30 years ago. Between 1971 and 1998, the share of wealth held by the richest 1% of households grew from 19.9% to 38.1%. Within this top 1%, the largest wealth gains accrued to people with household net worth over $50 million. As New York University economist Edward N. Wolff has observed: "The 1990s also saw an explosion in the number of millionaires and multimillionaires. The number of households worth $1,000,000 or more grew by almost 60%; the number worth $10,000,000 or more almost quadrupled."

Meanwhile, almost one in five households reported zero or negative net worth (excluding the value of their automobiles) throughout the 1990s "boom" years—and racial wealth disparities continued to widen. According to the most recent Survey of Consumer Finances, median net worth for whites rose 16.9% to $120,900 between 1998 and 2001. But median nonwhite and Hispanic household net worth actually fell 4.5%, to $17,100, during the same period.

British commentator Will Hutton observes that "U.S. society is polarizing and its social arteries hardening. The sumptuousness and bleakness of the respective lifestyles of rich and poor represent a scale of difference in opportunity and wealth that is almost medieval."

SHRINK, SHIFT, AND SHAFT

The drive to abolish the estate tax is just one part of a much broader attack on the progressive tax system. Neo-conservatives are pushing their "shrink, shift, and shaft" fiscal agenda: Shrink the regulatory and welfare states (while enlarging the "warfare" and the "watchtower" states); shift the tax burden from progressive taxes (like the estate tax) to regressive payroll and sales taxes; and shaft the overwhelming majority of the population that depends on government programs and services like public schools, libraries, and roads.

In contrast to the period after World War II, when the federal government carried out massive public investment in wealth-broadening initiatives like the GI Bill, the last three years have seen the Bush administration and Congress institute historic federal tax cuts that disproportionately benefit the very wealthy. In five decades, we've gone from a system of progressive taxation that funded America's biggest middle-class expansion to an increasingly regressive tax system inadequate to fund the most basic of social services.

Democrats have been loath to support anything that looks like a tax hike. Many actually voted for the estate tax phase-out. But taxing wealth is good policy, and in the context of a major wealth-building program, it would make good politics.

Consider how such a program would work: By simply freezing the estate tax at its 2009 level (taxing inherited fortunes in excess of $3.5 million at a rate of 45%), the tax could initially generate $20 to $25 billion a year for a wealth opportunity fund. But in the coming decades, an enormous intergenerational transfer of wealth will occur and estate tax revenue will grow to between $157 billion and $750 billion a year, depending on which estimated annual growth rate one uses. (The lower projection assumes 2% real growth in wealth. The higher figure assumes a 4% growth rate. See <www.bc.edu/research/swri> for more information about these assumptions.) If the estate tax were made more progressive, with a top rate returning to 70% on fortunes over $100 million, it would generate enough revenue for a wealth-broadening program of GI Bill-scale.

ASSET BUILDING SOLUTIONS

How should these revenues be spent? Good proposals and pilot projects already exist to broaden assets and reduce wealth disparities. Taken together, these ideas form the modest beginning of a policy agenda for greater wealth equality.

One example is a new wealth-broadening initiative in England, sponsored by Tony Blair's Labor Party. In 2003, the British Parliament established what have become known as "baby bonds"—small government-financed trust funds for each newborn in the country. Small sums will be deposited and invested for each new-born infant, and available for withdrawal at age 18.

In 1998, then-U.S. Senator Robert Kerrey introduced similar legislation to create what he called "KidSave" accounts. The KidSave initiative would guarantee every child $1,000 at birth, plus $500 a year for children ages one to five, to be invested until retirement. Through compound returns over time, the accounts would grow substantially, provide a significant supplement to Social Security and other retirement funds, and enable many more Americans to leave inheritances to their children.

Another important program is the national Individual Development Account (IDA) demonstration project. This project gives low-income people matching funds for their savings. While the number of households that benefit from IDAs has been small to date, and the amounts that low-income people have managed to save have been modest, the idea is to ramp up this concept, through expanded public funding, to assist many more households.

Nationwide, many community-based organizations are working to expand homeownership opportunities using a patchwork of development subsidies, low-interest mortgages, and down-payment assistant programs.

A challenge for all of these wealth-broadening programs, including the British baby bonds, is that they don't have an adequate or dedicated source of revenue to bring the efforts to a meaningful scale. Here is where some interesting theoretical proposals are emerging as to how to pay for asset programs.

Yale professors Bruce Ackerman and Anne Alstott put forward an "equality of opportunity" proposal in their 2001 book, *The Stakeholder Society*. They advocate imposing an annual 2% tax on wealth, to be paid by the wealthiest 41% of the country. The wealth tax would fund an $80,000 "stake" given to every American at age 21, conditioned on graduating from high school. This notion of "stakeholding," or providing people a piece of the nation's wealth as they come of age, has a long history. In 1797, Tom Paine argued that all new democratic republics, including France and the United States, should guarantee every 21-year old citizen a wealth stake. And in the United States, land grants and subsidized housing loans have been among the ways that the government has helped individuals build personal property.

Sources other than a wealth tax could provide an additional stream of revenue for wealth building—one interesting example is a proposed "sky trust," which addresses both the need for asset building and the problem of environmental degradation. Recognizing that the environmental "commons" is being destroyed, Peter Barnes, in *Who Owns the Sky*, proposes a trust capitalized by pollution credits. Polluting companies would purchase carbon and sulfur permits and the permit revenue would be paid into the trust. Barnes compares the idea to the Alaska Permanent Fund, which pays annual dividends to Alaska residents from the state's oil wealth.

By directly contradicting the thrust of the Bush fiscal agenda, which aims to reduce taxation on the wealthiest and dismantle the ladder of economic opportunity for the rest, a wealth-broadening initiative could move progressive constituencies and candidates off of the defense ("We want just half of Bush's tax cut") and behind a positive agenda.

Such an initiative would recapture the possibility of affirmative, activist government, reconnecting the people with the potential for positive government spending —as the GI Bill and homeownership expansion programs did for the post-war generation—and dramatize the limitations of Bush's "want another tax cut?" social policy.

At the same time, this emerging movement must defend existing safety nets and investments in opportunity as a foundation for moving forward. Broadening individual wealth alone has its limitations and is not a substitute for a robust social safety net and adequately funded Social Security program.

THE WEALTH-BROADENING MOVEMENT

From a constituency mobilization perspective, the proposal solves a problem: From the outset, there has been a fundamental imbalance in the estate tax debate. The wealthy individuals and business interests that pay the tax are highly motivated to abolish it. On the other side, the constituencies that would benefit from retaining it are immobilized.

Eliminating the estate tax will lead to budget cuts and a shifting of the tax burden onto those less able to pay—but this has been hard for the public to see. Because the revenues go into the general treasury, its benefits appear remote.

Linking estate tax revenue to a public "trust fund" would help secure support from the vast majority of Americans who are on the wrong side of today's wealth divide by addressing fundamental aspirations of the middle class and the poor alike:

LAST CENTURY'S WEALTH BROADENING PROGRAM

In the two decades after World War II, federal education and housing programs moved millions of families onto the multigenerational wealth-building train. Between 1945 and 1968, the percentage of American families living in owner-occupied dwellings rose from 44% to 63%, thanks in large part to a massive public commitment to subsidized and insured mortgages from the Federal Housing Authority (FHA), the Veteran's Administration (VA), and the Farmers Home Administration (FmHA).

Prior to the 1940s, mortgages averaged only 58% of property value, excluding all but those with substantial savings from owning homes. FHA and other mortgage subsidies enabled lenders to lengthen the terms of mortgages and dramatically lower down payments to less than 10%. Government guarantees alone enabled interest rates to fall two or three points.

Between World War II and 1972, 11 million families bought homes and another 22 million improved their properties, according to Kenneth T. Jackson's history of the FHA, Crabgrass Frontier. The FHA also insured 1.8 million dwellings in multi-family projects. The biggest beneficiary was white suburbia, where half of all housing could claim FHA or VA financing in the 1950s and 1960s. All these housing-subsidy programs helped finance private wealth in the form of homeownership for 35 million families between 1933 and 1978. The home mortgage interest deduction also benefited suburban homeowners, and interstate highway construction served as an indirect subsidy, as it opened up inexpensive land for suburban commuters.

Unfortunately, for a host of reasons—including racial discrimination in mortgage lending practices, housing settlement patterns, income inequality, and unequal educational opportunities—many nonwhite and Latino families were left standing at the wealth-building train station.

Today, racial wealth disparities persist, and are far more extreme even than disparities in income. Homeownership rates for blacks and Latinos are currently stalled at the level where whites were at the end of World War II. And while over 70% of non-Latino whites own their own homes today, homeownership rates for blacks and Latinos combined average just 48%.

The post-World War II investment in middle-class wealth expansion was paid for by a system of progressive taxation. The top income-tax rate coming out of the war was 91% (it's 38.6% today)—and the estate tax included a provision that taxed fortunes over $50 million at a 70% rate. In turn, many of the widely shared benefits of post-war spending meant that the progressivity of the tax system enjoyed widespread political support.

the desire for a degree of economic security, a foothold of opportunity, and the means to pass along assets to the next generation.

On the ground, a nascent "wealth broadening movement" already exists, made up of community-development corporations and agencies that promote affordable housing and homeownership, credit unions, and IDAs, as well as savings and investment clubs within religious congregations. These groups aspire to broaden their programs through state and federal legislation, but are hampered by the absence of sizable funding streams. They could provide organizational infrastructure and resources for the effort.

The cumulative impact of a program to broaden wealth by taxing wealth would be to dramatically reduce, over a generation, the disparities of wealth in the United States. This agenda is particularly important for people of color who were themselves excluded, or whose parents or ancestors were excluded, from previous government-led wealth- building opportunities. (See "Last Century's Wealth Broadening Program.")

Wealth is a great equalizing force. Cutting across racial lines, families with equal wealth have similar educational results, economic practices, and health conditions. Asset assistance will be all the more meaningful to those who possess few or no assets, who are disproportionately people of color. Over 11% of African Americans have no assets, compared to 5.6% of white non-Latino households.

In a sense, this agenda would fulfill the next phase of the American civil rights movement. The movement was able to push through legislation that outlawed gross white supremacist practices, but the reforms never adequately addressed the economic dimension of white supremacy. Efforts such as Dr. Martin Luther King's Poor People's Campaign and the War on Poverty were never fully institutionalized. The implementation of asset-building policies that are racially and ethnically inclusive will strengthen the social fabric for future generations.

Obviously, questions about how to design a program to tax wealth in order to broaden wealth remain. Should wealth-broadening go beyond these notions of individual wealth ownership to include community wealth? For instance, public or community-owned housing units with low monthly fees may not represent private wealth for an individual, but are a tremendous source of economic stability and security. Should the wealth-creation vehicles have strings attached, with funds restricted to education, homeownership, and retirement? How should we recognize, in some financial way, the legacy of racial discrimination in wealth-building? How do we protect the ideas from being co-opted by neo-conservatives and avoid risking greater erosion of the welfare state? And what are the politically winnable forms of wealth taxation?

Wealth-building efforts need a revenue stream in order to have a real impact. Organizations working at the state and national levels to defend the estate tax, and progressive taxes more generally, need a positive, galvanizing policy agenda. In sum, wealth taxation and asset development need one another. Taxing concentrated wealth and linking the revenues to programs that will spread wealth in the next generation is the political heart of a winning strategy to expand wealth ownership and build a more equitable society.

Closing the racial wealth divide will require that we not only take strong measures to spread wealth to the poor and middle class regardless of race, but that we also target and address the particular needs of historically disadvantaged groups. Only large-scale redistributive reforms can reduce persistent racial wealth disparities.

CLOSING THE RACIAL WEALTH GAP FOR THE NEXT GENERATION

BY MEIZHU LUI
August 2004

I t was only after the civil rights movement opened up new opportunities for people of color that Judith Roderick, an African-American woman, landed a union job in the defense industry in Boston. She worked hard, and, for many years, earned high wages and enjoyed health and retirement benefits.

She saved her money and bought a home in a predominantly black neighborhood. When the local bank denied her a conventional loan to rehab the house, Judith resorted to taking a high-interest loan. She set to work on the home repairs and began making loan payments.

All of that changed in the early 1990s, when company managers, seeking to cut labor costs, laid her off.

As Judith struggled to find a job with a similar wage, the loan caused her to spiral into deeper debt. A few years later, the bank took her house.

As Judith's fortunes declined, the fortunes of many other Boston-area residents—people with advanced degrees, professional jobs, and stock investments—soared. For them, the 1990s economy was booming.

White professionals poured into her neighborhood (which, thanks to her own efforts and those of other local activists, had been fixed up and rid of crime)—sending her rent soaring to $2,000 a month. The bank sold her old house for more than four times what she had originally paid for it.

Judith, who had taken over the care of her grandson, received temporary transitional assistance from the state and managed to get medical benefits for the child. She also qualified for Section 8, a federal rental subsidy. Today, she struggles to pay her bills and keep a roof over her own and her grandson's head.

Unfortunately, Judith's story is not an unusual one among people of color. Better economic times bring small gains, thanks to immense organizing efforts and personal sacrifice. But when there's an economic downturn, racial and ethnic minorities are the first to be, well, turned down.

Whites and people of color move along different economic tracks. Because of past and present discrimination, people of color begin several paces behind the starting line and face more hurdles along the course.

Activists, scholars, and policymakers must bear this in mind as they work to address the national problem of wealth inequality. Policy strategies, whether universal (applying equally to all regardless of race or ethnicity), or targeted to disadvantaged groups, should be examined for their intended and unintended consequences for people of color.

Too often, nonwhites have been excluded from supposedly universal programs. For example, the federal government backed $120 billion in home loans through the Federal Housing Administration between 1934 and 1962, enabling millions of families to attain homeownership. But because of rules that tied mortgage eligibility to race, the vast majority of FHA-backed loans went to whites.

Strategies to close the wealth gap should ensure that minorities have equal access to program benefits, and that programs target not just the overall wealth gap, but the racial wealth gap specifically. Attaining parity will require some catch up.

What follows is a partial list of policies that, if implemented, would go a long way toward putting people of all ethnic and racial backgrounds on the same economic track.

1. HOMEOWNERSHIP

It is said that it is better to have loved and lost than to never have loved at all. The same doesn't hold for homeownership. It's worse to save and purchase a home, only to lose it.

Did Judith really have to lose her home? This question is legitimate given that the federal government props up and protects the nation's two largest mortgage lenders, the Federal National Mortgage Corporation and the Federal Home Loan Mortgage Corporation (better known as Fannie Mae and Freddie Mac). These for-profit corporations were chartered by the government specifically to provide affordable housing for low- and moderate-income people.

These corporations don't make loans directly to individuals; rather, they buy small and medium-sized mortgages from banks, package them together into tradeable securities, and sell these mortgage packages to pension funds and other investors. This arrangement encourages local banks to issue home mortgage loans in low-income communities (because they know they'll be able to resell the loan to these corporations). Fannie Mae and Freddie Mac also work with community organizations to provide credit counseling and other information services in low-income neighborhoods.

The federal government heavily supports Fannie Mae and Freddie Mac with billion-dollar low-interest lines of credit from the Treasury, tax exemptions, and federal insurance, and the federal government could certainly require more of them.

To ensure that Fannie Mae and Freddie Mac reach their mandated quotas of services to low-income people, stronger enforcement mechanisms are needed. In addition, explicit quotas for assistance to people of color and immigrants should be introduced.

Too many immigrants still lack access to information about available housing programs. Many are unfamiliar with the process of purchasing a home, or for that matter, starting a business. This could be reversed if Fannie Mae and Freddie Mac worked with banks to target underserved immigrant communities with multilingual, culturally competent outreach programs. If financial institutions knew they would face repercussions for underserving non-English speaking households, they would design services to better meet their needs.

The 1977 Community Reinvestment Act (CRA) was a major victory for community members mobilized to combat discrimination in home financing. The law requires banks to offer low- and moderate-income people equal access to loans. However, almost 30 years after passage of the CRA, people of color remain less likely than comparable whites to be approved for home mortgages.

Because they buy so many mortgage loans, Fannie Mae and Freddie Mac wield great influence over home-lending practices nationwide. They could impose stricter anti-discrimination requirements on lenders and permit consumers who lack credit histories to submit alternative evidence of their capacity to save and pay bills on time.

Just as important, all regulated lenders should be required to take measures to protect low- and moderate-income borrowers from foreclosure through loan forgiveness programs, payment reductions, and payment waivers. For Judith, the foreclosure took away the asset she had saved to build and literally pushed her from the middle class back into poverty. Rather than profit from layoffs and other economic misfortunes that fall disproportionately on people of color, banks ought to make it their mission to build wealth in households of color and disadvantaged communities.

If Judith could have held on to her home for a few more years, she would have been able to sell the house herself when the market turned, regain her initial investment, and save enough to begin rebuilding her assets.

2. HIGHER EDUCATION

Today, higher education is more important than ever. The wage gap between those with a high school diploma and those with a college degree has continued to widen. Yet the cost of tuition at public and private universities alike has skyrocketed over the last few decades, making college less affordable for those who most need the leg up it provides. At the same time, the mix of federally funded scholarships and loans has shifted: today, 77% of student aid is in loans, so that even those low- and moderate-income students who manage to complete college will start their work lives with tens of thousands of dollars of debt. What's more, aid has become less needs-based and more merit-based, disproportionately benefiting white and wealthier students.

In contrast to today's students, who are left to bear the cost of college largely on their own or with loans, a whole generation of white men in the post-World War II generation got help from the federal government. The 1944 GI Bill subsidized college education for white war veterans, enabling large numbers to move into professional jobs. While African-American and Latino veterans also had formal rights to GI Bill aid, discrimination by universities blocked many from actually using those benefits.

In the 1960s and 1970s, civil rights legislation and affirmative action finally opened college doors for nonwhites—but the rising cost of college, and court challenges to affirmative action, are putting those advances at risk.

We need a new education initiative on the scale of the GI Bill—a massive effort to make higher education affordable to all college-ready students. Short of that, more investment in publicly funded higher education, increased funding for Pell grants and need-based scholarships, and strengthened affirmative action programs would be a good start. Without this sort of educational assistance, Judith's grandson will be unable to pay for college and will likely find himself struggling to get by in a low-wage job.

3. NATIONAL HEALTH CARE

Almost half of all personal bankruptcy filings are due to a lack of adequate health insurance or other health-related expenses. People of color, who make up a third of the nonelderly population, comprise over half of the uninsured, according to the Kaiser Family Foundation. It's no wonder that one of the top policy priorities of the Black Congressional Caucus in 2004 is the provision of health insurance for all.

There is nothing magic about insurance—insurance is basically a system for sharing the risk of unexpected losses. It's an idea that grew from longstanding community practice. Before companies like Blue Cross were formed, extended families would pitch in when any family member had doctors' bills he couldn't pay. In other words, families shared each individual family member's risk of ill health. Today, we're going backwards—each individual is supposed to take care of his or her own costs. When one premature baby can require a half-million dollars of care, this makes no sense. A universal health program would create a huge risk pool comprised of everyone in the country. The more people who share the risk, the more efficient the program, and the more affordable the cost of care.

4. UNIONIZATION AND FAIR TRADE

Union members have higher wages and better benefits than nonunion workers. This is not because union members have better skills, but because they exert collective pressure on employers and thereby gain a greater share of the wealth created by their labor.

Heavy unionization in manufacturing industries like steel and autos gave some African-American workers a foothold of economic security in the middle of the last century, enabling them to earn decent wages, with benefits and pensions, and to begin to realize the American dream.

The decline of U.S. manufacturing began in the 1970s and is accelerating today as global free-trade agreements give corporations the "freedom" to search the world for those most desperate for work at any wage.

During the same period, employers have used increasingly militant tactics to crush the labor movement, with the help of a multibillion dollar industry of anti-union consulting firms. Today, just 13% of the workforce belongs to unions, down from a peak of 35% in the 1950s.

Strengthening workers' right to organize unions would help restart the stalled process of building an African-American middle class—and also benefit immigrant workers. Fair trade agreements guaranteeing worker rights worldwide would, over the long run, also protect workers' job security at home.

5. ASSET DEVELOPMENT POLICIES

Various proposals for asset "starter kits" have been floated in the United States and elsewhere. Independent Development Accounts (IDAs) were launched by a 1998 federal pilot program. Children's Savings Accounts (CSAs) have been established in the United Kingdom, but remain at the proposal stage in the United States.

IDAs are a form of matched savings account in which savings may be withdrawn only for asset-building investments (for example, to buy a home, start a business, or go to school). The matching funds come from the government or a nonprofit organization. IDAs are administered by community-based organizations in partnership with financial institutions that hold deposits. There are now over 500 IDA initiatives across the country, according to the Center for Social Development.

CSAs ensure that every child starts life with a trust fund. At a child's birth, an account is established for her with perhaps $500 to $1,000 of public funds. Parents are encouraged to add roughly that amount to the fund every year, matched by more public and private funds, for up to five years. When the child reaches 18, she would have around $40,000 to use for education, to start a business, or as a down payment on a home.

IDAs should be expanded and funded more heavily and CSAs made available. Both programs should have a progressive matching system to provide larger matching funds to lower-income people. This would enable someone like Judith, who has worked hard all her life but has no cushion of savings, to pass along a financial nest egg to her grandchild. (You never know—he could be an African-American Bill

Gates!) Asset starter kits ensure all children, including poor children, have opportunities to develop their talents.

Asset-building programs like these must be designed with and for communities of color and immigrant communities. Many groups already form informal rotating savings and credit associations: individuals put in a certain amount of money every month, and then, in rotation, each has a turn at using all the money in the pot. These accounts have helped to start and expand many businesses, for example, in Korean communities. But "ROSCAs" face certain barriers. Most significantly, banks treat personal deposits as belonging to an individual or household, reporting any deposit of more than $10,000 to the Internal Revenue Service. Reforms should at minimum create a tax exemption for these collective savings pools, and, better still, bolster them with matching funds.

When Martin Luther King traveled to Washington, D.C., in 1963, he didn't go to tell people about a dream. He went to "cash a promissory note"—the Constitution's promise of life, liberty, and the pursuit of happiness for all. This promise cannot be kept without a government commitment to provide some measure of financial opportunity and security for all of us. For centuries, vast private wealth was created from a human rights disaster: the African slave trade. While this is an uncomfortable topic that most white Americans would just as well put under "file closed," slavery left a legacy that is still very much with us today. African Americans like Judith, whether descended from slaves or not, still suffer from the accumulated effects of the historical social and economic exclusion of their people, and the barriers to wealth creation that persist. If, as a society, we truly believe in equal opportunity for all, then we cannot claim there is a fair race being run when some people have not even approached the starting line. Call it reparations, or restitution, or a chance to catch up—or simply call it justice.

If, by the time Judith Roderick's grandchild is grown, he has access to a good education, health insurance, a financial nest egg, encouragement from an entire society cheering his success, and a guarantee that the color of his skin will not have any bearing on his future, then this nation will at last be on the road to closing the racial wealth gap.

The distribution of wealth in the United States is not likely to change dramatically unless the institutional framework for creating and distributing it is altered. A wide range of community economic development institutions, created by visionary activists and government officials across the country, is beginning to point the way.

COMMUNITY ECONOMIC DEVELOPMENT

An Alternative Vision for Creating and Distributing Wealth

BY THAD WILLIAMSON
August 2004

Inequalities of wealth in the United States result from an economic system that encourages individuals and corporations to accumulate private wealth for private ends. Corporations may rule the world today, but even within modern capitalist economies, there are counter-examples of public, quasi-public, and community-based institutions generating shared, common wealth and using it for shared, common ends. Although these institutions are minute relative to those of the mainstream economy, taken together they are beginning to achieve sufficient size and maturity so as to be able to suggest the outlines of an entirely different economic system.

The most obvious—and perhaps still the most important—example of publicly held wealth is the federal government itself, which owns over 3 billion square feet of building space and millions of acres of undeveloped land. Total federal assets, including land, buildings, infrastructure, and equipment, are estimated to exceed $1.4 trillion. The public also owns the airwaves, a priceless commodity. (Radio and TV networks are tenants of the airwaves, not owners.)

Recognizing just how much federally controlled wealth remains in the United States even today is important—not least because some conservatives and libertarians would like to see the government sell off (or give away) its vast assets. But these assets are of little or no direct value to the people on the wrong side of the wealth gap. The fact that the government owns vast tracts in Wyoming means little in low-income communities around the country where savings and steady work are scarce.

That's where local-scale, community-based economic institutions come in. Under the radar of mainstream media attention, an impressive array of alternative wealth-holding and job-creating institutions has evolved and matured in the past 30 years. While the mechanics of these institutions vary widely, all are built on the principle that profits accumulated through economic activity should be invested in the community or otherwise used to benefit all its members.

Perhaps the best known of these institutional innovations is the **community development corporation** (CDC). CDCs are nonprofit organizations governed by representatives from particular communities (neighborhoods, or entire cities or counties), charged with trying to stimulate economic development in depressed areas. Many CDCs focus on housing development; for example, they may buy abandoned or dilapidated properties, renovate them, then sell them to moderate-income families under special equity rules designed to keep the housing permanently affordable.

Other CDCs have branched out and established their own businesses. CDC-owned businesses both provide jobs to local residents and create a revenue stream that can be used to finance other activities (for example, anti-drug education, child care, or job training) that enhance the local quality of life.

Two CDCs that have been particularly successful in developing a portfolio of community-controlled businesses are the New Community Corporation in Newark, N.J., which employs 2,300 people and generates over $200 million a year in economic activity, and The East Los Angeles Community Union (TELACU), with assets of over $300 million. TELACU employs more than 700 people in businesses such as construction management, telecommunications, and roofing supply.

Closely related to the growth of CDCs are a range of **community development financial institutions** (CDFIs)—banks, credit unions, and microlenders that focus explicitly on assisting community development in depressed areas. Two of the best known examples are Shorebank, a network of financial institutions that invests over $150 million a year in low-income neighborhoods in Chicago, Cleveland, Michigan, and the Pacific Northwest; and Self-Help in Durham, N.C., which has provided over $3.5 billion in assistance to poor people since 1980 in the form of personal loans, business loans, and mortgages. Self-Help also played a critical role in helping pass landmark anti-predatory lending legislation in North Carolina in 1999.

In the 1990s, the federal government established the Community Development Financial Institutions Fund to provide badly needed capital support and technical assistance to fledgling CDFIs. The Bush administration has cut funding for the CDFI Fund; restoring and indeed dramatically expanding support for the fund should be a major policy priority.

Nonprofit-owned businesses are another promising model for broadening wealth. In the last decade, more and more nonprofits have sought to become financially independent by launching business activities. One is Pioneer Human Services in Seattle, a $55 million organization that employs over 1,000 people—most of whom are disadvantaged—in eight businesses, including a precision light-metal fabricator. Pioneer uses revenues from its enterprises to fund a wide range of social services for homeless people and addicts. Another example is Rubicon Programs in Richmond, Calif., which uses revenues from a bakery, a landscaping service, and a home care agency to fund about half of its $14 million budget. The funds are used to provide job training and other assistance to poor people.

Employee ownership is another powerful vehicle for broadening wealth. Over 11,000 firms in the United States are now at least partially employee-owned, and majority employee-owned firms have been successful in a range of sectors, from steel to supermarkets. Research conducted by Peter Kardas, Adria Scharf, and Jim Keogh shows that workers in majority employee-owned firms are better paid than workers in comparable traditional firms, and that these employees get nearly $20,000 more in pension benefits on average than their counterparts in conventional firms. Majority employee-owned firms where workers have full voting rights are unlikely to abandon local communities in search of a higher profit elsewhere; evidence suggests that employee-owned firms are also less likely to declare bankruptcy.

Local public enterprise is surprisingly widespread in the United States, and offers yet another way communities can create jobs and public wealth at the same time. The United States has a long tradition of publicly held electric utilities, which consistently offer lower rates and are generally credited with much more responsible and proactive environmental policies than private, for-profit utilities. The Sacramento Municipal Utility District, which employs more than 2,000 people, spends over $25 million a year on energy efficiency initiatives, discounts to low-income users, and other public programs.

The public utility approach now extends far beyond electricity. Glasgow, Ky., a small rural community, pioneered the concept of a publicly owned and operated telecommunications system. In 1988, the town's electric utility began constructing a citywide communications network to provide cable television, computer networking, and eventually high-speed Internet access. The town's citizens and businesses now enjoy high-speed Internet access and cable television service at a fraction of the rate charged by private providers: residents have saved an estimated $14 million in cable bills alone since 1989. Glasgow's investment in information-technology infrastructure has also attracted many new employers to the city.

By the year 2000, over 250 municipalities had plans in place to own and operate telecommunications systems. One of the largest is in Tacoma, Wash., which in the late 1990s created the Click! Network, part of the public utility Tacoma Power, to compete against AT&T Broadband and other private cable and high-speed Internet providers. By 2001, Click! began turning a profit and now helps bolster Tacoma

Power's overall financial position. As in Glasgow, in addition to saving Tacoma residents money, the Click! network has benefited local businesses and helped bolster local economic development. Utility officials also plan to use detailed information transmitted by the network to improve energy management and encourage energy conservation by residents.

Telecommunications is not the only game in town for cities and states wishing to boost revenues and hold down tax rates by establishing public enterprises. Other cities, including Hartford, Seattle, and Oakland, run real estate businesses, using city-owned land to leverage other forms of local economic development. San Diego generates some $43 million a year in revenues from the over 400 properties it leases. Municipalities are also generating revenue through composting systems, methane recovery operations, and retail activities. In addition to the jobs for local residents and other social benefits of many of these ventures, the additional revenue they generate helps pay for vital city services.

Perhaps the most dramatic example of how a public entity can reshape the accumulation and distribution of wealth is the Alaska Permanent Fund. Revenues from oil extraction not only pay for almost the entire Alaska state government, they also fund an annual "dividend" payout to each Alaskan of roughly $1,000 to $2,000. The dividend checks are a major boost to working-class and lower-income Alaskans and are one of the largest sources of income in the state economy as a whole.

Alaska's situation is unique, but its experience points to broader possibilities for asserting public control over natural resources and other public goods in order to provide everyone a steady stream of income and—at least slightly—to level the wealth distribution. It is easy to imagine entrepreneurial cities establishing public control over downtown land and then using revenues from leasing the land to fund dividends for city residents and other public purposes. Or the federal government devoting fees from broadcasters' use of the public airwaves to particular public goods. (Reading programs funded by revenue from TV networks might be appropriate!)

Advocates for a more egalitarian society in which wealth is less concentrated have to do more than critique today's disturbing trends. They must consider alternative mechanisms for producing and distributing wealth that really do lift all boats. Community-based economic institutions have an important role to play: they provide tangible benefits to people right now, they offer models that can be replicated and expanded, and, more broadly, they highlight a new understanding of wealth as a public, shared good that can and should be used for public, shared purposes.

Predatory lenders who charge usurious rates, write loans full of pitfalls in fine print, and push homeowners into foreclosure are literally stripping the wealth out of poor communities and communities of color. Activist David Swanson shows how a grassroots campaign forced the nation's largest predatory lender to pay back the people it swindled and adopt permanent reforms.

FLAME-BROILED SHARK

How Predatory Lending Victims Fought Back and Won

BY DAVID SWANSON
July/August 2004

If someone told you that a number of low-income people, most of them African-American or Latino, most of them women, most of them elderly, had been robbed of much of their equity or of their entire homes by a predatory mortgage lender, you might not be surprised. But if you heard that these women and men had brought the nation's largest high-cost lender to its knees, forced it to sell out to a foreign company, and won back a half a billion dollars that had been taken from them, you'd probably ask what country this had happened in. Surely it couldn't have been in the United States, land of unbridled corporate power.

And yet it was. In 2001, these families, all members of the Association of Community Organizations for Reform Now (ACORN), launched a campaign against the nation's largest and most notorious predatory lender, Household International (also known as Household Finance or Beneficial). The 2003 settlement included a ban on talking about the damage Household had inflicted on borrowers and neighborhoods. That's one reason many people haven't heard this story—the families who defeated Household are in effect barred from publicly criticizing the corporation and teaching others the lessons they learned. (I was ACORN's communications coordinator during much of the Household campaign but left before it ended. No one asked me not to tell this story.)

In low-income minority neighborhoods in the United States, the little wealth that exists lies in home equity (see "Home Equity as a Percent of Net Worth"). People

HOME EQUITY AS A PERCENT OF NET WORTH, BY INCOME QUINTILE, 2000

	Lowest	Next-Lowest	Middle	Next-to-Highest	Highest
Non-Hispanic Whites	85.6	77.7	70.8	62.9	44.4
Hispanics	90.0	73.5	76.3	70.9	64.9
African Americans	NA	78.7	70.9	73.5	67.8

Source: U.S. Census Bureau, May 2003.

of color have made gains in home ownership during the past few decades, thanks in part to efforts by community groups like ACORN and National People's Action to force banks to make loans in communities of color (see "Minority Homeownership Is Growing"). Overall, these gains have been good for the new homeowners and good for their neighborhoods.

But low-income home ownership is fragile. Half of all extremely low-income homeowners pay more than half of their income for housing, according to the National Low Income Housing Coalition. Because low-income homeownership is not protected by additional savings, a temporary loss of income or a sudden large expense, such as a medical bill, can mean the loss of the home.

High-cost lenders—including large national operations like Household, Wells Fargo, and Citigroup, as well as small-time local sharks—strip away, rather than build up, equity in poor neighborhoods. Predatory high-cost lenders turn the usual logic of lending upside down. They make their money by intentionally issuing loans that borrowers will be unable to repay. Their loans invariably leave borrowers worse off, not better off.

Most high-cost (also called "subprime") loans are home-mortgage refinance loans. They carry excessive, and sometimes variable, interest rates and exorbitant fees. The more abusive lenders bundle bogus products like credit insurance into their loans, which accrue more interest and fees. Some lenders quietly omit taxes and insurance costs from monthly mortgage statements, causing crises when the yearly tax and insurance bills arrive. Others encourage borrowers to consolidate credit card and other debt within the mortgage, which further decreases home equity and places the home at greater risk. Loans may even exceed the value of the home, trapping people in debt they cannot refinance with a responsible lender. Hidden balloon payments force repeated refinancing (with fees each time). When borrowers find themselves unable to meet payments, the predatory lender refinances them repeatedly and ultimately seizes the house. Borrowers often have little recourse, as mandatory arbitration clauses written into their loan contracts prevent them from taking lenders to court.

High-cost loans are not made only to people with poor credit. Fannie Mae estimates that as many as half of all subprime borrowers could have qualified for a lower-cost mortgage. After British financial corporation HSBC bought Household International in March 2003, it announced that 46% of Household's real estate-backed loans had been made to borrowers with 'A' credit. But Household had made no 'A' (standard low-cost) loans. In fact, Household was a leading cause of the rows of vacant houses appearing in ACORN neighborhoods in the 1990s.

FIGHTING BACK

ACORN members didn't take this abuse lying down. Their grassroots effort against Household relied on numerous strategies, including shareholder activism, political advocacy, and the old stand-by of direct action. It offers a model for low-income communities seeking to challenge exploitative corporations.

In 2001, ACORN members launched the campaign with simultaneous protests inside Household offices in cities around the country, and then began work to pass anti-predatory lending legislation at local, state, and federal levels.

Later that year, ACORN, together with the advocacy group Coalition for Responsible Wealth, introduced a shareholder resolution that proposed to tie Household executives' compensation to the termination of the company's predatory lending practices. When Household held its annual meeting in a suburb of Tampa, Fla., a crowd of ACORN members arrived at the event wearing shark suits and holding shark balloons. The resolution won 5% of the shareholders' vote. In 2002, Household held its meeting an hour and a half from the nearest airport in rural Kentucky. ACORN members weren't deterred by the remote location—they came from all over the country by car. The protest may have been the biggest thing the town of London, Ky., had ever seen. This time, 30% of the shareholders supported the resolution.

ACORN also helped borrowers file a number of class-action suits against Household for practices that were clearly illegal under existing law, and it let Wall Street analysts know what Household stood to lose from these lawsuits. ACORN urged state attorneys general and federal regulators to investigate the firm, and simultaneously put pressure on stores, including Best Buy, that issued Household credit cards. As a result of ACORN agitation, various local and state governments passed resolutions urging their pension funds to divest from the firm.

In the summer of 2002, ACORN members did something that really got the attention of Household executives and board members. On a beautiful day, thousands of Household borrowers poured out of buses onto the lawns of the company CEO and board members in the wealthy suburbs north of Chicago. They knocked on the officials' doors, speaking directly to the people whose policies had hurt them from a distance. When forced to leave, ACORN members plastered "Wanted" posters all over the neighborhood.

Through all of this, ACORN worked the media. It kept a database of borrowers' stories, and put reporters in touch with them, generating several hundred national print articles and television and radio spots. It also maintained an enormous website about Household (which has since been removed as part of the gag-order agreement).

Meanwhile, ACORN Housing Corporation, a nonprofit loan-counseling agency created by ACORN, helped many borrowers cancel rip-off services, such as credit insurance, that were built into their loans, and, when possible, refinance out of their Household loans altogether.

HOUSEHOLD'S CONCESSIONS

For more than two years, a small handful of ACORN staff organized thousands of members in an unrelenting effort, until Household International could no longer sustain the negative attention, shareholder discontent, and legal and regulatory pressures. In early 2003, the lender agreed to pay $489 million in restitution to borrowers through the 50 state attorneys general. The company later agreed to pay millions more to ACORN to fund new financial literacy programs. This was one of the largest consumer settlements in history, but it amounted to only a fraction of what Household had taken from people, and it could not undo all the damage done to families who had lost their homes. In addition to the payments, the company will:

- Ensure that new loans actually provide a benefit to consumers prior to issuing the loans.
- Reform and improve disclosures to consumers.
- Reimburse states to cover the costs of the investigations into Household's practices.
- Limit prepayment penalties to the first two years of a loan.
- Limit points and origination fees, upfront charges built into the loan, to 5%. (A "point" is one percentage point of the loan amount.)
- Eliminate "piggyback" second mortgages. (When Household issued home loans, it would simultaneously issue a second, smaller, loan at an even higher rate. It often labeled these second loans "lines of credit" in order to avoid federal regulations that limit the rate that can be charged.)
- Implement a "Foreclosure Avoidance Program" to provide relief to borrowers who are at risk of losing their homes due to delinquent payments (for example, reducing interest rates, waiving unpaid late charges, deferring interest, and reducing the principal).

ACORN-led efforts won legislative and corporate reforms as well. Several cities and states (including Arkansas, California, New Mexico, New Jersey, and New York)

PHOTOGRAPHY BY ACORN

ACORN members from 27 states protest Wells Fargo's predatory lending practices as part of the ACORN national convention in Los Angeles, 2004.

have banned abusive practices that were once routine. One practice ACORN targeted aggressively was "single-premium credit insurance," a nearly useless and overpriced insurance policy that predatory lenders added to many loans (often falsely describing it as a requirement or failing to tell borrowers it had been included). In 2002, Household and other major lenders announced they would drop the product. This was one of several corporate reforms ACORN won during the course of the campaign.

This campaign demonstrates that a well-organized grassroots effort can combat corporate exploitation and extract significant concessions. By pursuing different strategies at once, ACORN repeatedly hit Household with the unexpected, and put it on the defensive. The outcome is good news for low-income neighborhoods, and bad news for Wells Fargo, the predatory lender who is next on ACORN's list.

Pension wealth is one of the most powerful and underused weapons of working people. Most pension wealth is invested by the financial industry with no concern for the impact on working people or their communities. But among union and public-employee pension trustees, there's a growing movement to direct a portion of workers' pension wealth toward worker-friendly investments that bolster the labor movement, save jobs, and build affordable housing.

LABOR'S CAPITAL

Putting Pension Wealth to Work for Workers

BY ADRIA SCHARF
September/October 2005

Pension fund assets are the largest single source of investment capital in the country. Of the roughly $17 trillion in private equity in the U.S. economy, $6 to 7 trillion is held in employee pensions. About $1.3 trillion is in union pension plans (jointly trusteed labor-management plans or collectively bargained company-sponsored plans) and $2.1 trillion is in public employee pension plans. Several trillion more are in defined contribution plans and company-sponsored defined benefit plans with no union representation. These vast sums were generated by—and belong to—workers; they're really workers' deferred wages.

Workers' retirement dollars course through Wall Street, but most of the capital owned *by* working people is invested with no regard *for* working people or their communities. Pension dollars finance sweatshops overseas, hold shares of public companies that conduct mass layoffs, and underwrite myriad anti-union low-road corporate practices. In one emblematic example, the Florida public pension system bought out the Edison Corporation, the for-profit school operator, in November 2003, with the deferred wages of Florida government employees—including public school teachers. (With just three appointed trustees, one of whom is Governor Jeb Bush, Florida is one of the few states with no worker representation on the board of its state-employee retirement fund.)

The custodians of workers' pensions—plan trustees and investment managers—argue that they are bound by their "fiduciary responsibility" to consider only narrow financial factors when making investment decisions. They maintain they have a singular obligation to maximize financial returns and minimize financial risk for beneficiaries—with no regard for broader concerns. But from the perspective of the teachers whose dollars funded an enterprise that aims to privatize their jobs, investing in Edison, however promising the expected return (and given Edison's track record, it wasn't very promising!), makes no sense.

A legal concept enshrined in the 1974 Employee Retirement Income Security Act (ERISA) and other statutes, "fiduciary responsibility" does constrain the decision-making of those charged with taking care of other people's money. It obligates fiduciaries (e.g., trustees and fund managers) to invest retirement assets for the exclusive benefit of the pension beneficiaries. According to ERISA, fiduciaries must act with the care, skill, prudence, and diligence that a "prudent man" would use. Exactly what that means, though, is contested.

The law does *not* say that plan trustees must maximize short-term return. It does, in fact, give fiduciaries some leeway to direct pension assets to worker- and community-friendly projects. In 1994, the U.S. Department of Labor issued rule clarifications that expressly permit fiduciaries to make "economically targeted investments" (ETIs), or investments that take into account collateral benefits like good jobs, housing, improved social service facilities, alternative energy, strengthened infrastructure, and economic development. Trustees and fund managers are free to consider a double bottom line, prioritizing investments that have a social pay-off so long as their expected risk-adjusted financial returns are equal to other, similar, investments. Despite a backlash against ETIs from Newt Gingrich conservatives in the 1990s, Clinton's Labor Department rules still hold.

Nevertheless, the dominant mentality among the asset management professionals who make a living off what United Steelworkers president Leo Gerard calls "the deferred-wage food table" staunchly resists considering any factors apart from financial risk and return.

This is beginning to change in some corners of the pension fund world, principally (no surprise) where workers and beneficiaries have some control over their pension capital. In jointly managed union defined-benefit (known as "Taft-Hartley") plans and public-employee pension plans, the ETI movement is gaining ground. "Taft-Hartley pension trustees have grown more comfortable with economically targeted investments as a result of a variety of influences, one being the Labor Department itself," says Robert Pleasure of the Center for Working Capital, an independent capital stewardship-educational institute started by the AFL-CIO. Concurrently, more public pension fund trustees have begun adopting ETIs that promote housing and economic development within state borders. Most union and public pension trustees now understand that, as long as they follow a careful process and protect returns, ETIs do not breach their fiduciary duty, and may in certain cases actually be sounder investments than over-inflated Wall Street stocks.

SAVING JOBS: HEARTLAND LABOR CAPITAL NETWORK

During the run-up of Wall Street share prices in the 1990s, investment funds virtually redlined basic industries, preferring to direct dollars into hot public technology stocks and emerging foreign markets, which despite the rhetoric of fiduciary responsibility were often speculative, unsound, investments. Even most collectively bargained funds put their assets exclusively in Wall Street stocks, in part because some pension trustees feared that if they didn't, they could be held liable. (During an earlier period, the Labor Department aggressively pursued union pension trustees for breaches of fiduciary duty. In rare cases where trustees were found liable, their personal finances and possessions were at risk.) But in the past five years, more union pension funds and labor-friendly fund managers have begun directing assets into investments that bolster the "heartland" economy: worker-friendly private equity, and, wherever possible, unionized industries and companies that offer "card-check" and "neutrality." ("Card-check" requires automatic union recognition if a majority of employees present signed authorization cards; "neutrality" means employers agree to remain neutral during organizing campaigns.)

The Heartland Labor Capital Network is at the center of this movement. The network's Tom Croft says he and his allies want to "make sure there's an economy still around in the future to which working people will be able to contribute." Croft estimates that about $3 to $4 billion in new dollars have been directed to worker-friendly private equity since 1999—including venture capital, buyout funds, and "special situations" funds that invest in financially distressed companies, saving jobs and preventing closures. Several work closely with unions to direct capital into labor-friendly investments.

One such fund, New York-based KPS Special Situations, has saved over 10,000 unionized manufacturing jobs through its two funds, KPS Special Situations I and II, according to a company representative. In 2003, St. Louis-based Wire Rope Corporation, the nation's leading producer of high carbon wire and wire rope products, was in bankruptcy with nearly 1,000 unionized steelworker jobs in jeopardy. KPS bought the company and restructured it in collaboration with the United Steelworkers International. Approximately 20% of KPS's committed capital is from Taft-Hartley pension dollars; as a result, the Wire Rope transaction included some union pension assets.

The Heartland Labor Capital Network and its union partners want to expand this sort of strategic deployment of capital by building a national capital pool of "Heartland Funds" financed by union pension assets and other sources. These funds have already begun to make direct investments in smaller worker-friendly manufacturing and related enterprises; labor representatives participate alongside investment experts on their advisory boards.

"It's simple. Workers' assets should be invested in enterprises and construction projects that will help to build their cities, rebuild their schools, and rebuild America's infrastructure," says Croft.

"CAPITAL STEWARDSHIP": THE AFL-CIO

For the AFL-CIO, ETIs are nothing new. Its Housing Investment Trust (HIT), formed in 1964, is the largest labor-sponsored investment vehicle in the country that produces collateral benefits for workers and their neighborhoods. Hundreds of union pension funds invest in the $2 billion trust, which leverages public financing to build housing, including low-income and affordable units, using union labor. HIT, together with its sister fund the Building Investment Trust (BIT), recently announced a new investment program that is expected to generate up to $1 billion in investment in apartment development and rehabilitation by 2005 in targeted cities including New York, Chicago, and Philadelphia. The initiative will finance thousands of units of housing and millions of hours of union construction work. HIT and BIT require owners of many of the projects they help finance to agree to card-check recognition and neutrality for their employees.

HIT and BIT are two examples of union-owned investment vehicles. There are many others—including the LongView ULTRA Construction Loan Fund, which finances projects that use 100% union labor; the Boilermakers' Co-Generation and Infrastructure Fund; and the United Food and Commercial Workers' Shopping Center Mortgage Loan Program—and their ranks are growing.

Since 1997, the AFL-CIO and its member unions have redoubled their efforts to increase labor's control over its capital through a variety of means. The AFL-CIO's Capital Stewardship Program promotes corporate governance reform, investment manager accountability, pro-worker investment strategies, international pension fund cooperation, and trustee education. It also evaluates worker-friendly pension funds on how well they actually advance workers' rights, among other criteria. The Center for Working Capital provides education and training to hundreds of union and public pension fund trustees each year, organizes conferences, and sponsors research on capital stewardship issues including ETIs.

PUBLIC PENSION PLANS JOIN IN

At least 29 states have ETI policies directing a portion of their funds, usually less than 5%, to economic development within state borders. The combined public pension assets in ETI programs amount to about $55 billion, according to a recent report commissioned by the Vermont state treasurer. The vast majority of these ETIs are in residential housing and other real estate.

The California Public Employees' Retirement System (CalPERS) is an ETI pioneer among state pension funds. The single largest pension fund in the country, it has $153.8 billion in assets and provides retirement benefits to over 1.4 million members. In the mid-1990s, when financing for housing construction dried up in California, CalPERS invested hundreds of millions of dollars to finance about 4% of the state's single-family housing market. Its ETI policy is expansive. While it requires economically targeted investments earn maximum returns for their level of risk and fall within geographic and asset-diversification guidelines, CalPERS also considers the investments' benefits to its members and to state residents, their job creation potential, and the economic and social needs of different groups in the state's population. CalPERS directs about 2% of its assets—about $20 billion as of May 2001—to investments that provide collateral social benefits. It also requires construction and maintenance contractors to provide decent wages and benefits.

Other state pension funds have followed CalPERs' lead. In 2003, the Massachusetts treasury expanded its ETI program, which is funded by the state's $32 billion pension. Treasurer Timothy Cahill expects to do "two dozen or more" ETI investments in 2004, up from the single investment made in 2003, according to the *Boston Business Journal.* "It doesn't hurt our bottom line, and it helps locally," Cahill explained. The immediate priority will be job creation. Washington, Wisconsin, and New York also have strong ETI programs.

In their current form and at their current scale, economically targeted investments in the United States are not a panacea. Pension law does impose constraints. Many consultants and lawyers admonish trustees to limit ETIs to a small portion of an overall pension investment portfolio. And union trustees must pursue ETIs carefully, following a checklist of "prudence" procedures, to protect themselves from liability. The most significant constraint is simply that these investments must generate risk-adjusted returns equal to alternative investments—this means that many deserving not-for-profit efforts and experiments in economic democracy are automatically ruled out. Still, there's more wiggle room in the law than has been broadly recognized. And when deployed strategically to bolster the labor movement, support employee buyouts, generate good jobs, or build affordable housing, economically targeted investments are a form of worker direction over capital whose potential has only begun to be realized. And (until the day that capital is abolished altogether) that represents an important foothold.

As early as the mid-1970s, business expert Peter Drucker warned in *Unseen Revolution* of a coming era of "pension-fund socialism" in which the ownership of massive amounts of capital by pension funds would bring about profound changes to the social and economic power structure. Today, workers' pensions prop up the U.S. economy. They're a point of leverage like no other. Union and public pension funds are the most promising means for working people to shape the deployment of capital on a large scale, while directing assets to investments with collateral benefits. If workers and the trustees of their pension wealth recognize the power they hold, they could alter the contours of capitalism.

Are communities powerless against mega-corporations? Adam Sacks describes a struggle between corporate agribusiness and small towns in rural Pennsylvania, in which citizens have organized to protect their environment, their economy, and the social fabric of their community against factory pig farms and the politicians who love them.

RIGHTS FIGHT

Small Town Values vs. Corporate Agriculture

BY ADAM SACKS
July/August 2005

> They hang the man and flog the woman,
> Who steals the goose from off the common,
> Yet let the greater villain loose,
> That steals the common from the goose.
> > —*17th-century English protest rhyme*

In the late 1990s, life was getting tough for agribusiness in North Carolina. Over the previous decade or so, the state had risen from the number 15 hog producer in the country to number two. With more hogs than people, North Carolina's largely African-American Duplin and Sampson counties were the two largest pork-producing counties in the nation. By 1997, pollution, public health, and environmental justice problems were causing such widespread outcry that the state imposed a moratorium on all new pig farms that would last for almost six years. Soon factory farm corporations went on the prowl for greener pastures, so to speak.

Central Pennsylvania looked like an attractive target. It has an excellent system of roadways and accessible distribution centers. Land is relatively cheap. Many small farmers were, as usual, struggling. The Pennsylvania Farm Bureau, nominally a farmer advocacy organization, is firmly in the pocket of big agribusiness and highly influential in the state legislature. The central part of the state is rural, with township populations ranging from several hundred to a few thousand. This means there were no zoning regulations—the townships didn't think they needed them—to get in the way of large-scale hog farming. Rural township governments had no idea how to deal with powerful businesses. In short, the townships between Philadelphia in the east and Pittsburgh in the west were sitting ducks. Or so the ag boys thought.

ONSLAUGHT

The phone was ringing off the hook in the office of Thomas Linzey, a young attorney at the nonprofit organization he founded, the Community Environmental Legal Defense Fund (CELDF). Three years out of law school, Linzey was one of a rare breed of lawyer dedicated full time to public interest law. Idealistic and determined, he had set up a regulatory practice to help communities appeal permits issued to businesses they didn't want in their backyards. And he was good at it. In hearing after hearing, he pointed out defects in permit applications and convinced regulators and judges that these irresponsible corporate entities shouldn't be allowed to ply their noxious trades. Permits were rescinded, communities celebrated victories, Linzey and CELDF won prizes and kudos and were invited to Environment Day at the White House as guests of Vice President Al Gore. But there was a problem.

A few months after a community victory, the heretofore unpermitted corporation would return, permit in hand, ready to do business. What had happened? The only relevant issue in the regulatory appeal, whether all the bureaucratic dotted i's and crossed t's were in place, was resolved: the community had unearthed the problems with the permit, and the corporation proceeded to fix them. By challenging the permit and exposing the defects, the community had unwittingly done the corporation's work for free. Since townships of a few thousand people generally don't stand much of a chance against corporate legal budgets, practically speaking there was no further recourse.

Linzey had been puzzling over the battles won and wars lost in his first three years when the factory farm onslaught began. Local township officials, farmers, and concerned citizens were calling him, desperate, saying, "They're telling us that all we can do is regulate manure odor—but we don't want these toxic and destructive factory farms in our community *at all!* Please help us figure this out."

Factory pig farm operations produce tons of manure a day, which ends up in lakes, rivers, and drinking water. They not only seriously damage the environment—they also wreak havoc on the local economy and put independent family farmers out of business. Struggling farmers enter into one-sided output contracts with agribusiness corporations, agreeing to sell only to them. On their face, these contracts appear to be a way of guaranteeing a small farmer a market. But farmers soon find themselves trapped. The contracts hook them into expensive capital improvements that can cost hundreds of thousands of dollars, often paid for with loans issued by the corporations themselves. The contracts give the corporation ownership over all of the farm's animals—unless some die, in which case responsibility for the carcasses reverts to the farmers for disposal. And they allow the corporations to evade responsibility for environmental damage, since the giant firms don't technically own the property.

TAKING THE CONSTITUTION AWAY FROM CORPORATIONS

In 2002, Licking and Porter Townships in Clarion County, Pa., passed ordinances that strip corporations of their constitutional rights. The ordinances arose from residents' concern about a corporation suing them over their right to regulate sewage sludge. By abolishing corporate constitutional rights, the township eliminated the corporation's right to go to court against it, in effect returning the corporation to its status in the late 18th and early 19th centuries, before the courts began granting corporations the constitutional rights of people.

The ordinance reads, in part:

An Ordinance by the Second Class Township of _____, _____ County, Pennsylvania, Eliminating Legal Personhood Privileges from Corporations Doing Business Within _____ Township to Vindicate Democratic Rights

Section 5. Statement of Law. Corporations shall not be considered to be "persons" protected by the Constitution of the United States or the Constitution of the Commonwealth of Pennsylvania within the Second Class Township of _____, _____ County, Pennsylvania.

Section 6. Statement of Law. Corporations shall not be afforded the protections of the Commerce Clause (Article I, §8) of the United States Constitution; or the Contracts Clause of the United States Constitution (Article I, §10) and the Constitution of the Commonwealth of Pennsylvania (Article I, §17), as interpreted by the Courts, within the Second Class Township of _____, _____ County, Pennsylvania.

The result is an unequal arrangement in which the farmers own their land, but are so in hock to their corporate buyers, and utterly dependent on them, that they effectively lose control of their operations. The corporate party can unilaterally terminate the contract at any time, leaving the farmers to bail themselves out if they can. Most lose everything.

Like the township officials, Linzey was at a loss at first, but figured it was worth looking around to see what the possibilities were. He discovered that nine states, from Oklahoma in 1907 to South Dakota in 1998, had passed laws or constitutional amendments against corporate ownership or control of farms. Some of these laws contained exceptions for incorporated farms that were family owned and operated on a daily basis by one or more family members. That is, they didn't affect real farmers—people who wake up before sunrise, mingle with cows and pigs, and get their hands and boots dirty—but did cover the farms owned by corporate executives. Linzey converted text from these existing laws into a "Farm Ownership Ordinance" that many townships considered, and some passed. The ordinance template stated: "No corporation or syndicate may acquire, or otherwise obtain an interest, whether legal, beneficial, or otherwise, in any real estate used for farming in this Township, or engage in farming."

WHAT HAPPENED TO OUR LOCAL DEMOCRACY?

Although the citizens of rural Pennsylvania townships would be the last to call themselves activists or revolutionaries, their battles to preserve the health and integrity of their lives and homes against corporate assault have the makings of a sociopolitical earthquake. These mostly conservative Republican communities found themselves asking what had happened to their democracy.

How did it come to pass that a small handful of corporate directors a thousand miles away got to decide what takes place in their backyards? Why does the democratic decision of hundreds or thousands of citizens to keep out dangerous and destructive activity get trumped by distant interests whose only concern is how much of the community's wealth they can run away with, regardless of the collateral damage to the environment, economy, and social fabric of the community? As one town supervisor put it, "What the hell are rights of corporations?"

In short, the townspeople began having conversations about what it means to be a sovereign people, with inalienable rights, whose government operates only with their consent—conversations that hadn't been heard in the town commons or around kitchen tables for a long, long time. Organized by community leaders among friends and neighbors who had never before been active in civic affairs, their meetings took various forms. There were formal county-wide gatherings of hundreds of people, small conclaves in living rooms, and backyard barbecue chats. Armed with copies of the Constitution and Declaration of Independence, they asked and tried to answer basic questions, such as: What is a democracy? What are the people's rights, responsibilities, and privileges? What is the law? Who makes it and who enforces it? What are the courts? Whose side are they on?

Citizens realized that the issue was not really the factory farm or the sludged field. The issue was who has the right to decide what happens in our communities: we the people, or the corporations that have taken over our economy and our government for the benefit of the very few to the detriment of the rest of us. Farms are just one of a thousand different fronts to fight harms from pollution to corruption to war. But after all, in a democracy—and perhaps in human society in general—there's only one fundamental issue, from which all governing process derives: the right to decide.

People in many central Pennsylvania townships had these conversations. They began shunning the regulatory system and instead passed ordinances to control both factory farms and another threat that appeared at around the same time: land-applied sewage sludge (which had caused the tragic deaths of two teenagers in 1995). Seventy townships passed antisludge ordinances, which imposed a fee to render land application of sewage sludge unprofitable. They remain sludge-free. Eleven townships passed factory farm ordinances, which outlawed nonfamily corporate ownership and control of farming operations. None has a factory farm to date. Two townships, Licking and Porter, even passed ordinances stripping corporations of their constitutional rights outright. Within their towns, corporations would no longer have the status of "persons" (see "Taking the Constitution Away from Corporations").

All of this exercise of local control began to cause some serious discomfort among agribusiness interests. Of course, corporations could go ahead and sue the townships, which they did, claiming that their constitutional rights as legal persons had been abrogated. Such outrageous but judicially and legislatively supported claims infuriated the people in targeted communities: citizen response to the corporate claim of personhood became a crucial component in the subsequent organizing. But soon corporations were pursuing a more efficient tactic than lawsuits. It involved having elected officials do their heavy lifting.

POLITICAL BLOWBACK

On May 2, 2001, Pennsylvania Senate Bill 826 was filed with the Agriculture and Rural Affairs Committee. Couched as an amendment to a 1982 act protecting agricultural operations from nuisance suits and ordinances under certain circumstances, the bill aimed to crack down on township efforts. The amendment further limited the ability of localities to pass ordinances, and it wasn't the least bit subtle, reading: "No municipality shall adopt or enact a frivolous ordinance that would prohibit, restrict, or regulate an agricultural operation." What counts as "frivolous"? Any attempt to "regulate the type of business that may own or conduct an agricultural operation." Just to drive home the point and punish any township that tried to protect itself, the bill entitles the aggrieved party to recover costs and attorney fees from lawsuits they file to challenge the ordinances.

When Linzey heard about 826, he set out to rally the people. An unprecedented coalition formed to oppose this assault on local democracy. The Sierra Club, the United Mine Workers of America, Common Cause, the Pennsylvania Farmers Union, the Pennsylvania Association for Sustainable Agriculture, and 400 rural township governments all joined to defeat 826. Groups that ordinarily wouldn't be talking to each other found common ground not because they were fighting sewage sludge or factory farms or some other single issue, but because they could all agree that the state was out of bounds in usurping basic democratic rights. Senate Bill 826 never made it out of committee.

But it wasn't over yet.

In one of those dark backrooms of the statehouse where corporate politics thrive, the bill was renumbered, and on May 2, 2002, it was slipped back into the Senate, where it passed 48 to 2. A leaked Pennsylvania Farm Bureau memorandum said that the renumbering was necessary to avoid any bad publicity. People told Linzey, "Nice try—but you'll never win against a vote like that." Undaunted, the coalition stormed into action, and threatened enough legislators with loss of a job that the bill never came to a vote in the House.

And it still wasn't over—illustrating the Jeffersonian wisdom that the price of liberty is constant vigilance.

This time, in 2003, the agribusiness forces attached the substance of the bill to an anti-sexual predator law on the last day of the legislative session. They figured that in an election year no legislator would want to be vulnerable to charges of favoring molesting children (although the freshman sponsor of that bill withdrew her sponsorship, saying that the bill was intended to protect children, not corporations). As soon as the bill landed on the desk of Democratic Governor Ed Rendell, the local democracy forces barraged him. He backed down and didn't sign the bill, but explained that this was only because better top-down regulatory protection was in order. With better state rules, he implied, it would be okay to strip municipalities of their rights.

In 2004, Rendell unveiled his ACRE initiative (Agriculture, Communities, and Rural Environment), under which an appointed political board would have the authority to overturn local laws. In other words, laws passed democratically by a majority of citizens in a community could be struck down by an unelected collection of corporate appointees. The coalition has beat that one back too for now—it will likely come up again in the next legislative session.

So the vigilance continues. Each time the state government attempts such probusiness shenanigans, it increasingly reveals on whose behalf it is working. And each time, more people see with growing clarity how relentlessly their lives and rights are sold and legislated away, and begin to understand how the failure of democracy leads to very real harms in their communities.

There is broader significance to such fights to save the sustainable family farm. It's about the underlying political power structure and its links to economic power. It's about who decides the fate of communities, and in whose interest those decisions are made. Just as past empires established colonies—including those that rebelled to form our nation—for the purposes of expropriating resources to feed and entertain the nobility and the rising merchant class, so today do corporate-driven governments sustain a culture of expropriation of the commons, with a blindness and ferocity that threatens to render the earth unlivable.

Saving the sustainable family farm is also about uniting all of us who are fighting important single-issue battles. As long as we are divided and scattering our energies in a thousand different directions, we will continue to lose. When we finally unite on the common terra firma of local control over sustainability, health, well-being, and democracy, we will be in a position to create an irresistible force.

A version of this article was published by Food First/Institute for Food and Development Policy (www.food-first.org) in April 2005.

For most poor farmers in South Africa, the end of the apartheid era has not produced many tangible economic benefits. But in the South African wine industry, a small but growing number of worker-owned vineyards have helped to promote land redistribution, more egalitarian labor arrangements, and black empowerment. William Mosely looks at three worker co-owned vineyards, and how their efforts are helping to make a better life for the working poor.

POST-APARTHEID VINEYARDS

BY WILLIAM MOSELY
January/February 2006

A s I walked through the rows of grape vines with a representative of one of South Africa's few worker co-owned vineyards, I could tell that he was proud of what his group had accomplished. Nearly all of the 60 members of the Bouwland partnership trust are coloured or black farm workers. They own a controlling share of the Bouwland vineyard and wine label, producing 17,000 bottles of wine per year, with exports to Europe and Canada. By all accounts, this is an amazing achievement for an effort that is only three years old. But the group is also nervous. They are still heavily dependent on the expertise and equipment of their white partners, and they must repay a substantial commercial bank loan. This project and others like it represent a small but growing number of worker-owned vineyards in post-Apartheid South Africa. These efforts embody the hopes, dreams, and challenges of those who aspire to make the new South Africa a reality for the working poor.

In 1994, the African National Congress (ANC) took power in South Africa under the leadership of Nelson Mandela, formally ending decades of state-sponsored discrimination. Among a wide range of exclusionary policies during the Apartheid era were restrictions on the ownership of farmland by non-whites outside of the homelands or Bantustans—a policy that left only 13% of the country's land for the entire majority black population. This led to complete white domination of commercial agriculture, particularly in the Western Cape Province, an area often thought of as the historical hearth of white farming. Of all of South Africa's provinces, agriculture in the Western Cape is the most commercialized and export-oriented. Wine exports in particular have skyrocketed since Apartheid ended and the international community lifted sanctions. While South African wines were once unheard-of in North American and European supermarkets, they now compete with wines from their southern hemisphere counterparts, mainly Chile and Australia, for a share of the "good value" wine market (i.e., reasonable-quality wines of low to moderate price). In fact, South Africa's wine production nearly quadrupled between 1994 and 2004, and the country is now the eighth or ninth largest wine producer in the world. But what has this growth meant for South Africa's historically disadvantaged groups, particularly the farm workers who comprise one of the poorest segments of the country's population? What is the ANC government doing, if anything, to ensure that the wealth from growing wine exports trickles down to the poorest workers?

While many North Americans are familiar with the struggle against Apartheid and the subsequent political opening in the 1990s, fewer may be aware of efforts to transform South Africa's economy. The ANC has promised to redress the legacy of discriminatory land ownership policies in the farming sector through a land reform program that facilitates the transfer of land from whites to blacks (a generic term in South Africa that encompasses people of African, mixed race and Indian origin). In fact, the government has pledged to redistribute 30% of the country's agricultural land by 2014. Land reform is part of a broader transformation strategy for South Africa's agricultural sector aimed at increasing black participation in decision-making. The wine industry in the Western Cape is one instance where the effects of that strategy are visible, and this is significant given its economic importance to the province, its growing export potential, and the history of white dominance.

THE COLOURED FARM WORKER POPULATION
AND THE SOUTH AFRICAN WINE INDUSTRY

Wine production in South Africa's Western Cape Province dates back to the 17th century, when the Dutch established an outpost at Cape Town to provision ships sailing from Europe to the Far East. Because the area's local Khoisan population was sparse and unaccustomed to agricultural labor, the Dutch brought slaves from East Africa, Madagascar, and the East Indies to work their farms. The farm laborer population evolved into a mixed race or mulatto group, locally referred to as coloureds, who now comprise 60% of the Western Cape's population.

Even though slavery was abolished in 1834, conditions on farms remained difficult and wages were low. The historic relationship between white farmers and farm workers has often been described in terms of paternalism and dependency. Permanent farm workers (as opposed to seasonal laborers) lived on the farms, often for multiple generations. In addition to meager wages, permanent workers typically received housing, food, and wine. Many farm workers bought goods on credit at the company stores their bosses owned and fell into the classic debt-bondage cycle. The provision of cheap wine to workers as a component of compensation, known as the "tot or dop" system, was used to attract and retain workers in a low-wage industry (and the poorest white farmers were often the greatest abusers of this practice). While this practice has been illegal since the 1960s, and more strictly monitored in the post-Apartheid era, alcoholism continues to be a major problem among farm workers.

Raising grapes required a tremendous amount of labor, so those farms with larger areas in grape production often employed 30 to 60 permanent workers who lived on the farm with their families. Spouses and children would then join the workforce at key moments in the agricultural season. Until the end of Apartheid, wine production remained limited because international sanctions blocked exports. Furthermore, other than the dreg wine reserved for the coloured farm workers in the Western Cape, wine consumption was reserved largely for whites—blacks in other parts of the country were encouraged to drink beer.

POST-APARTHEID AGRICULTURE

Since the end of Apartheid, shifts in the international political economy, as well as a number of policies and programs at the national level, have had a profound impact on commercial agriculture and on the wine industry in particular. At the international level, the biggest change was the end of sanctions on products that were clearly South African. This change had little impact on exports whose origin was ambiguous, such as table fruit, whose sale continued unabated in Europe during the Apartheid era. But as origin and label are extremely important for all but the cheapest wines, the end of sanctions represented a huge opening of markets for the South African wine industry. As a result, South African wine production went from 38.9 million liters in 1994 to 153.4 million liters in 2004. Today, there are some 4,400 farming units that produce wine grapes in South Africa. Almost all are in the Western Cape because the Mediterranean climate in this region favors their production . The livelihoods of over 108,000 South Africans depend on the wine industry.

Once Apartheid ended, international financial institutions such as the World Bank and the IMF pressed South Africa to adopt neoliberal economic policies that encouraged export orientation and free trade. Key donors, including the United States, pushed the ANC government to focus narrowly on establishing a procedural democracy, rather than pursuing a broader vision of democracy involving economic justice. The ANC would also come under pressure from the World Bank to adopt a policy of negotiated land reform based on the principle of willing seller/willing buyer, rather than a more radical alternative.

Within this international context, the formerly Marxist ANC government developed five sets of policies that would affect wine farming: 1) liberalizing agricultural trade and deregulating the marketing of agricultural products; 2) abolishing certain tax concessions and reducing direct subsidies to farmers; 3) introducing a minimum wage and other protections for farm workers; 4) implementing land reform policies and programs; and 5) setting broad goals for black empowerment and transformation in the agricultural sector.

In order to ensure food self-sufficiency at the national level, and to cater to an important constituency of the conservative National Party, Apartheid-era governments provided white commercial farms with a range of subsidies and tariff protections. The ANC government subsequently moved toward a dramatic liberalization of South African agricultural policy. This shift was motivated not only by external pressures, but also by the need to redirect resources away from agricultural subsidy programs to other areas, and by little sympathy in the new government for the situation of white commercial farmers. The increasingly competitive commercial agriculture sector has led to the loss of smaller and more marginal farms. With farms going out of business —and with commercial farmers seeking to avoid offering newly required legal protections to workers—the number of permanent farm laborer positions has dropped.

LAND REDISTRIBUTION AND TRANSFORMATION IN THE AGRICULTURAL SECTOR

Since the late 1990s, land redistribution programs have provided government grants to help blacks and coloureds acquire land when they are not in a position to benefit from land restitution. This program provides approximately $3,080 per eligible individual for the purchase of farmland (or more if the beneficiary contributes additional capital). In the Western Cape, the majority of land redistribution beneficiaries are current or former farm workers. Because farmland is relatively expensive in the province (especially vineyard appropriate land), large groups of beneficiaries, often 50 to 100 people, must pool their grants in order to buy a farm. In some instances, farms are purchased outright at market prices from willing sellers and then run independently by the land redistribution beneficiaries. In other instances, people use their grants to buy a portion of an existing farm, going into partnership with a white farmer. This second approach, known as a share equity scheme, is the only approach used to date with vineyards.

The reasons why vineyards have not been purchased outright number at least two: the purchase price of most vineyards is so high that it would take a vast number of grantees to purchase one; and there are certain advantages to going into partnership with an established wine grape farmer who presumably already has the know-how and contacts needed to run a successful vineyard. As of early 2005, there were 101 government land redistribution projects in the Western Cape, and of these nine were share equity schemes producing wine grapes. To put this in perspective, there are 7,185 commercial farms in the Western Cape, of which roughly 2,372 produce 100 tons or more of grapes annually. As such, land redistribution projects only constitute 1.4% of all farms in the Western Cape, and projects focused on the production of

A SAMPLING OF SOUTH AFRICA'S WORKER CO-OWNED VINEYARDS AND WINERIES

Bouwland

Description: Formed in 2003, this farm outside of Stellenbosch is 74% owned by farm workers.

Contact Information: Tel: +27 21 865-2135; Fax: +27 21 865-2683; Email: bouwland@adept.co.za; Website: www.bouwland.co.za. Address: P.O. Box 62, Koelenhof 7605 South Africa

Wines: Chenin Blanc, Cabernet-Sauvignon-Merlot

Export destinations: U.K., the Netherlands, Belgium, Denmark, Germany and Canada. They are working with their Canadian distributor to expand exports to the United States.

New Beginnings

Description: The oldest and most celebrated worker co-owned vineyard in South Africa, this project began in 1997 when the owner of Nelson's Creek winery and vineyard gave 9.5 hectares of land to 18 of his workers as an expression of thanks for their efforts on his farm.

Contact Information: Tel: +27 21 869-8453; Fax: +27 21 869-8424; Email: newbeginnings @nelsonscreek.co.za. Website: www.nelsonscreek.co.za/new_beginnings/new_beginnings.htm. Address: P.O. Box 2009, Windmeul, 7630 Paarl, South Africa

Wines: Chardonnay, Cabernet Sauvignon, Pinotage

Export Destinations: Germany and the Netherlands. Export opportunities to the United States are being explored.

Thandi

Description: This is the label under which Nuutbegin and three other worker co-owned vineyards sell their wine. Thandi became the first wine brand in the world to achieve fair trade status.

Contact information: Tel: +27 21 886 6458; Fax: +27 21 886 6589; Email: rydal@thandi.com; Website: www.thandi.com/. Address: R310, Lynedoch, P.O. Box 465, Stellenbosch 7613, South Africa

Wines: Pinot Noir, Cabernet Sauvignon, Chardonnay, Sauvignon Blanc-Semillon, Merlot-Cabernet

Export Destinations: U.K., the Netherlands, Belgium, Germany, Japan, and the United States. The label will be introduced to Canada and Scandinavia shortly.

wine grapes make up less than half of one percent of all farms in this category. However, in addition to the nine government supported share equity schemes, there are also a number of worker co-owned vineyards that have been privately financed by progressive commercial farmers, international donors, foundations, and local wine industry groups.

South Africa's land redistribution program has been criticized from both right and left. Many conservative white South Africans believe that black or coloured farmers are incapable of effectively managing commercial farms. They see land redistribution as a waste of the government's money at best and, at worst, a program that could lead to collapse of the agricultural sector. Current problems with neighboring Zimbabwe's land reform process, including a series of disputed farm occupations by black war veterans, have only further fueled these fears.

Critics of the program from the political left, and even center, have focused on several issues. First, the pace at which the program is redistributing land has been exceptionally slow. By mid-2005, a little less than 3% of the formerly white-owned land had been redistributed to black or coloured South Africans, a long way from the 30% targeted for redistribution by 2014. Second, critics are questioning the "willing seller/willing buyer" principle that relies on the voluntary sale of commercial farms at market value, as the government does not have anything close to the level of resources needed to purchase 30% of white-owned farmland at market prices by 2014. Third, whether the large-scale, commercial orientation of the land redistribution program is appropriate has come into question at a time when so many commercial farms are going under. Finally, there are some specific concerns about share equity schemes because this mechanism may be manipulated by white farmers to obtain capital without actually relinquishing control. Furthermore, some have questioned how realistic it is to go into partnership with someone who may previously have been the autocratic "boss."

In addition to land redistribution, the South African government has a broader plan for transformation in the agricultural sector. This includes setting targets to increase the representation of blacks in management positions, to increase black ownership of agro-enterprises, and to increase the supply of produce to supermarkets by black-owned farms. Increasing black participation in the management of farms is key because farm workers have been excluded for years from the business and management side of farming. While farm workers are highly skilled in certain tasks, such as the pruning of grape vines, under Apartheid few blacks and coloureds were able to develop the managerial and business skills needed to run commercial farms. Moving farm workers into management positions will develop a cadre of black people who could go on to run successful commercial farms of their own.

While encouraging ownership of wineries and wine labels by black business interests is important for economic equality in South Africa, this is not the same as ownership by farm workers. Farm ownership by the emerging black upper class of business entrepreneurs does not automatically help the poor; worker-owned wineries and vineyards have a better chance of doing so.

THREE WORKER CO-OWNED VINEYARDS
The Bouwland partnership trust, the Nelson's Creek New Beginnings project and

the Nuutbegin trust represent three different models of worker co-owned vineyards. The Bouwland partnership trust came into being in 2003, when 60 land redistribution beneficiaries (of whom 55 are farm workers from the nearby Beyerskloof and Kanonkop vineyards) bought a 76% share of the 56-hectare Bouwland vineyard from Beyerskloof outside of Stellenbosch (of which 40 hectares is planted in Pinotage, Cabernet Sauvignon, and Merlot grapes). The trust's membership is roughly half male and half female, a split that is not only required by the government to receive grants, but that reflects the significant presence of women as farm workers in the South African wine industry. The group went into partnership with the winemaker for Beyerskloof and Kanonkop and with the owner of a London-based wine distribution firm. Using land redistribution grants from the government, and a commercial bank loan, they purchased both a majority share of the vineyard and a stake in the established Bouwland wine label.

The Bouwland trust operates with a somewhat complicated labor arrangement. Rather than working on their land during off hours, the trust shares the cost of a team of workers with Beyerskloof (which includes many trust members) that spends 40% of its time on the Bouwland land. The Bouwland property has no infrastructure, but rather relies on Beyerskloof for the use of its equipment and tasting room. With the exception of one full time employee who is involved in marketing and management, nearly of all of the group's shareholders have kept their day jobs as farm laborers on the nearby Beyerskloof and Kanonkop vineyards. The group currently produces and sells 17,000 cases of wine annually but is just breaking even, largely because they are paying off a loan. Their wine is sold in local supermarkets and exported to the UK, the Netherlands, Belgium, Denmark, Germany, and Canada. They currently are working with their Canadian distributor to expand exports to the United States. This is a solid project with a bright future, but the group is wrestling with the fact that it has yet to turn a profit, as well as some concerns about its dependence on Beyerskloof.

The Nelson's Creek New Beginnings Project is the oldest and most celebrated worker-owned vineyard in South Africa. This project began in 1997 when the owner of Nelson's Creek winery and vineyard gave 9.5 hectares of land to 18 of his workers as an expression of thanks for their efforts on his farm. The vineyard has subsequently grown to 13.5 hectares (the additional land was purchased from Nelson's Creek), producing Chardonnay, Cabernet Sauvignon and Merlot grapes. The group has its own wine label, New Beginnings, and sells wines to local supermarkets, along with exports to Germany and the Netherlands. Export opportunities to the United States are being explored. The group is reliant on Nelson's Creek for equipment, management, and winemaking expertise. The New Beginnings project is turning a profit and its members are using the money to buy food and consumer goods and pay their children's school fees.

The Nuutbegin trust began in 2000 when 99 farm workers from the Waterskloof and Fransmanskloof vineyards obtained land redistribution grants to purchase a 50% share of a long-term lease from the municipality for 25 hectares of prime vineyard land. The other two partners, the owners of the Waterskloof and Fransmanskloof vineyards, each have a 25% stake in the project. The group produces Merlot, Shiraz, and Cabernet Sauvignon grapes which are sold to the Thandi winery, in which the Nuutbegin trust has a 7% stake. Thandi produces a variety of wines, sourcing its grapes from four different worker co-owned vineyards in the area. Significantly, this is the first wine label to be fair-trade accredited in the world. While this accreditation should allow Thandi to fetch a small premium on the global market, Nuutbegin's 7% share in the label means that its returns from this end of the business are more limited. All of the shareholders have maintained their day jobs as farm workers, and they coordinate with the owners of Waterskloof and Fransmanskloof to schedule time to work the vines at Nuutbegin. Like Bouwland, this group has yet to turn a profit, and they are somewhat concerned about their continuing dependence on their white partners.

THE WAY FORWARD

As these case studies make clear, land redistribution and black empowerment in the wine industry are extremely challenging. High land prices and capital costs, not to mention the need for sophisticated business and wine-making expertise, mean that worker co-owned vineyards and wine labels are few in number, slow to start, and often dependent on the good graces of white employers and partners. It is important to note that the real money to be made in viticulture is in the selling of wine, not in the production of grapes. So vineyards with their own labels, such as the Bouwland and New Beginnings projects, have an advantage. Furthermore, because land, investment, and capital costs are so high, new projects must take on significant debt obligations that severely limit profits in the early years. Unlike Bouwland and Nuutbegin, New Beginnings did not incur significant debt; thus it can generate dividends for its membership more quickly and so benefit from a higher level of worker interest in the project.

The role of government land redistribution initiatives in the viticulture sector may always be minimal because the costs are so high. Interestingly, there has been more private support for black empowerment in viticulture than any other agricultural subsector, probably because the opportunity for new markets and profits is so high. This presents both an opportunity and a danger. On the positive side, private money means additional support for projects such as New Beginnings. But there is also a danger that private backers may see black empowerment and fair trade solely as means to earning greater profits rather than as paths toward economic justice. The key to lasting change will be having policy makers, academics, and consumers who are attuned to the difference between vineyards and wine labels that are truly co-owned by workers and those that are co-owned by black business interests with no or nominal participation of the workers.

Alas, what should North American and European wine consumers with a conscience do? I say seek out, and demand that your local wine market order, those South African labels that are co-owned and produced by farm workers (see "A Sampling of South Africa's Worker Co-Owned Vineyards and Wineries"). Yes, the South African land redistribution program is not perfect, but a growing market for worker-friendly wines will make existing ventures more profitable and encourage more white wine-makers to go into partnership with their workers. This is more than just fair trade—it is about creating a marketplace that rewards those working for change and economic justice, a world where workers really benefit from the fruits of their labor.

Resources: 2006; Mather, C. 2002. "The Changing Face of Land Reform in Post-Apartheid South Africa." *Geography.* 87(4): 345-354; Scully, P. 1992. "Liquor and Labor in the Western Cape, 1870-1900." In: Crush, J. and C. Ambler (eds). *Liquor and Labor in Southern Africa.* Athens: Ohio University Press, 56-77; Williams, G. 2005. "Black Economic Empowerment in the South African Wine Industry." *Journal of Agrarian Change.* 5(4): 476-504; Zimmerman, F.J. 2000. "Barriers to Participation of the Poor in South Africa's Land Redistribution." *World Development.* 28(8): 1439-1460.

Many small farmers have lost their land to big developers. Conservation land trusts provide an option for tenant farmers to take more control over their land, resist corporate consolidation of agricultural production, and help to protect communities and the environment.

THE LAND TRUST SOLUTION

BY MICHELLE SHEEHAN
March/April 2005

I t was back in the early 1970s that Steven and Gloria Decater of Covelo, Calif., first started farming an unused plot of land belonging to a neighbor. Over many years, they turned the fallow plot into fertile farmland that yielded a bounty of organic vegetables. They named it "Live Power Community Farm" and launched California's first successful community supported agriculture (CSA) program there in 1988. But the Decaters' hold on the land was vulnerable. Without ownership rights, they risked losing the farm to encroaching development. The couple wanted to buy the property but could not afford the land into which they had poured their lives.

The Decaters found a solution to their land-tenure challenge that gave them ownership rights *and* ensured the land would remain an active organic farm. Their solution creates an important precedent—and a possible path for other small tenant farmers.

With the help of Equity Trust Inc., a Massachusetts-based organization that promotes property ownership reform, the Decaters gained ownership rights to the land in 1995—without having to pay the full value themselves. The couple purchased just its "agricultural use value," while Equity Trust, acting as a conservation land trust (a nonprofit institution that controls land for the benefit of current and future generations), purchased "easements," or deed restrictions, that were equal in value to the land's development rights. Together, the two payments amounted to the original asking price.

Agricultural easements are a good way for small farmers to gain ownership control over land when they're not looking to develop or sell it anyway, because they limit the property's market price to its working agricultural value, making it more affordable—while conserving it.

In transferring development rights to the conservation land trust, the Decaters forever forfeited their rights to subdivide or develop the land for anything other than farming; the terms cannot be changed unless both parties agree through a court process. The transaction unpacked the bundle of property rights associated with land ownership, dividing ownership between two entities and placing deliberate restrictions on how the land could be used in the future.

RAMPED UP LAND-USE RULES

This approach made sense for the Decaters, because they were interested in more than just owning the farm for themselves. "We wanted to have some sort of relationship where it wasn't merely privatized ownership," Gloria explains, "but a socially and economically responsible form of land tenure." They also wanted to make certain that the land would continue to be cultivated by resident farmers with sustainable methods well into the future.

Their vision for the farm was secured by designing easement provisions that went beyond any existing precedent. For example, most easements on farmland define agriculture rather loosely. As Equity Trust's Ellie Kastanopoulos notes, "anyone willing to put a few cows on their property and call it a farm" could exploit many agricultural easements. The Decaters and Equity Trust built in a "ramped up" agriculture requirement: Live Power Community Farm must be farmed continually by resident farmers and remain organic or "biodynamic" (a farming philosophy that treats the land as a balanced and sustainable unit and uses the rhythms of nature to maintain the health of the farm).

The Decaters' other major concern was the affordability of their land for future farmers. They see a lot of young farmers for whom "one of the biggest stumbling blocks is getting access to land," Gloria says. While traditional conservation easements ban developers, they do not curb the upward pressure on the price of the land from individual home or estate buyers. Steve worried that when he and Gloria were ready to pass on the land, market forces could "spike the cost of the land so high that any farmer would be bid clear out of the picture." To prevent this, the Decaters and Equity Trust crafted limitations on the resale price of the land into the easement.

Today, Live Power is an active 40-acre horse-powered community supported agriculture (CSA) farm, thriving amidst encroaching development and the huge corporate farms that dominate California agriculture. Not only do the Decateown their land, but their unique conservation easement ensures that it will permanently remain an affordable, active, and ecologically sustainable farm. The Decaters are true stewards of the land, and the land trust's easement provisions reflect their commitment.

NEW WAYS OF LOOKING AT LAND OWNERSHIP

In addition to conservation land trusts, Equity Trust and others have implemented a second land trust model. So-called "community land trusts" usually focus on low-income housing in urban areas, but have in some cases included agricultural interests. They operate by purchasing tracts of land and then leasing them on a long-term basis to tenants who agree to a detailed land-use agreement. Although a farmer who enters into such a relationship would not own the land, he or she would have agricultural control and would own any improvements made to the land. In the tenant contract, the land trust would retain a purchase option for those improvements so that when the farmer was ready to move on, the land trust could ensure the lands remained affordable for new farmers. The land-use agreement could also include provisions to ensure the land remains in production. This option works well in areas where land is exorbitantly expensive, prohibiting the farmer from purchasing even restricted land, or when easements are not available.

In both land trust models, Equity Trust stresses, there is flexibility in how the relationship between the land trust and farmer is defined. Key to the definition is the land use agreement, which can be tailored for the particular situation according to either party's wishes. Kastanopolous notes that these are complex arrangements and "there is no black and white way of doing things." Indeed, one of Equity Trust's missions is to "change the way people think about and hold property." Their goal is to provide models that can be replicated and adapted to varied situations.

These partnerships and new ways of looking at land ownership acknowledge that there are diverse interests in a piece of land. The farmers, the community, the environment, and future users are all considered. Steven Decater is excited by the prospect of agricultural land trusts catching on. "We'll have permanent farms," he

FIGURE 1

Average Real Estate Value of U.S. Farms

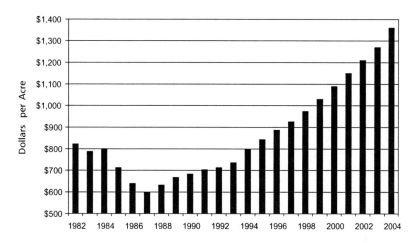

Source: U.S. Department of Agriculture National Agricultural Statistics Service <*www.usda.gov/nass*>

WHAT ARE CONSERVATION LAND TRUSTS?

Conservation land trusts are nonprofit organizations designed to protect ecologically fragile environments, open space, or small farms. According to the 2003 National Land Trust Census, there are 1,537 local and national conservation land trusts in operation nationwide, protecting approximately 9 million acres of land, an area four times the size of Yellowstone National Park. This is twice the acreage protected by conservation land trusts just five years ago. New conservation land trusts are formed at the rate of two per week, according to the Land Trust Alliance. They exist in every state; California leads with 173 land trusts, followed by Massachusetts (154) and Connecticut (125). While land trusts protect land in a variety of ways, two of the most common approaches are acquiring land and acquiring conservation easements, legal agreements that permanently restrict the use of land, shielding it from development to ensure its conservation.

For more information on land trusts, see: Land Trust Alliance <*www.lta.org*>, Equity Trust, Inc. <www.equitytrust.org>, and Vermont Land Trust <*www.vlt.org*>.

says, "and they're going to be needed." He's right about that. Farm real estate values have risen by 70% in the last 20 years (see figure). Across the country, massive mechanized and chemically sustained corporate-controlled farms are rapidly replacing small-time farmers.

The most vulnerable small farmers are ones who sink tremendous energy and resources into improving their soil but are unable to afford the market value of the land they work. Their lack of ownership control puts their land, and their investment, in jeopardy. This is a particularly common experience for operators of CSA farms, in which producers sell "shares" directly to consumers who receive regular harvest portions during the growing season. According to an informal survey conducted by Equity Trust in the late 1990s, 70% of CSA farms operated on rented land.

Land trusts allow small tenant farms to access land, resist rising property values, and conserve small agricultural tracts. They provide an alternative to unchecked development and farm consolidation, while helping to preserve communities, shield the environment from development, and protect the livelihoods of small farmers. But they are underutilized—in part because the strategy poses certain challenges. It requires:

- resources to purchase the agricultural value of the land,
- willingness by current landowners to sell or donate the land to a land trust,
- technical expertise, and
- in the conservation land trust model, the presence of a conservation land trust

FIGURE 2

Number of Land Trusts Whose Primary Purpose is to Protect this Land Type*

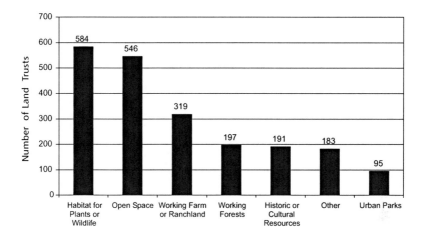

*One land trust may choose more than one primary land type.

Source: "National Land Trust Census," Land Trust Alliance, 2004

with enough resources to pay for easements—which has become more difficult with skyrocketing property values.

Yet thanks to the hard work of the Decaters, Equity Trust, and other organizations including the Vermont Land Trust (VLT) and the Institute of Community Economics (ICE), this innovative approach to land ownership has taken hold in several parts of the country (see "What Are Conservation Land Trusts?"). The VLT oversees many similar transactions every year; it has worked with more than 1,000 landowners and conserved more than 400 farms. Although the group has not quite figured out how to meet the high demand for affordable land as demand pressure drives land prices up across the state, it is nevertheless successfully managing to preserve large areas of farmland in Vermont—and writing affordability restrictions into their easements wherever possible.

Steve Getz, a dairy farmer assisted by the VLT through an easement purchase, says, "We would not have been able to afford the land without the VLT." He and his wife Karen say they respect how the land trust model challenges the "it's my land and I'll do whatever I please with it" mantra that reflects the dominant conception of private land ownership in this country. They now own a successful pasture-based dairy farm in Bridport that will be forever preserved.

Daniel Fireside looks at what happens when communities decide to treat affordable housing as a right, rather than just another speculative commodity. It turns out that this approach not only keeps prices affordable in rising markets, but also protects homeowners when prices crash.

HOUSING LAND TRUSTS KEEPS PRICES AFFORDABLE— FOR NOW AND FOREVER

BY DANIEL FIRESIDE
July 2008

Since the recent housing boom went bust, the news has been filled with stories of panic-stricken homeowners, skyrocketing foreclosure rates, and multi-billion-dollar taxpayer bailouts.

It's especially striking, then, that not a single owner of a house, condo, or co-op purchased through the Vermont-based Champlain Housing Trust (CHT) has experienced a foreclosure in the past year. Nor do any of the renters in the more than 1,600 CHT apartments have to fear eviction because of the mortgage melt-down. It's the kind of track record that has brought the CHT international accolades and sparked an affordable housing revolution.

Over the past 25 years, the CHT has become one of the largest providers of affordable housing in the tri-county area surrounding Burlington, the state's largest city, and home to its priciest homes and tightest rental market.

The genesis of the idea took form in the late 1970s, when environmentalist Rick Carbin formed the Vermont Land Trust to preserve open space as developers bought up farms. Instead of buying and holding land, as some land trusts do, the trust bought undeveloped properties at the edge of urban areas and resold them, often at a profit, but with strict limits on future development.

Then, in the early 1980s, wealthy out-of-town speculators began driving up the cost of housing in Burlington. Longtime working-class residents were being priced out of their homes and neighborhoods. Frustration reached a boiling point when the political establishment cut a deal with big-time developers to put upscale apartments on the city's scenic waterfront. Voter disgust with this plan to privatize public space led to an upset mayoral victory in 1981 by socialist gadfly Bernie Sanders and his ragtag Progressive Coalition.

Sanders and the coalition quickly sought to develop institutions that would have a lasting impact. They established the Burlington Community Land Trust as an independent nonprofit corporation in 1984 with backing from the Burlington City Council and $200,000 in seed money. While the land trust was designed primarily to promote sustainable home ownership in the city, the Lake Champlain Housing Development Corporation, set up at the same time, focused on rental properties in the areas surrounding Burlington. The two organizations merged in 2006 to form the nonprofit CHT.

The trust became a central part of the area's affordable housing effort—one that bridges the ideological divide between a flawed free-market approach and heavy-handed government intervention. Both Democratic and Republican politicians found it difficult to oppose a program that promotes homeownership and offers life-long renters a "piece of the American Dream."

HOUSING TRUST 101

Buying land through a housing trust starts when the trust acquires a parcel through purchase, foreclosure, tax abatements, or donation. The trust arranges for a housing unit to be built on the parcel if one does not yet exist, then sells the building but retains ownership of the land beneath. The new homeowner leases the land for a nominal sum (for example, $25 per month), generally for 99 years or until the house is resold.

This model supports affordable housing in several ways. First, homebuyers have to meet low-income requirements. Second, the buying price of the home is reduced because it does not include the price of the land. Third, the trust works with lenders to reduce mortgage costs by using the equity of the land as part of the mortgage calculation. This reduces the size of the down payment and other closing costs, and eliminates the need for private mortgage insurance. In all, the trust can cut the cost of home ownership by 25 percent or more.

For longtime CHT member Bob Robbins, purchasing a home through the trust was the only affordable option. "We did not have access to money for a down payment on a regular home, and at our income level, we wouldn't have qualified for a mortgage," Robbins says. "Through the CHT, we were able to purchase a $99,000 home with just $2,500 down."

Unlike federal programs that only help the initial buyer, the CHT keeps the property affordable in perpetuity by restricting the profit buyers are able to take when they sell the house. According to the terms of the CHT leases, homeowners get back all of their equity plus the market value of any capital improvements they made. However, they only get 25 percent of any increase in the value of the house, and none of the increase in the value of the land.

This model gives the buyer access to the benefits of homeownership otherwise beyond her means, including tax deductions, wealth accumulation through equity, and stable housing costs. In return, she gives up her chance at windfall profits. A study of trust homes sold to a second generation of buyers showed that members were realizing a net gain of 29 percent on the money they had invested. "These aren't sky-high returns," says CHT executive director Brenda Torpy. But most CHT homeowners would never have been able to buy homes otherwise.

"We're trying to stop the concentration of land in the hands of a wealthy minority," says Torpy.

The CHT has become an increasingly important force in Burlington's housing market as well as in the surrounding counties, even as city administrations have come and gone. After 25 years, the trust has over 2,100 households living in its homes, condos, and apartments, not concentrated in pockets of poverty, but spread through-out the area. Since the 2006 merger of the Burlington Community Land Trust and the Lake Champlain Community Development Corporation into the CHT, the trust has become one of the region's largest managers of rental property.

The CHT is remarkable not only for its size, but for its promotion of community empowerment. CHT tenants and owners vote for and serve on its governing board, along with government officials and other city residents with technical expertise, such as architects and urban planners. The system is designed so that all interested parties have a voice and a vote, making it an experiment in democratic self-governance as well as an affordable housing program.

BOOMS WITHOUT THE BUST

CHT employs several strategies to make sure their model succeeds, even during tough times. They offer homes below the market rate—typically half the price of a comparable open-market unit. Unlike shady mortgage brokers, "we're not going to let people take risky mortgage products," says Chris Donnelly, CHT's director of community relations. And if residents run into trouble, the land trust works with them. "It's not hand-holding," Donnelly says. "It's standing next to the homeowner."

A study conducted in December showed that foreclosure rates among members of 80 housing trusts across the United States were 30 times lower than the national average.

Tenants in the trust's rental properties are also benefiting from CHT's commitment to affordability and community building. By leveraging grants and subsidies, and because they aren't seeking a profit, CHT is able to keep rents up to 30 percent below market rate, even though they use the most environmentally rigorous building standards and set aside funds to cover future maintenance and repairs. The trust fixes up the buildings that for-profit companies won't touch. "When a fire destroys a block, we're the ones who come running in to restore the neighborhood," says Donnelly.

"We're going to steward these places forever," says Donnelly.

Housing advocates in Burlington have created a sustainable model for affordable housing through shrewd politics and a belief that housing is a fundamental human right rather than a commodity. Their model is being emulated across the country. There are 200 community land trusts in the United States today, including in large cities like Atlanta and Cincinnati. Washington, D.C., is in the midst of creating a 1,000-home land trust with advice and support from the CHT. Half of these trusts started up in just the past seven years.

Back in Burlington, the main obstacle to CHT's expansion is money. The trust relies on government programs, grants, and donations to bring new properties into its model. "We're doing about 25 new homes each year, and about 25 to 30 resales. We could easily do 100 sales a year if we just had enough cheap capital. The model has been proven to work. It's gone to scale. It would be a great way to fill the need without the problems we're seeing nationally," says Donnelly. But public funding has been flat or falling in recent years, and the economic downturn will make other funding harder to find.

Donnelly hopes that the recent troubles in the conventional housing market and some international accolades will help spur more interest in the land trust model.

In October, CHT will be honored with a World Habitat Award at the annual gathering of UN-HABITAT, the global agency dedicated to sustainable living. The award is one of only two given out each year. Donnelly is proud of the achievement. "It's like the Nobel Prize for sustainable development and housing."

Reprinted with permission from *Yes! Magazine*.

Land is the most important form of wealth for the over 1.3 billion people who work in agriculture around the globe. Both traditional, hierarchical land-ownership patterns and new commercial pressures related to globalization are squeezing many of these farmers' rights and access to land, as this article examines in the case of Nepal.

REFORMING LAND REFORM

Nepal's land-rights movement moves beyond failed market-based approaches.

BY RAVI BHANDARI AND ALEX LINGHORN
July/August 2009

Land lies at the heart of many of the world's most compelling contemporary issues: from climate change to armed conflict, from food security to social justice. Since the turn of the millennium, land issues have reclaimed center stage in national and international development debates, which increasingly focus on the role access to land plays in promoting economic growth and alleviating poverty.

The distribution of agricultural land in many poor countries is profoundly inequitable, giving rise to social tension, impaired development, and extreme poverty. As legacies of colonialism and institutionalized feudalism, these inequities pose serious threats to future prosperity and sustainable peace in many poor agrarian societies. Donor-driven development projects focusing on land governance have sought to impose market-led capitalist ideals, further polarizing power and marginalizing the poor. Exacerbating this dire situation are new commercial pressures on land, rapidly transforming it into a commodity to be traded between international banks, multinational companies, governments and speculators. Looming large is the paradigm-shifting presence of globalization, reinforced by international financial institutions seeking to unilaterally impose their macroeconomic policies. This toxic blend of national feudalism and international hegemony has placed the nearly one billion farmers worldwide who lack secure land tenure in peril, condemned to a life of extreme poverty and exploitation. In some countries, basic livelihood needs such as access to potable water and firewood, or education and even citizenship, are denied to those without land ownership certificates.

Land reform, or agrarian reform, is the process of transforming prevailing policies and laws that govern land ownership and access with the aim of instituting a more equal distribution of agricultural land while improving productivity. It can range from modest tinkering with land tenure and administration systems to wholesale redistribution of land from rich to poor.

In the last century, no fewer than 55 countries initiated programs of redistributive land reform, with many more altering their rural land ownership systems in more modest ways. In the early period of land reform (1950s–1970s), many nations sought to reallocate land from those who owned it to those who worked it. These "land to the tiller" programs were particularly prevalent in post-colonial South America, with its high levels of landlessness and gross inequity in land holdings. Overall these reforms failed; in many cases land became concentrated in the hands of the state, and in feudal countries real reform rarely occurred. China's land reform was directly responsible for a famine which killed over 40 million people.

Meanwhile, international institutions such as the World Bank were keenly promoting Western-style land-tenure laws, which proved incongruous in many developing countries where customary land ownership systems had long protected indigenous and other groups' access to their traditional lands.

Land reform entered a new phase in the 1980s and 1990s. Under the banner of "market-assisted land reform," the World Bank pushed countries toward a new, neoliberal approach: facilitating a land market of "willing buyers" and "willing sellers." In this model, the World Bank provided loans to the buyers, who were then required to pay full market price and display the clear intention of maximizing productivity. These land markets generously rewarded the rich, who often took the opportunity to off-load marginal land, and imposed an enormous debt burden on the poor.

Market-assisted land reform has largely been a failure as well. Commoditizing land has contributed to a rise in landlessness, widening and entrenching the gap between rich and poor. The fundamental flaws of market-assisted reform lie in its failure to address existing inequalities or to appreciate the gamut of issues associated with land in developing countries, including conflict, minority and gender discrimination, and environmental degradation.

In recent years, rising landlessness and inequality have continued to fuel tensions and contribute to conflict. In response, landless farmers' organizations have begun to build powerful social movements to challenge the status quo and demand their rights to land. Governments and international institutions have finally begun to realize that authentic land reform is a prerequisite to alleviating poverty and achieving sustainable peace and economic prosperity.

Nepal is one of the most relevant countries today in the debate over land reform. Nepal's legacy of highly unequal land ownership and its failed land reform policies helped lead the country into a decade of civil war, from 1996 to 2006. Nepal made global headlines in 2001 when the crown prince embarked on a murderous rampage through the palace in Kathmandu, slaughtering the king and queen and most of the royal family before killing himself. However, it is the deeper question of land ownership in relation to political and economic power that is actually shaping developments in Nepal—as in so many other poor, agrarian countries around the globe.

The small, mountainous nation of Nepal, landlocked and sandwiched between the giants of China and India, is home to 30 million people. Half the population lives below the poverty line, making it is one of the world's poorest countries. Nepal's dramatic topography renders 80% of the land uncultivable, yet three-quarters of the population depend on agriculture for their livelihood, one third of whom are marginal tenants and landless farmers.

Nepal's pattern of land ownership is the corollary of over 200 years of autocratic monarchy, with successive kings treating the land as their personal property and distributing large tracts to military leaders, officials, and family members in lieu of salaries or as gifts. This feudal system allowed non-farmer elites to accumulate considerable land holdings while deliberately precluding ordinary people from owning land, ensuring their continued position as agricultural servants.

Nepal's land governance was subject to the whims of capricious rulers until, in response to a fledgling land-rights movement initiated by tenant farmers, the monarchy introduced the first land act in 1964. The act imposed ceilings (maximum limits) on individual land holdings, with redistribution of the surplus to needy farmers; it also pledged to end the ritual of offering vast land grants to royal favorites. In practice ceilings were not enforced, little land was redistributed, and landlords rather than tenants often benefited.

No further significant land reform measures occurred for the next 30 years; even today the 1964 Land Act remains at the center of Nepal's land reform legislation. In 1996, amendments to the original act stipulated that tenant farmers who had cultivated a piece of land continuously for at least three years would be given the right of tenancy and the right to receive half the land they farmed. As the majority of tenants were unregistered, landlords reacted predictably to the new law by evicting them and refusing to grant secure tenancy contracts. In a country as poorly developed as Nepal, where it can take many days walk to the nearest road and even longer to reach a centralized bureaucracy, the new law served to terminate tenancy rights for over half a million families.

The World Bank's mission to proselytize market-assisted land reform had by now reached Nepal. The bank proposed establishing a national land bank to assist the poor in buying land from the rich. Matching willing buyers with willing sellers is an expensive and difficult process and leaves the door wide open to corruption at multiple levels. The concept of landless farmers borrowing huge sums of money to purchase land from feudal elites who had not acquired their lands through fair means did little to imbue a sense of justice. The land bank proposal has so far remained on the table, postponed by years of conflict and civil-society resistance.

Decades of land reform policies in Nepal have failed to significantly redistribute land, improve agricultural productivity, or correct socio-economic power imbalances. The main reason for this lies in the decision makers' conflicts of interest. Government leaders are closely tied to landlords, if they are not landlords themselves. This corrupt nexus of power has ensured the continued failure of land reform and the perpetuation of a feudal society. The primary result of imposing land ceilings was concealment of ownership; the primary result of land records reform

A COMMUNITY-LED APPROACH TO LAND REFORM

An innovative model for land reform is rising from the ashes of market-led agendas and centralized state bureaucracies, one loosely termed "community-based land reform." Borrowing from success stories over the past half century and incorporating new insights into sustainable rural development, the model offers a democratized, devolved approach that involves communities in the planning, implementation, and ongoing management of land reform.

In this model, each rural community is authorized to control its own land relations, including redistribution, working within a clear set of parameters laid out by the state. Governments typically fear relinquishing power, but it is precisely through this process of devolution that the majority poor can be included, empowered, and mobilized to ensure the effectiveness and sustainability of the reform. This bottom-up approach is often more cost-effective than top-down methods because of its potential to harness the administrative powers of existing local institutions (in Nepal's case, Village Development Committees). Plus, accurate data on land ownership, tenancy, and other factors such as idle land—an important starting point for any reform program—is more likely to emerge from community-level institutions. Devolved reform offers more room for flexibility across varying ecological zones and social contexts, while locally tested pilot schemes can provide valuable feedback.

Community-led reform is not simply a development buzzword or the latest fad. It has proven success, notably, the elected Land Committees that facilitated Japan's successful reform. Landless populations are pressing for greater inclusion, rightly asserting that they hold the knowledge required to design the most viable model for land reform. Even the World Bank has admitted that "greater community involvement" may be required; the bank now describes market-assisted land reform as only one "option."

was authenticating elite ownership; the primary result of tenancy registration was eviction; and the primary result of modernization was abuse of customary rights.

The increasing dispossession of the majority poor and the escalating autocracy of the king led the country into civil war in 1996. Land reform was the rallying cry of the opposition Maoists, who declared themselves saviors of the poor and enemies of feudalism, colonialism, and foreign imperialism.

Over the next decade the Maoists came to control over half the country's rural areas. With public and political opinion turning against the king, the war ended with the signing of the Comprehensive Peace Accord in 2006, paving the way for multi-party elections. The Maoists swept to victory in the 2008 election, confounding the international community but not the Nepalese voters. Under intense popular pressure, the king was forced to abdicate and a new Federal Republic of Nepal was declared on May 28, 2008. The People's Movement, as the popular political agitation against the king became known, played a significant role in the Maoist victory, and that same civil society is clamoring for the Maoist-led government to deliver on its promises of land reform.

The land rights movement in Nepal has built a significant democratic power base in the form of the National Land Rights Forum, which has over 1.6 million landless members. United, democratic, people-led, inclusive, and peaceful, Nepal's land-rights movement should serve as a model for similar movements across the globe. The movement pursues a rights-based approach, advocating the intrinsic link between land rights and the fundamental human rights of subsistence, protection, participation and identity. This approach leverages existing international conventions, laws, and constitutions which protect fundamental rights and is an effective way to ensure a framework for land reform that will address the structural causes of poverty.

Civil society pressure has led Nepal's government to embark on a revolutionary program of "scientific" (i.e., comprehensive) land reform. Exactly how revolutionary or scientific it will be remains to be seen. Following two weeks of mass demonstrations by the land-rights movement, the government recently established the Scientific Land Reform Commission to investigate available options and provide concrete recommendations. They have pledged to closely involve landless people in the process and to end feudal control over Nepal's land once and for all.

Redistribution of land, either through awarding new land to the landless or granting ownership rights to existing occupants, is just the first step toward creating a viable and sustainable model for rural economies. In many developing countries there is a trend towards abandoning, selling or mortgaging awarded lands, often to raise money for medical expenses or because of a lack of credit to finance production. With rising land prices and a dearth of government support services, poor farmers will understandably focus on solving their immediate food and economic security problems, reversing the land reform process and undermining the whole basis of a sustainable livelihood model.

In the case of Nepal, where broader macroeconomic policies do not support agriculture in general or small-scale producers in particular, land reform alone will not bring substantial income gains to the poor or a reduction in poverty and inequality. Indeed, if the macroeconomic context is adverse to agriculture, for example if exchange rate overvaluation and trade policies make agricultural imports too cheap for local growers to compete with, then to encourage the poor to seek a living in farming is to lure them into debt and penury.

Nepal is in the process of integrating into regional and global trading platforms which require a series of profound economic policy commitments. As a member of the World Trade Organization, Nepal has a legal obligation to align its economic policy with global requirements. The landless, near landless, and smallholders face an uncertain future in this era of globalization.

Both land reform and protective measures against unfair trade practices must be in place before Nepal agrees to open its markets and resource wealth to international speculators. Indeed, the revenues of many transnational companies now far exceed those of the countries in which they operate. Such a concentration of lightly regulated power in international profit-seeking hands is ominous for small producers and even more so for the most marginalized members of agrarian societies. While genuine community-based agricultural investment is welcome, the neocolonial pacts favored by foreign investors often pose a serious threat to tenure security and marginal farmers, many of whom could be pushed out of food production and forced to join the ranks of the rural hungry or the urban unemployed.

In addition to the globalization of trade, there are new powerful commercial pressures for landless and marginalized farmers to contend with. Catalyzed by soaring food prices in 2008 and compounded by worldwide financial uncertainty, import-reliant, often oil-rich, countries have begun scrambling to secure food sources for their domestic markets, in what has been called "the last great global land grab." Concurrent with this is the rampant growth of subsidized biofuel production to meet ambitious renewable fuel targets in the West, and the inception of carbon trading, which places a commercial value on standing forests and rangelands. Extractive mining and "ecotourism" add to the perilous predicament for vulnerable landless and marginal farmers.

The scramble for land often occurs in countries with a weak legal framework where farmers are not protected by secure land tenure systems. This results in the fertile land of the world's poorest countries becoming privatized and concentrated, creating a direct threat to food sovereignty, local production, and rural livelihoods. The increase in biofuel production is certain to intensify competition for land between indigenous forest users, land-poor farmers, agribusinesses and financial speculators.

Land reform is a pressing issue in many developing countries that are shackled by entrenched inequities in land access and ownership. While each country faces its own particular land-related issues, some common themes prevail: lack of political will to carry out effective land reform; entrenched, inequitable power structures; exclusive legal systems; poor dissemination of information; and the age-old millstones of corruption and excessive bureaucracy.

The rising discontent among landless and small holder farmers has forced open an ideological debate between neo-liberalism, centralized elite domination and pro-people policy making. The majority of the rural poor have begun to find their voice; Nepal's civil war will act as a warning that their land grievances can quickly turn to violence.

Today, the billions of dollars of potential investment from multinational corporations and from food-hungry, oil-rich nations is enormously tempting to impoverished states at a time when the worldwide financial crisis threatens aid from the West and the demand for exports is shrinking. Governments must not be lured into exclusive market mechanisms that generate ever-greater inequalities and create a profoundly negative effect upon community governance, food sovereignty and peace building. Effective redistributive land reform, ensuring secure tenancy and ownership systems for marginal farmers, must occur in poor agrarian societies before opening their doors to global trade.

Land reform is beginning to emerge from the vortex of market-led ideology to find itself at the epicenter of topical discourses on poverty alleviation, sustainable rural development, conflict transformation, food security and fundamental human rights. International financial institutions continue to push reforms that consolidate and authenticate inequity, but land rights organizations are now enjoying a higher profile with increasing solidarity from a wide variety of state and non-state actors.

It is abundantly clear that the best approaches to land reform are those that integrate security, livelihood, resource management, and community empowerment. Land reform must redistribute land widely enough to preclude any dominant landowning class and be accompanied by a support structure to sustain productivity. The expansion of rural markets that will follow will generate growth, and this will lead to stable peace and national development. All eyes are on Nepal to see if the new government seizes the unique chance to institute such an innovative and rational process of land reform.

Sources: Ravi Bhandari, "The Peasant Betrayed: Towards a Human Ecology of Land Reform in Nepal," in Roy Allen (ed.) *Human Ecology Economics: A New Framework for Global Sustainability*; Ravi Bhandari, "The Significance of Social Distance in Sharecropping Efficiency: The Case of Rural Nepal," *Journal of Economic Studies*, September,

2007; Ravi Bhandari, "Searching for a Weapon of Mass Production in Nepal: Can Market-Assisted Land Reform Live Up to its Promise?" *Journal of Developing Societies*, June 2006; Community Self-Reliance Centre Nepal, *Land and Tenurial Security Nepal*, 2008; Elizabeth Fortin, "Reforming Land Rights: The World Bank and the Globalization of Agriculture," *Social and Legal Studies*, 2005; Lorenzo Cotula, *Fuelling Exclusion? The Biofuels Boom and Poor People's Access to Land*, International Institute for Environment and Development, 2008; International Land Coalition, *Land and Vulnerable People in a World of Change*, Global Bioenergy Partnership, 2008; International Land Coalition, *Secure Access to Land for Food Security*, UNDP-OGC, November 24, 2008; Alex Linghorn, "Land Reform: An International Perspective," *Land First*, July 2008; Alex Linghorn, "Commercial Pressures on Land," *Land First*, April 2009; Oxfam International, *Another Inconvenient Truth: How Biofuel Policies are Deepening Poverty and Accelerating Climate Change*, 2008; Rights and Resources Initiative, *Seeing People Through Trees: Scaling Up Efforts to Advance Rights and Address Poverty, Conflict, and Climate Change*, 2008.

Amid the debate over the U.S. stimulus package, Ryan Dodd urges a more direct attack upon unemployment—a program in which the government guarantees the right to work by offering a minimum-wage job to anyone who may need one. Dodd argues that the costs of unemployment in the capitalist system more than justify government expenditures on such a program.

A NEW WPA?

BY RYAN A. DODD
March/April 2008

Dark clouds are now looming over America's economic future. As first the stock market boom and then the housing boom have come to an end, along with the fountains of cheap credit that were their mainspring, the perennial gale of unemployment is blowing in. The president and Congress have addressed the downturn with tax rebates and talk of "debt relief." Meanwhile, public infrastructure is crumbling. Workers' wages are stagnating while their work hours are rising. Health insurance is becoming less and less affordable for the typical family. And as U.S. military spending escalates, government spending on essential services is drastically reduced.

All of these facts serve to remind us that capitalist economies are inherently unstable and structurally incapable of creating full employment at decent wages and benefits. While tax rebates and debt relief may provide some minor protection from the coming economic storm, these measures are temporary—and inadequate—responses to a perpetual problem. As an alternative to these ad hoc policies or, worse yet, the free-market fundamentalism still widely preached in Washington, some economists and policymakers, in the United States and abroad, are touting a policy that seeks to end unemployment via a government promise to provide a job to anyone ready, willing, and able to work.

ARGENTINA'S EXPERIMENT IN DIRECT JOB CREATION

In early December 2001, following nearly two decades of neoliberal restructuring, the Argentine economy collapsed. Apparently, two decades of privatization, liberalization, and government austerity, ushered in by Argentina's brutal military junta (in power from 1976 to 1983), were not enough to sate the appetites of global financial capital: earlier that year the International Monetary Fund had withheld $1.3 billion in loans the country needed to service its $142 billion external debt. In response to the IMF's action, the government froze all bank accounts (although many wealthy Argentines managed to relocate their funds abroad before the freeze) and drastically cut government spending. As a consequence, the economy experienced a severe depression as incomes and expenditures fell through the floor. The unemployment rate shot up to a record 21.5% by May 2002, with over 50% of the population living in poverty.

The popular response to the crisis was massive. Protests and demonstrations erupted throughout the country. The government went through five presidents in the course of a month. Workers eventually reclaimed dozens of abandoned factories and created democratically run cooperative enterprises, many of which are still in operation today and are part of a growing co-op movement.

Reclaiming factories was a lengthy and difficult process, however, and the imme-diate problem of unemployment remained. In response, in April 2002 the Argentine government put into place a direct job creation program known as *Plan Jefes de Hogar* ("Heads-of-Household Plan"), which promised a job to all heads of households sat-isfying certain requirements. In order to qualify, a household had to include a child under the age of 18, a person with a disability, or a pregnant woman; the household head had to be unemployed; and each household was generally limited to only one participant in the program. The program provided households with 150 pesos a month for four hours of work a day, five days a week. Program participants mainly engaged in the provision of community services and/or participated in worker training programs administered by local nonprofits.

While limited in scope and viewed by many in the government as an emergency measure, the program was incredibly successful and popular with its workers. It pro-vided jobs and incomes to roughly two million workers, or 13% of Argentina's labor force, as well as bringing desperately needed goods and services—from community gardens to small construction projects—to severely depressed neighborhoods. The entry of many women into the program, while their husbands continued to look for jobs in the private sector, had a liberating effect on traditional family structures. And by some accounts, the program helped facilitate the cooperative movement that sub-sequently emerged with the takeover of abandoned factories. Not surprisingly, as Argentina's economy has recovered from the depths of the crisis, the government has recently made moves to discontinue this critical experiment in direct job creation.

"EMPLOYER OF LAST RESORT"

The Argentine experience with direct job creation represents a real-world example of what is often referred to as the *employer of last resort* (ELR) proposal by a number of left academics and public policy advocates. Developed over the course of the past two decades, the ELR proposal is based on a rather simple idea. In a capitalist economy, with most people dependent on private employment for their livelihoods, the government has a unique responsibility to guarantee full employment. This responsibility has been affirmed in the U.N. Universal Declaration of Human Rights, which includes a right to employment. A commitment to full employment is also official U.S. government policy as codified in the Employment Act of 1946 and the Humphrey-Hawkins Act of 1976.

Although many versions of the ELR proposal have been put forward, they all revolve around the idea that national governments could guarantee full employment by providing a job to anyone ready, willing, and able to work. The various proposals differ mainly on the wage and benefit packages they would provide to participants. The most common proposal calls for paying all participants a universal basic wage and benefit package, regardless of skills, work experience, or prior earnings. This wage and benefit package would then form the effective minimum for both the public and private sectors of the economy. After fixing a wage and benefit package, the government would allow the quantity of workers in the program to float, rising and falling in response to cyclical fluctuations in private-sector employment.

As with Argentina's program, ELR proposals typically call for participants to work in projects to improve their local communities—everything from basic infrastructure projects to a Green Jobs Corps. Most ELR proponents also advocate a decentralized approach similar to Argentina's, with local public or nonprofit institutions planning and administering the projects, though it is essential that the program be funded at the national level.

This raises an important question: How will governments pay for such a large-scale program? Wouldn't an ELR program require significantly raising taxes or else result in exploding budget deficits? Can governments really afford to employ everyone who wants a job but cannot find one in the private economy? Advocates of ELR address the issue of affordability in different ways, but all agree that the benefits to society vastly outweigh the expense. Many ELR advocates go even further, arguing that any talk of "costs" to society misrepresents the nature of the problem of unemployment. The existence of unemployed workers represents a net cost to society, in terms of lost income and production as well as the psychological and social stresses that result from long spells of unemployment. Employing them represents a net benefit, in terms of increased incomes *and* enhanced individual and social wellbeing. The real burden of an ELR program, from the perspective of society, is thus effectively zero.

Most estimates of the direct cost of an ELR program are in the range of less than 1% of GDP per year. For the United States, this was less than $132 billion in 2006, or about 5% of the federal budget. (By way of comparison, in 2006 the U.S. government spent over $120 billion on the wars in Iraq and Afghanistan—and that figure does not include the cost of lives lost or ruined or the future costs incurred, for example, for veterans' health care.) Furthermore, an ELR program provides benefits to society in the form of worker retraining, enhanced public infrastructure, and increased social output (e.g., cleaner parks and cities, free child care, public performances, etc.). By increasing the productivity of those participants who attend education or training programs, an ELR program would also decrease real costs throughout the economy. Estimates of program costs take into account a reduction in other forms of social assistance such as food stamps, cash assistance, and unemployment insurance, which would instead be provided to ELR participants in the form of a wage and benefit package. Of course, those who cannot work would still be eligible for these and other forms of assistance.

Today, the ELR idea is mostly confined to academic journals and conferences. Still, proponents can point to a number of little known real-world examples their discussions have helped to shape. For example, the Argentine government explicitly based its *Jefes de Hogar* program on the work of economists associated with the Center for Full Employment and Price Stability (CFEPS) at the University of Missouri-Kansas City. Daniel Kostzer, an economist at the Argentine Ministry of Labor and one of the main architects of the program, had become familiar with the CFEPS proposal and was attempting to create such a program in Argentina a few years before the collapse provided him with the necessary political support. Similar experiments are being considered or are currently underway in India, France, and Bolivia. Advocates of ELR proposals can also be found at the Levy Economics Institute (U.S.), the Center for Full Employment and Equity (Australia), and the National Jobs for All Coalition (U.S.).

THE CASE FOR DIRECT JOB CREATION

Involuntary unemployment is a fundamental and inherent feature of a capitalist economy left to its own devices. In a society where most people depend on employment in the private sector for their livelihood, the inability of a capitalist economy to consistently create enough jobs for all who seek work is deeply troubling, pointing to the need for intervention from outside of the private sector. ELR advocates view national governments—with their unique spending abilities, and with their role as, in principle, democratically accountable social institutions—as the most logical institutions for collective action to bring about full employment. In addition, government job creation is viewed as the simplest and most direct means for overcoming the problem of involuntary unemployment in a capitalist economy.

The standard mainstream response to the problem of unemployment is to blame the victims of capitalism for lacking the necessary talents, skills, and effort to get and keep a job. Hence, the mainstream prescription is to promote policies aimed at enhancing the "human capital" of workers in order to make them more "competitive" in a rapidly globalizing economy. The response of ELR advocates is that such policies, if they accomplish anything at all, simply redistribute unemployment and poverty more equitably. For example, according to the Bureau of Labor Statistics, the number of unemployed workers (including so-called "discouraged" and "under-employed" workers) in August 2007 was 16.4 million, while the number of job vacancies was 4.1 million. No amount of investment in human capital is going to change the fact that there simply aren't enough jobs to go around.

Advocates of ELR also consistently reject the Keynesian rubric, with its focus on demand-management strategies—that is, policies aimed at increasing aggregate demand for the output of the economy. This approach has been pursued either directly, through government spending on goods and services (including transfer payments to households), or indirectly, largely through policies intended to increase private investment. Such an approach exacerbates inequality by biasing policy in favor of the already well-to-do, through tax cuts and investment credits to wealthy individuals and powerful corporations. These policies also tend to privilege the more highly skilled and better-paid workers found in the industries that generally benefit from the government's largesse (often arms manufacturers and other military-related companies). For example, much of the increase in government spending during the Cold War era went into the high-tech, capital-intensive, and oligopolized sectors of the economy. Capital-intensive industries require relatively small amounts of labor, and, thus, produce little employment growth per dollar of government expenditure. Under this policy approach, the most that lower-paid or unemployed workers could hope for would be to snatch a few crumbs from the great corporate feast as the economy expanded over time.

In contrast to both the human-capital and demand-management approaches, ELR provides a means for rapidly achieving zero involuntary unemployment. By definition, any-one who is unemployed and chooses not to accept the ELR offer would be considered voluntarily unemployed. Many individuals with sufficient savings and decent job prospects may forgo the opportunity to participate in the ELR program, but ELR always provides them with a backup option.

In addition to the immediate effects of ELR on employment, the program acts as an "automatic stabilizer" in the face of cyclical fluctuations in the private sector of the economy. During a recession, the number of participants in the program can be expected to grow as people are laid off and/or find it increasingly difficult to find private-sector employment. The opposite happens during the recovery phase of the business cycle, as people find it easier to find private-sector employment at wages above the ELR minimum. As a result, ELR advocates argue, the existence of such a program would dampen fluctuations in private-sector activity by setting a floor to the decline in incomes and employment.

A final and less discussed benefit of the program is its socializing effect. The example of Argentina is instructive in this respect. The nature of employment in the *Jefes* program, oriented as it was toward community rather than market imperatives, created a sense of public involvement and responsibility. Participants reported increases in morale and often continued to work beyond the four hours a day for which they were getting paid; they appreciated the cooperative nature of most of the enterprises and their focus on meeting essential community needs as opposed to quarterly profit targets. By expanding the public sphere, the *Jefes* program created a spirit of democratic participation in the affairs of the community, unmediated by the impersonal relations of market exchange. These are the kinds of experiences that are essential if capitalist societies are to move beyond the tyranny of the market and toward more cooperative and democratic forms of social organization.

Some economists and advocates have pressed for a similar proposal, the *basic income guarantee* (BIG). Instead of guaranteeing jobs, under this proposal the government would guarantee a minimum income to everyone by simply giving cash assistance to anyone earning below that level, in an amount equal to the gap between his or her actual income and the established basic income. (Hence this proposal is sometimes referred to as a "negative income tax.") BIG is an important idea deserving wider discussion than it has so far received. But ELR advocates have a number of concerns. One is that a BIG program is inherently inflationary: by providing income without putting people to work, it creates an additional claim on output without directly increasing the production of that output. Another is that BIG programs are less politically palatable—and hence less sustainable—than ELR schemes, which benefit society at large through the provision of public works and other social goods, and which avoid the stigma attached to "welfare" programs. Finally, a job offers social and psychological benefits that an income payment alone does not: maintaining and enhancing work skills, keeping in contact with others, and having the satisfaction of contributing to society. When, for instance, participants in Argentina's *Jefes* program were offered an income in place of a job, most refused; they preferred to work. Consequently, ELR programs meet the same objectives as basic income guarantee schemes and more, without the negative side effects of inflation and stigmatization. Nonetheless, a BIG program may be appropriate for those who should not be expected to work.

LEARNING FROM THE PAST

The idea that the government in a capitalist economy should provide jobs for the unemployed is not new. In the United States, the various New Deal agencies created during the Great Depression of the 1930s offer a well-known example. Organizations such as the Works Progress Administration and the Civilian Conservation Corps were designed to deal with the massive unemployment of that period. Unemployment peaked at almost 25% of the civilian labor force in 1933 and averaged over

17% for the entire decade. These programs were woefully inadequate, largely due to their limited scale. It ultimately took the massive increases in government expenditure precipitated by the Second World War to pull the U.S. economy out of depression.

The onset of the postwar "Golden Age" and the dominance of Keynesian economics sounded the death knell of direct job creation as a solution to unemployment. The interwar public employment strategy was replaced with a "demand-management" strategy—essentially a sort of trickle-down economics in which various tax incentives and government expenditure programs, mainly military spending, were used to stimulate private investment. Policymakers believed that this would spur economic growth. The twin problems of poverty and unemployment would then be eliminated since, according to President Kennedy's famous aphorism, "a rising tide lifts all boats."

In the mid-1960s, the civil rights movement revived the idea of direct job creation as a solution to the problems of poverty and unemployment. Although the Kennedy and Johnson administrations had declared a so-called War on Poverty, the movement's call for direct job creation fell on deaf ears as the Johnson administration, at the behest of its Council of Economic Advisers, pursued a more conservative approach based on the standard combination of supply-side incentives to increase private investment and assorted strategies to "improve" workers' "human capital" so as to make them more attractive to private employers.

The rise to dominance of neoliberalism since the mid-1970s has resulted in a full-scale retreat from even the mildly social democratic policies of the early postwar period. While a commitment to full employment remains official U.S. policy, the concerns of central bankers and financial capitalists now rule the roost in government circles. This translates into a single-minded obsession with fighting inflation at the expense of all other economic and social ob-jectives. Not only is fighting inflation seemingly the only concern of economic policy, it is seen to be in direct conflict with the goal of full employment (witness the widespread acceptance among economists and policymakers of the NAIRU, or "non-accelerating inflation rate of unemployment" theory, which posits that the economy has a set-point for unemployment, well above zero, below which rapidly rising inflation must occur). Whenever falling unemployment leads to concerns about "excessive" wage growth, central banks are expected to raise interest rates in an attempt to force slack on the economy and thereby decrease inflationary pressures. The resulting unemployment acts as a kind of discipline, tempering the demands of working-class people for higher wages or better working conditions in favor of the interests of large commercial and financial institutions. The postwar commitment to full employment has finally been sacrificed on the altar of price stability.

ELR AND CAPITALISM

As demonstrated by the history of public employment programs in the United States and the example of Argentina, direct job-creation programs do not happen absent significant political pressure from below. This is the case whether or not those calling for change explicitly demand an ELR program. Given the hegemonic position of neoliberal ideology, there are many powerful forces today that would be hostile to the idea of governments directly creating jobs for the unemployed. These forces represent a critical barrier to the implementation of an ELR program. In fact, these forces represent a critical barrier to virtually any project for greater social and economic justice. The purpose of initiating a wider discussion of ELR proposals is to build them into more comprehensive programs for social and economic justice. As is always the case, this requires the building of mass-based social movements advocating for these and other progressive policies.

A significant objection to the ELR proposal remains: it's capitalism, stupid. If you don't like unemployment, poverty, and inequality—not to mention war, environmental destruction, and alienating and exploitative work—then you don't like capitalism, and you should seek alternatives instead of reformist employment policies. ELR advocates would not disagree. In the face of the overlapping and myriad problems afflicting a capitalist economy, the achievements of even a full-scale ELR program would be limited. The political difficulties involved in establishing an ELR program in the first place, in the face of opposition from powerful elements of society, would be immense. And certainly, the many experiments in non-capitalist forms of economic and social organization currently being carried out, for example, in the factories of Argentina and elsewhere, should be championed. But it is fair to ask: shouldn't we also champion living wage laws, a stronger social safety net for those who cannot or should not be expected to work, and universal health care— as well as an end to imperialist wars of aggression, environmentally unsustainable practices, and the degradation of work? In sum, shouldn't we seek to alleviate all of the symptoms of capitalism, even as we work toward a better economic system?

Sources: Joseph Halevi, "The Argentine Crisis," *Monthly Review*, (April 2002); Pavlina Tcherneva, "Macroeconomic Stabilization Policy in Argentina: A Case Study of the 2002 Currency Collapse and Crisis Resolution through Job Creation," (Bard College Working Paper, 2007); L. Randall Wray, *Understanding Modern Money: The Key to Full Employment and Price Stability*, (Edward Elgar, 1998); Congressional Research Service, "The Cost of Iraq, Afghanistan and Other Global War on Terror Operations Since 9/11," (www.fas.org/sgp/crs/natsec/RL33110. pdf, update 7/07); National Jobs for All Coalition, "September 2007 Unemployment Data," www.njfac.org/ jobnews.html); Nancy Rose, "Historicizing Government Work Programs: A Spectrum from Workfare to Fair Work," (Center for Full Employment and Price Stability, Seminar Paper No. 2, March 2000); Judith Russell, *Economics, Bureaucracy and Race: How Keynesians Misguided the War on Poverty*, (Columbia Univ. Press, 2004); Fadhel Kaboub, "Employment Guarantee Programs: A Survey of Theories and Policy Experiences," (Levy Econ. Inst., Working Paper No. 498, May 2007).

Taxing wealth is a sure way to address the growing wealth gap: it can prvide revenue to meet pressing social needs and at the same time slow or reverse the trend toward wealth concentration. But conventional political wisdom says sinificant wealth taxes simply won't fly in American politics. Political economist Gar Alperovitz takes on the conventional wisdom and explains why he is optimistic about the prospects for a new program of taxing large concentrations of wealth.

THE COMING ERA OF WEALTH TAXATION

BY GAR ALPEROVITZ
July/August 2004

Americans concerned with inequality commonly point to huge disparities in the distribution of income, but the ownership of wealth is far, far more concentrated. This fact is certain to bring the question of wealth taxation to the top of the nation's political agenda as the country's fiscal crisis deepens and, with it, the deterioration of public institutions and the pain of all those who rely on them.

Broadly, in any one year the top 20% garners for itself roughly 50% of all income, while the bottom 80% must make due with the rest. The top 1% regularly takes home more income than the bottom 100 million Americans combined.

When it comes to wealth, these numbers appear almost egalitarian. The richest 1% of households owns half of all outstanding stock, financial securities, trust equity, and business equity! A mere 5% at the very top owns more than two-thirds of the wealth in America's gigantic corporate economy, known as financial wealth—mainly stocks and bonds.

This is a medieval concentration of economic power. The only real question is when its scale and implications will surface as a powerful political issue. A wealth tax is "by definition, the most progressive way to raise revenue, since it hits only the very pinnacle of the income distribution," notes economist Robert Kuttner. But conventional wisdom says that it is impossible to deal with wealth head-on. The battle over repeal of the estate tax, in this view, demonstrated that even the most traditional of "wealth taxes" are no longer politically feasible.

Perhaps. However, a longer perspective reminds us that times can change—as, indeed, they often have when economic circumstances demanded it.

EMERGING SIGNS OF CHANGE

Indeed, times are already beginning to change. One sign: Although many Democrats were nervous about challenging George W. Bush in the first year after he took office, by early 2004 all the Democrats running for president had come to demand a repeal in some form of his tax giveaways to the elite.

It is instructive to trace the process of change. At the outset, only a few liberals challenged the president. The late Paul Wellstone, for instance, proposed freezing future income tax reductions for the top 1% and retaining the corporate Alternative Minimum Tax (AMT), for an estimated $134 billion in additional revenue over 10 years. Ted Kennedy proposed delaying tax cuts for families with incomes over $130,000 and keeping the estate tax (while gradually raising the value of exempted estates from a then-current $1 million to $4 million by 2010). Kennedy estimated this would generate $350 billion over 10 years.

By May 2002, even centrist Democrat Joseph Lieberman urged postponing both the full repeal of the estate tax and reductions in the top income-tax rates. Lieberman estimated his plan would save a trillion dollars over 20 years. The Bush tax cuts were simply unfair, he said, "giving the biggest benefit to those who needed it the least."

The Democrats failed to stop Bush's 2001 and 2003 rounds of tax cuts. But there are reasons to believe that politicians will ultimately come to accept the validity of maintaining and raising taxes on the wealthiest Americans. Just as many Democrats changed their stand on the Bush tax cuts, a similar progression is likely with regard to wealth taxation more generally over the next few years—and for two very good reasons. First, there is an extraordinary fiscal crisis brewing; and second, wealth taxes —like taxes on very high-income recipients—put 95% to 98% of the people on one side of the line and only 2% to 5% or so on the other.

GO WHERE THE MONEY IS

The hard truth is that it is now all but impossible to significantly raise taxes on the middle class. This reality flows in part from the ongoing decline of organized labor's political power, and in part from the Republicans' takeover of the South—another long and unpleasant political story. At any rate, it means that the only place to look for significant resources is where the remaining real money is—in the holdings of corporations and the elites who overwhelmingly own them. Put another way: Raising taxes first on the income and ultimately on the wealth of the very top groups is likely to become all but inevitable as, over time, it becomes clear that there is no way to get much more in taxes from the middle-class suburbs.

Moreover, as Democratic politicians have come increasingly to realize, the "logic of small versus large numbers" could potentially neutralize a good part of the suburbs politically, painting conservatives into a corner where they're forced to defend the very unreasonable privileges of the very rich.

The knee-jerk reaction that taxing wealth is impossible is based upon the kind of thinking about politics that "remembers the future"—in other words, thinking that assumes the future is likely to be just like the past, whether accurately remembered or not. Since wealth has not been taxed, it cannot be taxed now, goes the argument (or rather, assumption).

Of course, taxation of wealth has long been central to the American tax system for the kind of wealth most Americans own—their homes. Real estate taxes, moreover, are based on the market value of the home—not the value of a homeowner's equity: An owner of a $200,000 home will be taxed on the full value of the asset, even if her actual ownership position, with a mortgage debt of, say, $190,000, is only a small fraction of this amount. A new, more equitable form of wealth taxation would simply extend this very well established tradition and—at long last!—bring the elites who own most of the nation's financial wealth into the picture.

Many Americans once thought it impossible to tax even income—until the 1913 passage, after long debate and political agitation, of the 16th Amendment to the U.S. Constitution. Note, however, that for many years, the amendment in practice meant targeting elites: Significant income taxation was largely restricted to roughly the top 2% to 4% until World War II.

Even more important is a rarely discussed truth at the heart of the modern history of taxation. For a very long time now the federal income tax has, in fact, targeted elites—even in the Bush era, and even in a society preoccupied with terrorism and war. In 2000, the top 1% of households paid 36.5% of federal income taxes. The top 5% paid 56.2%. Although detailed calculations are not yet available, the massive Bush tax cuts are not expected to alter the order of magnitude of these figures. Estimates suggest that, ultimately, the tax reductions may modify the figures by no more than two or perhaps three percentage points.

In significant part this results from the rapidly growing incomes of the wealthiest: even at lower rates, they'll still be paying nearly the same share of total income tax. The simple fact is, however, that the record demonstrates it is not impossible to target elites. We need to take this political point seriously and act on it aggressively in the coming period.

FISCAL CRUNCH AHEAD

What makes wealth taxes even more likely in the coming period is the extraordinary dimension of the fiscal crisis, which will force government at all levels to adopt new strategies for producing additional resources. Projections for the coming decade alone suggest a combined federal fiscal deficit of more than $5 trillion—$7.5 trillion if Social Security Trust Fund reserves are left aside.

A worsening fiscal squeeze is coming—and it is not likely to be reversed any time soon. Critically, spending on Social Security benefits and Medicare will continue to rise as the baby-boom generation retires. So will spending on Medicaid. Recent studies project that by 2080 these three programs alone will consume a larger share of GDP than all of the money the federal government collects in taxes. And, of course, the ongoing occupation of Iraq will continue to demand large-scale financial support.

Nor are the trends likely to be altered without dramatic change: The truth is that the Bush tax and spending strategies, though particularly egregious, are by no means unique. Long before the Bush-era reductions, domestic discretionary spending by the federal government was trending down—from 4.7% of GDP a quarter century ago to 3.5% now, a drop during this period alone of roughly 25%.

A radically new context is thus taking shape which will force very difficult choices. Either there will be no solution to many of the nation's problems, or politicians and the public will have to try something new. Suburban middle-class voters, who rely on good schools, affordable health care, assistance for elderly parents, and public infrastructure of all kinds, will begin to feel the effects if the "beast" of government is truly starved. This pain is likely to redirect their politics back toward support for a strong public sector—one which is underwritten by taxes on the wealthiest. Quite simply, it is the only place to go.

TIME TO TAX WEALTH

Ideological conservatives like to argue that all Americans want to get rich and so oppose higher taxes on the upper-income groups they hope to join. In his recent history of taxation, *New York Times* reporter Steven Weisman has shown that this may or may not be so in normal times, but that when social and economic pain increase, politicians and the public have repeatedly moved to tax those who can afford it most. Bill Clinton, for one, raised rates on the top groups when necessity dictated. So did the current president's father! Now, several states—including even conservative Virginia—have seen pragmatic Republicans take the lead in proposing new elite taxation as the local fiscal crisis has deepened.

The likelihood of a political shift on this issue is also suggested by the growing number of people who have proposed direct wealth taxation. A large group of multimillionaires has launched a campaign opposing elimination of taxes on inherited wealth—paid only by the top 2%—as "bad for our democracy, our economy, and our society." Yale law professors Bruce Ackerman and Anne Alstott in their book *The Stakeholder Society* have proposed an annual 2% wealth tax (after exempting the first $80,000). Colgate economist Thomas Michl has urged a net-worth tax, and Hofstra law professor Leon Friedman has proposed a 1% tax on wealth owned by the top 1%. Even Donald Trump has proposed a one time 14.25% net-worth tax on Americans with more than $10 million in assets.

Wealth taxation is common in Europe. Most European wealth taxes have an exemption for low and moderate levels of wealth (especially the value of pensions and annuities). Economist Edward Wolff, who has studied these precedents carefully, suggests that America might begin with a wealth tax based on the very modest Swiss effort, with marginal rates between 0.05% and 0.3% after exempting roughly the first $100,000 of assets for married couples. He estimates that if this were done, only millionaires would pay an additional 1% or more of their income in taxes.

Europe also offers examples of much more aggressive approaches. Wealth taxation rates in 10 other European countries are much higher than Switzerland's— between 1% and 3%—and would yield considerable revenues if applied here. Wolff calculated that a 3% Swedish-style wealth tax in the United States would have produced $545 billion in revenue in 1998. Although an updated estimate is not available, nominal GDP increased about 19% between 1998 and 2002, and wealth taxes would likely produce revenues that roughly tracked that increase.

Some writers have held that wealth taxes are prohibited by the U.S. Constitution. There appear to be two answers to this. The first is legal: Ackerman, a noted constitutional expert, has argued at length in the Columbia Law Review that wealth taxes are not only constitutional, but represent the heart of both original and contemporary legal doctrine on taxation.

The second answer is political. We know that courts have a way of bending to the winds of political-economic reality over time. As the pain deepens, the courts are likely one day to recognize the validity of the legal arguments in favor of wealth taxation. Alternatively, political pressure may ultimately mandate further constitutional change, just as it did in 1913 with regard to income taxation.

There is no way of knowing for sure. But as with all important political change, the real answer will be found only if and when pressure builds up both intellectually and politically for a new course of action. The challenge, as always, is not simply to propose, but to act.

Americans are constantly exhorted to save—but also to spend! Social Securty alone is not enough to fund even a modestly comfortable retirement—but many families cannot save enough to fill the gap or meet a financial setback. How should the nation understand and address these dilemmas? Here, economist Ellen Frank looks at how we can both meet individuals' need for economic security and maintain the stability of a modern market economy. Her answer: forget about legislating ever more vehicles for tax-advantaged individual savings, and instead expand the institutions of social wealth.

NO MORE SAVINGS!

The Case for Social Wealth

BY ELLEN FRANK
May/June 2004

Pundits from the political left and right don't agree about war in Iraq, gay marriage, national energy policy, tax breaks, free trade, or much else. But they do agree on one thing: Americans don't save enough. The reasons are hotly disputed. Right-wingers contend that the tax code rewards spenders and punishes savers. Liberals argue that working families earn too little to save. Environmentalists complain of a work-spend rat race fueled by relentless advertising. But the bottom line seems beyond dispute.

Data on wealth-holding reveal that few Americans possess adequate wealth to finance a comfortable retirement. Virtually none have cash sufficient to survive an extended bout of unemployment. Only a handful of very affluent households could pay for health care if their insurance lapsed, cover nursing costs if they became disabled, or see their children through college without piling up student loans. Wealth is so heavily concentrated at the very top of the income distribution that even upper-middle class households are dangerously exposed to the vagaries of life and the economy.

With low savings and inadequate personal wealth identified as the problem, the solutions seem so clear as to rally wide bipartisan support: Provide tax credits for savings. Encourage employers to establish workplace savings plans. Educate people about family budgeting and financial investing. Promote home ownership so people can build home equity. Develop tax-favored plans to pay for college, retirement, and medical needs. More leftish proposals urge the government to redistribute wealth through federally sponsored "children's development accounts" or "American stakeholder accounts," so that Americans at all income levels can, as the Demos-USA website puts it, "enjoy the security and benefits that come with owning assets."

But such policies fail to address the paradoxical role savings play in market economies. Furthermore, looking at economic security solely through the lens of personal finance deflects focus away from a better, more direct, and far more reliable way to ensure Americans' well-being: promoting social wealth.

THE PARADOX OF THRIFT

Savings is most usefully envisaged as a physical concept. Each year, businesses turn out automobiles, computers, lumber, and steel. Households (or consumers) buy much, but not all, of this output. The goods and services they leave behind represent the economy's savings.

Economics students are encouraged to visualize the economy as a metaphorical plumbing system through which goods and money flow. Firms produce goods, which flow through the marketplace and are sold for money. The money flows into peoples' pockets as income, which flows back into the marketplace as demand for goods. Savings represent a leak in the economic plumbing. If other purchasers don't step up and buy the output that thrifty consumers shun, firms lay off workers and curb production, for there is no profit in making goods that people don't want to buy.

On the other hand, whatever consumers don't buy is available for businesses to purchase in order to expand their capacity. When banks buy computers or developers buy lumber and steel, then the excess goods find a market and production continues apace. Economists refer to business purchases of new plant and equipment as "investment." In the plumbing metaphor, investment is an injection—an additional flow of spending into the economy to offset the leaks caused by household saving.

During the industrial revolution, intense competition meant that whatever goods households did not buy or could not afford would be snatched up by emerging businesses, at least much of the time. By the turn of the 20th century, however, low-paid consumers had become a drag on economic growth. Small entrepreneurial businesses gave way to immense monopolistic firms like U.S. Steel and Standard Oil whose profits vastly exceeded what they could spend on expansion. Indeed expansion often looked pointless since, given the low level of household spending, the only buyers for their output were other businesses, who themselves faced the same dilemma.

As market economies matured, savings became a source of economic stagnation. Even the conspicuous consumption of Gilded Age business owners couldn't provide enough demand for the goods churned out of large industrial factories. Henry Ford was the first American corporate leader to deliberately pay his workers above-market wages, reasoning correctly that a better-paid work force would provide the only reliable market for his automobiles.

Today, thanks to democratic suffrage, labor unions, social welfare programs, and a generally more egalitarian culture, wages are far higher in industrialized economies than they were a century ago; wage and salary earners now secure nearly four-fifths of national income. And thrift seems a quaint virtue of our benighted grandparents. In the United States, the personal savings rate—the percentage of income flowing to households that they did not spend—fell to 1% in the late 1990s. Today, with a stagnant economy making consumers more cautious, the personal savings rate has risen—but only to around 4%.

Because working households consume virtually every penny they earn, goods and services produced are very likely to find buyers and continue to be produced. This is an important reason why the United States and Europe no longer experience the devastating depressions that beset industrialized countries prior to World War II.

Yet there is a surprisingly broad consensus that these low savings are a bad thing. Americans are often chastised for their lack of thrift, their failure to provide for themselves financially, their rash and excessive borrowing. Politicians and economists constantly exhort Americans to save more and devise endless schemes to induce them to do so.

At the same time, Americans also face relentless pressure to spend. After September 11, President Bush told the public they could best serve their country by continuing to shop. In the media, economic experts bemoan declines in "consumer confidence" and applaud reports of buoyant retail or auto sales. The U.S. economy, we are told, is a consumer economy—our spendthrift ways and shop-til-you-drop culture the motor that propels it. Free-spending consumers armed with multiple credit cards keep the stores hopping, the restaurants full, and the factories humming.

Our schizophrenic outlook on saving and spending has two roots. First, the idea of saving meshes seamlessly with a conservative ideological outlook. In what author George Lakoff calls the "strict-father morality" that informs conservative Republican politics, abstinence, thrift, self-reliance, and competitive individualism are moral virtues. Institutions that discourage saving—like Social Security, unemployment insurance, government health programs, state-funded student aid—are by definition socialistic and result in an immoral reliance on others. Former Treasury Secretary Paul O'Neill bluntly expressed this idea to a reporter for the *Financial Times* in 2001. "Able-bodied adults," O'Neill opined, "should save enough on a regular basis so that they can provide for their own retirement and for that matter for their health and medical needs." Otherwise, he continued, elderly people are just "dumping their problems on the broader society."

This ideological position, which is widely but not deeply shared among U.S. voters, receives financial and political support from the finance industry. Financial firms have funded most of the research, lobbying, and public relations for the campaign to "privatize" Social Security, replacing the current system of guaranteed, publicly-funded pensions with individual investment accounts. The finance industry and its wealthy clients also advocate "consumption taxes"—levying taxes on income spent, but not on income saved—so as to "encourage saving" and "reward thrift." Not coincidentally, the finance industry specializes in committing accumulated pools of money to the purchase of stocks, bonds and other paper assets, for which it receives generous fees and commissions.

Our entire economic system requires that people spend freely. Yet political rhetoric combined with pressure from the financial services industry urges individuals to save, or at least to try to save. This rhetoric finds a receptive audience in ordinary households anxious over their own finances and among many progressive public-interest groups alarmed by the threadbare balance sheets of so many American households.

So here is the paradox. People need protection against adversity, and an ample savings account provides such protection. But if ordinary households try to save and protect themselves against hard times, the unused factories, barren malls, and empty restaurants would bring those hard times upon them.

SOCIAL WEALTH

The only way to address the paradox is to reconcile individuals' need for economic security with the public need for a stable economy. The solution therefore lies not in personal thrift or individual wealth, but in social insurance and public wealth.

When a country promotes economic security with dependable public investments and insurance programs, individuals have less need to amass private savings. Social Security, for example, provides the elderly with a direct claim on the nation's economic output after they retire. This guarantees that retirees keep spending and reduces the incentive for working adults to save. By restraining personal savings, Social Security improves the chances that income earned will translate into income spent, making the overall economy more stable.

Of course, Americans still need to save up for old age; Social Security benefits replace, on average, only one-third of prior earnings. This argues not for more saving, however, but for more generous Social Security benefits. In Europe, public pensions replace from 50% to 70% of prior earnings.

Programs like Social Security and unemployment insurance align private motivation with the public interest in a high level of economic activity. Moreover, social insurance programs reduce people's exposure to volatile financial markets. Proponents of private asset-building seem to overlook the lesson of the late 1990s stock market boom: that the personal wealth of small-scale savers is perilously vulnerable to stock market downswings, price manipulation, and fraud by corporate insiders.

It is commonplace to disparage social insurance programs as "big government" intrusions that burden the public with onerous taxes. But the case for a robust public sector is at least as much an economic as a moral one. Ordinary individuals and households fare better when they are assured some secure political claim on the economy's output, not only because of the payouts they receive as individuals, but because social claims on the economy render the economy itself more stable.

Well-funded public programs, for one thing, create reliable income streams and employment. Universal public schooling, for example, means that a sizable portion of our nation's income is devoted to building, equipping, staffing, and maintaining schools. This spending is less susceptible than private-sector spending to business cycles, price fluctuations, and job losses.

Programs that build social wealth also substantially ameliorate the sting of joblessness and minimize the broader economic fallout of unemployment when downturns do occur. Public schools, colleges, parks, libraries, hospitals, and transportation systems, as well as social insurance programs like unemployment compensation and disability coverage, all ensure that the unemployed continue to consume at least a minimal level of goods and services. Their children can still attend school and visit the playground. If there were no social supports, the unemployed would be forced to withdraw altogether from the economy, dragging wages down and setting off destabilizing depressions.

In a series of articles on the first Bush tax cut in 2001, the *New York Times* profiled Dr. Robert Cline, an Austin, Texas, surgeon whose $300,000 annual income still left him worried about financing college educations for his six children. Dr. Cline himself attended the University of Texas, at a cost of $250 per semester ($650 for medical school), but figured that "his own children's education will likely cost tens of thousands of dollars each." Dr. Cline supported the 2001 tax cut, the *Times* reported. Ironically, though, that cut contributed to an environment in which institutions like the University of Texas raise tuitions, restrict enrollments, and drive Dr. Cline and others to attempt to amass enough personal wealth to pay for their children's education.

Unlike Dr. Cline, most people will never accumulate sufficient hoards of wealth to afford expensive high-quality services like education or to indemnify themselves against the myriad risks of old age, poor health, and unemployment. Even when middle-income households do manage to stockpile savings, they have little control over the rate at which their assets can be converted to cash.

Virtually all people—certainly the 93% of U.S. households earning less than $150,000—would fare better collectively than they could individually. Programs that provide direct access to important goods and services—publicly financed education, recreation, health care, and pensions—reduce the inequities that follow inevitably from an entirely individualized economy. The vast majority of people are better off with the high probability of a secure income and guaranteed access to key services such as health care than with the low-probability prospect of becoming rich.

The next time a political candidate recommends some tax-exempt individual asset building scheme, progressively minded people should ask her these questions: If consumers indeed save more and the government thus collects less tax revenue, who will buy the goods these thrifty consumers now forgo? Who will employ the workers who used to manufacture those goods? Who will build the public assets that lower tax revenues render unaffordable? And how exactly does creating millions of little pots of gold substitute for a collective commitment to social welfare?

Most proposals to address today's yawning wealth gap aim to rechannel more of the world's privately held wealth into the hands of people who now have little or none of it. That is necessary. But in this visionary article, Working Assets founder Peter Barnes reminds us that there is another, vast source of wealth that people are barely aware of and that institutions neglect and abuse: the commons. And in it, he sees the potential to restore a modicum of both equity and ecological sanity to modern capitalist economies.

SHARING THE WEALTH
OF THE COMMONS

BY PETER BARNES
November/December 2004

We're all familiar with private wealth, even if we don't have much. Economists and the media celebrate it every day. But there's another trove of wealth we barely notice: our common wealth.

Each of us is the beneficiary of a vast inheritance. This common wealth includes our air and water, habitats and ecosystems, languages and cultures, science and technologies, political and monetary systems, and quite a bit more. To say we share this inheritance doesn't mean we can call a broker and sell our shares tomorrow. It *does* mean we're responsible for the commons and entitled to any income it generates. Both the responsibility and the entitlement are ours by birth. They're part of the obligation each generation owes to the next, and each living human owes to other beings.

At present, however, our economic system scarcely recognizes the commons. This omission causes two major tragedies: ceaseless destruction of nature and widening inequality among humans. Nature gets destroyed because no one's unequivocally responsible for protecting it. Inequality widens because private wealth concentrates while common wealth shrinks.

The great challenges for the 21st century are, first of all, to make the commons visible; second, to give it proper reverence; and third, to translate that reverence into property rights and legal institutions that are on a par with those supporting private property. If we do this, we can avert the twin tragedies currently built into our market-driven system.

DEFINING THE COMMONS

What exactly is the commons? Here is a workable definition: *The commons includes all the assets we inherit together and are morally obligated to pass on, undiminished, to future generations.*

This definition is a practical one. It designates a set of assets that have three specific characteristics: they're (1) inherited, (2) shared, and (3) worthy of long-term preservation. Usually it's obvious whether an asset has these characteristics or not.

At the same time, the definition is broad. It encompasses assets that are natural as well as social, intangible as well as tangible, small as well as large. It also introduces a moral factor that is absent from other economic definitions: it requires us to consider whether an asset is worthy of long-term preservation. At present, capitalism has no interest in this question. If an asset is likely to yield a competitive return to capital, it's kept alive; if not, it's destroyed or allowed to run down. Assets in the commons, by contrast, are meant to be preserved regardless of their return.

This definition sorts all economic assets into two baskets, the market and the commons. In the market basket are those assets we want to own privately and manage for profit. In the commons basket are the assets we want to hold in common and manage for long-term preservation. These baskets then are, or ought to be, the yin and yang of economic activity; each should enhance and contain the other. The role of the state should be to maintain a healthy balance between them.

THE VALUE OF THE COMMONS

For most of human existence, the commons supplied everyone's food, water, fuel, and medicines. People hunted, fished, gathered fruits and herbs, collected firewood and building materials, and grazed their animals in common lands and waters. In other words, the commons was the source of basic sustenance. This is still true today in many parts of the world, and even in San Francisco, where I live, cash-poor people fish in the bay not for sport, but for food.

Though sustenance in the industrialized world now flows mostly through markets, the commons remains hugely valuable. It's the source of all natural resources and nature's many replenishing services. Water, air, DNA, seeds, topsoil, minerals, the protective ozone layer, the atmosphere's climate regulation, and much more, are gifts of nature to us all.

Just as crucially, the commons is our ultimate waste sink. It recycles water, oxygen, carbon, and everything else we excrete, exhale, or throw away. It's the place we store, or try to store, the residues of our industrial system.

The commons also holds humanity's vast accumulation of knowledge, art, and thought. As Isaac Newton said, "If I have seen further it is by standing on the shoulders of giants." So, too, the legal, political, and economic institutions we inherit—even the market itself—were built by the efforts of millions. Without these gifts we'd be hugely poorer than we are today.

To be sure, thinking of these natural and social inheritances primarily as economic assets is a limited way of viewing them. I deeply believe they are much more than that. But if treating portions of the commons as economic assets can help us conserve them, it's surely worth doing so.

How much might the commons be worth in monetary terms? It's relatively easy to put a dollar value on private assets. Accountants and appraisers do it every day, aided by the fact that private assets are regularly traded for money.

This isn't the case with most shared assets. How much is clean air, an intact wetlands, or Darwin's theory of evolution worth in dollar terms? Clearly, many shared inheritances are simply priceless. Others are potentially quantifiable, but there's no current market for them. Fortunately, economists have developed methods to quantify the value of things that aren't traded, so it's possible to estimate the value of the "priceable" part of the commons within an order of magnitude. The surprising conclusion that emerges from numerous studies is that *the wealth we share is worth more than the wealth we own privately.*

This fact bears repeating. Even though much of the commons can't be valued in monetary terms, the parts that *can* be valued are worth more than all private assets combined.

It's worth noting that these estimates understate the gap between common and private assets because a significant portion of the value attributed to private wealth is in fact an appropriation of common wealth. If this mislabeled portion was subtracted from private wealth and added to common wealth, the gap between the two would widen further.

Two examples will make this point clear. Suppose you buy a house for $200,000 and, without improving it, sell it a few years later for $300,000. You pay off the mortgage and walk away with a pile of cash. But what caused the house to rise in value? It wasn't anything you did. Rather, it was the fact that your neighborhood became more popular, likely a result of the efforts of community members, improvements in public services, and similar factors.

Or consider another fount of private wealth, the social invention and public expansion of the stock market. Suppose you start a business that goes "public" through an offering of stock. Within a few years, you're able to sell your stock for a spectacular capital gain.

Much of this gain is a social creation, the result of centuries of monetary-system evolution, laws and regulations, and whole industries devoted to accounting, sharing information, and trading stocks. What's more, there's a direct correlation between the scale and quality of the stock market as an institution and the size of the private gain. You'll fetch a higher price if you sell into a market of millions than into a

FIGURE 1

Approximate Value of Natural, Private, and State Assets, 2001
(Trillions of U.S. Dollars)

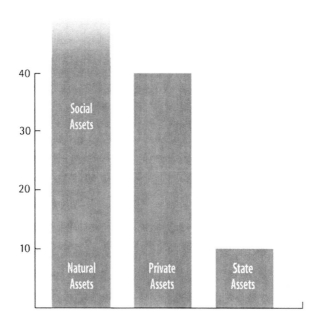

market of two. Similarly, you'll gain more if transaction costs are low and trust in public information is high. Thus, stock that's traded on a regulated exchange sells for a higher multiple of earnings than unlisted stock. This socially created premium can account for 30% of the stock's value. If you're the lucky seller, you'll reap that extra cash—in no way thanks to anything you did as an individual.

Real estate gains and the stock market's social premium are just two instances of common assets contributing to private gain. Still, most rich people would like us to think it's their extraordinary talent, hard work, and risk-taking that create their well-deserved wealth. That's like saying a flower's beauty is due solely to its own efforts, owing nothing to nutrients in the soil, energy from the sun, water from the aquifer, or the activity of bees.

THE GREAT COMMONS GIVEAWAY

That we inherit a trove of common wealth is the good news. The bad news, alas, is that our inheritance is being grossly mismanaged. As a recent report by the advocacy group Friends of the Commons concludes, "Maintenance of the commons is terrible, theft is rampant, and rents often aren't collected. To put it bluntly, our common wealth—and our children's—is being squandered. We are all poorer as a result."

Examples of commons mismanagement include the handout of broadcast spectrum to media conglomerates, the giveaway of pollution rights to polluters, the extension of copyrights to entertainment companies, the patenting of seeds and genes, the privatization of water, and the relentless destruction of habitat, wildlife, and ecosystems.

This mismanagement, though currently extreme, is not new. For over 200 years, the market has been devouring the commons in two ways. With one hand, the market takes valuable stuff from the commons and privatizes it. This is called "enclosure." With the other hand, the market dumps bad stuff into the commons and says, "It's your problem." This is called "externalizing." Much that is called economic growth today is actually a form of cannibalization in which the market diminishes the commons that ultimately sustains it.

Enclosure—the taking of good stuff from the commons—at first meant privatization of land by the gentry. Today it means privatization of many common assets by corporations. Either way, it means that what once belonged to everyone now belongs to a few.

Enclosure is usually justified in the name of efficiency. And sometimes, though not always, it does result in efficiency gains. But what also results from enclosure is the impoverishment of those who lose access to the commons, and the enrichment of those who take title to it. In other words, enclosure widens the gap between those with income-producing property and those without.

Externalizing—the dumping of bad stuff into the commons—is an automatic behavior pattern of profit-maximizing corporations: if they can avoid any out-of-pocket

FIGURE 2

The Market Assault on the Commons

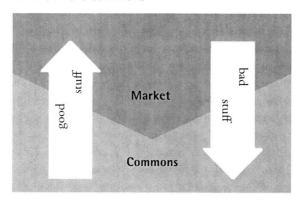

costs, they will. If workers, taxpayers, anyone downwind, future generations, or nature have to absorb added costs, so be it.

For decades, economists have agreed we'd be better served if businesses "internalized" their externalities—that is, paid in real time the costs they now shift to the commons. The reason this doesn't happen is that there's no one to set prices and collect them. Unlike private wealth, the commons lacks property rights and institutions to represent it in the marketplace.

The seeds of such institutions, however, are starting to emerge. Consider one of the environmental protection tools the U.S. currently uses, pollution trading. So-called cap-and-trade programs put a cap on total pollution, then grant portions of the total, via permits, to each polluting firm. Companies may buy other firms' permits if they want to pollute more than their allotment allows, or sell unused permits if they manage to pollute less. Such programs are generally supported by business because they allow polluters to find the cheapest ways to reduce pollution.

Public discussion of cap-and-trade programs has focused exclusively on their trading features. What's been overlooked is how they give away common wealth to polluters.

To date, all cap-and-trade programs have begun by giving pollution rights to existing polluters for free. This treats polluters as if they own our sky and rivers. It means that future polluters will have to pay old polluters for the scarce—hence valuable—right to dump wastes into nature. Imagine that: because a corporation polluted in the past, it gets free income forever! And, because ultimately we'll all pay for limited pollution via higher prices, this amounts to an enormous transfer of wealth—trillions of dollars—to shareholders of historically polluting corporations.

In theory, though, there is no reason that the initial pollution rights should not reside with the public. Clean air and the atmosphere's capacity to absorb pollutants are "wealth" that belongs to everyone. Hence, when polluters use up these parts of the commons, they should pay the public—not the other way around.

TAKING THE COMMONS BACK

How can we correct the system omission that permits, and indeed promotes, destruction of nature and ever-widening inequality among humans? The answer lies in building a new sector of the economy whose clear legal mission is to preserve shared inheritances for everyone. Just as the market is populated by profit-maximizing orporations, so this new sector would be populated by asset-preserving trusts.

Here a brief description of trusts may be helpful. The trust is a private institution that's even older than the corporation. The essence of a trust is a fiduciary relationship. A trust holds and manages property for another person or for many other people. A simple example is a trust set up by a grandparent to pay for a grandchild's education. Other trusts include pension funds, charitable foundations and university endowments. There are also hundreds of trusts in America, like the Nature Conservancy and the Trust for Public Land, that own land or conservation easements in perpetuity.

If we were to design an institution to protect pieces of the commons, we couldn't do much better than a trust. The goal of commons management, after all, is to preserve assets and deliver benefits to broad classes of beneficiaries. That's what trusts do, and it's not rocket science.

Over centuries, several principles of trust management have evolved. These include:

- Trustees have a fiduciary responsibility to beneficiaries. If a trustee fails in this obligation, he or she can be removed and penalized.
- Trustees must preserve the original asset. It's okay to spend income, but don't invade the principal.
- Trustees must assure transparency. Information about money flows should be readily available to beneficiaries.

Trusts in the new commons sector would be endowed with rights comparable to those of corporations. Their trustees would take binding oaths of office and, like judges, serve long terms. Though protecting common assets would be their primary job, they would also distribute income from those assets to beneficiaries. These beneficiaries would include all citizens within a jurisdiction, large classes of citizens (children, the elderly), and/or agencies serving common purposes such as public transit or ecological restoration. When distributing income to individuals, the allocation formula would be one person, one share. The right to receive commons income would be a nontransferable birthright, not a property right that could be traded.

Fortuitously, a working model of such a trust already exists: the Alaska Permanent Fund. When oil drilling on the North Slope began in the 1970s, Gov. Jay Hammond, a Republican, proposed that 25% of the state's royalties be placed in a mutual fund to be invested on behalf of Alaska's citizens. Voters approved in a referendum. Since then, the Alaska Permanent Fund has grown to over $28 billion, and Alaskans have received roughly $22,000 apiece in dividends. In 2003 the per capita dividend was $1,107; a family of four received $4,428.

What Alaska did with its oil can be replicated for other gifts of nature. For example, we could create a nationwide Sky Trust to stabilize the climate for future generations. The trust would restrict emissions of heat-trapping gases and sell a declining number of emission permits to polluters. The income would be returned to U.S. residents in equal yearly dividends, thus reversing the wealth transfer built into current cap-and-trade programs. Instead of everyone paying historic polluters, polluters would pay all of us.

Just as a Sky Trust could represent our equity in the natural commons, a Public Stock Trust could embody our equity in the social commons. Such a trust would capture some of the socially created stock-market premium that currently flows only to shareholders and their investment bankers. As noted earlier, this premium is sizeable—roughly 30% of the value of publicly traded stock. A simple way to share it would be to create a giant mutual fund—call it the American Permanent Fund—that would hold, say, 10% of the shares of publicly traded companies. This mutual fund, in turn, would be owned by all Americans on a one share per person basis (perhaps linked to their Social Security accounts).

To build up the fund without precipitating a fall in share prices, companies would contribute shares at the rate of, say, 1% per year. The contributions would be the price companies pay for the benefits they derive from a commons asset, the large, trusted market for stock—a small price, indeed, for the hefty benefits. Over time, the mutual fund would assure that when the economy grows, everyone benefits. The top 5% would still own more than the bottom 90%, but at least every American would have *some* property income, and a slightly larger slice of our economic pie.

SHARING THE WEALTH

The perpetuation of inequality is built into the current design of capitalism. Because of the skewed distribution of private wealth, a small self-perpetuating minority receives a disproportionate share of America's nonlabor income.

Tom Paine had something to say about this. In his essay "Agrarian Justice," written in 1790, he argued that, because enclosure of the commons had separated so many people from their primary source of sustenance, it was necessary to create a functional equivalent of the commons in the form of a National Fund. Here is how he put it:

> There are two kinds of property. Firstly, natural property, or that which comes to us from the Creator of the universe—such as the earth, air, water. Secondly, artificial or acquired property—the invention of men. In the latter, equality is impossible; for to distribute it equally, it would be necessary that all should have contributed in the same proportion, which can never be the case. ... Equality of natural property is different. Every individual in the world is born with legitimate claims on this property, or its equivalent.

Enclosure of the commons, he went on, was necessary to improve the efficiency of cultivation. But:

> The landed monopoly that began with [enclosure] has produced the greatest evil. It has dispossessed more than half the inhabitants of every nation of their natural inheritance, without providing for them, as ought to have been done, an indemnification for that loss, and has thereby created a species of poverty and wretchedness that did not exist before.

The appropriate compensation for loss of the commons, Paine said, was a national fund financed by rents paid by land owners. Out of this fund, every person reaching age 21 would get 15 pounds a year, and every person over 50 would receive an additional 10 pounds. (Think of Social Security, financed by commons rents instead of payroll taxes.)

A PROGRESSIVE OFFENSIVE

Paine's vision, allowing for inflation and new forms of enclosure, could not be more timely today. Surely from our vast common inheritance—not just the land, but the atmosphere, the broadcast spectrum, our mineral resources, our threatened habitats and water supplies—enough rent can be collected to pay every American over age 21 a modest annual dividend, and every person reaching 21 a small start-up inheritance.

Such a proposal may seem utopian. In today's political climate, perhaps it is. But consider this. About 20 years ago, right-wing think tanks laid out a bold agenda. They called for lowering taxes on private wealth, privatizing much of government, and deregulating industry. Amazingly, this radical agenda has largely been achieved.

It's time for progressives to mount an equally bold offensive. The old shibboleths —let's gin up the economy, create jobs, and expand government programs—no longer excite. We need to talk about *fixing* the economy, not just growing it; about *income* for everyone, not just jobs; about nurturing *ecosystems, cultures,* and *communities,* not just our individual selves. More broadly, we need to celebrate the commons as an essential counterpoise to the market.

Unfortunately, many progressives have viewed the state as the only possible counterpoise to the market. The trouble is, the state has been captured by corporations. This capture isn't accidental or temporary; it's structural and long-term.

This doesn't mean progressives can't occasionally recapture the state. We've done so before and will do so again. It does mean that progressive control of the state is the exception, not the norm; in due course, corporate capture will resume. It follows that if we want lasting fixes to capitalism's tragic flaws, we must use our brief moments of political ascendancy to build institutions that endure.

Programs that rely on taxes, appropriations, or regulations are inherently transitory; they get weakened or repealed when political power shifts. By contrast, institutions that are self-perpetuating and have broad constituencies are likely to last. (It also helps if they mail out checks periodically.) This was the genius of Social Security, which has survived—indeed grown—through numerous Republican administrations.

If progressives are smart, we'll use our next New Deal to create common property trusts that include all Americans as beneficiaries. These trusts will then be to the 21st century what social insurance was to the 20th: sturdy pillars of shared responsibility and entitlement. Through them, the commons will be a source of sustenance for all, as it was before enclosure. Life-long income will be linked to generations-long ecological health. Isn't that a future most Americans would welcome?

What is wealth? No doubt our basic material needs must be met. Still, many would say their true wealth lies not in material goods but in family, friends, and community; social and economic security; and other non-material assets. Can an economic system that excels in the production of material goods be reoriented toward these other kinds of wealth?

AMERICA BEYOND CONSUMERISM

Has capitalist economic growth outlived its purpose?

BY THAD WILLIAMSON
May/June 2008

One of the great benefits of studying the history of economic ideas is coming to the recognition that the founding figures of capitalist economics, and in particular Adam Smith, author of the pivotal *Wealth of Nations*, were often deeply ambivalent about the acquisitive way of life. Consider the famous parable of the poor man's son, presented by Smith in his *Theory of Moral Sentiments*:

> The poor man's son, whom heaven in its anger has visited with ambition, when he begins to look around him, admires the condition of the rich. He finds the cottage of his father too small for his accommodation, and fancies he should be lodged more at his ease in a palace. He is displeased with being obliged to walk a-foot, or to endure the fatigue of riding on horseback. He sees his superiors carried about in machines, and imagines that in one of these he could travel with less inconveniency. ... He thinks if he had attained all these, he would sit still contentedly, and be quiet, enjoying himself in the thought of the happiness and tranquility of his situation. He is enchanted with the distant idea of this felicity. It appears in his fancy like the life of some superior rank of beings, and, in order to arrive at it, he devotes himself forever to the pursuit of wealth and greatness. To obtain the conveniencies which these afford, he submits in the first year, nay in the first month of his application, to more fatigue of body and more uneasiness of mind than he could have suffered through the whole of his life from want of them. He

studies to distinguish himself in some laborious profession. With the most unrelenting industry he labours night and day to acquire talents superior to all his competitors. He endeavours next to bring those talents into public view, and with equal assiduity solicits every opportunity of employment. For this purpose he makes his court to all mankind; he serves those whom he hates, and is obsequious to those whom he despises. Through the whole of his life he pursues the idea of a certain artificial and elegant repose which he may never arrive at, for which he sacrifices a real tranquility that is at all times in his power, and which if in the extremity of old age, he should at last attain to it, he will find to be in no respect preferable to that humble security and contentment which he had abandoned for it. It is then ... that he begins at last to find that wealth and greatness are mere trinkets of frivolous utility, no more adapted for procuring ease of body or tranquility of mind than the tweezer-cases of the lover of toys; and like them too, more troublesome to the person who carries them about with him than all the advantages they can afford him...

In his heart he curses ambition, and vainly regrets the ease and the indolence of youth, pleasures which are fled for ever, and which he has foolishly sacrificed for what, when he has got it, can afford him no real satisfaction.

Adam Smith, traditionally regarded as the patron saint of capitalist economics, here avers that the fundamental engines of the market economy—ambition and acquisitiveness—rest on what he terms a "deception," the illusion that all the objects we spend our days striving for will make us happy.

Fast forward over 200 years. Here is how a contemporary economist, Juliet Schor of Boston College, describes "Greg," a sixth grader in a Boston suburb, in her 2004 book *Born to Buy: The Commercialized Child and the New Consumer Culture*:

Greg is an avid consumer. He loves professional wrestling, Gameboy, Nintendo, television, movies, junk food, and CDs (especially those with parental advisories). Since he came to live with his [father and step-mother], they've had a succession of incidents, most of which resulted in Greg's losing privileges to one or another of these things. He isn't allowed to do wrestling moves on his younger sister, but he does, and he loses the right to watch wrestling. He's supposed to do his homework, but he has lied and said he doesn't have any so he can spend his time playing a new Gameboy. He's supposed to tell the truth, but he stole [his stepmom's] Snickers bar and denied it. He knows he's not allowed to have CDs with parental advisories, but he went behind [his parents]' back and asked his [biological] mother to buy them for him...

Another couple described their son Doug as "the ultimate consumer." He wanted to buy every product he saw advertised on television. Doug was now in sixth grade, and they were fighting constant battles. He would stay on the computer all day if they let him. He has a weakness for fast food. He has a lot of trouble holding on to money. His mother even described trying to sneak out to the store without him to avoid conflicts about buying stuff.

Schor was stunned to find that persistent parent-child conflicts over money and goods were widespread, not confined to a few severe cases like Greg and Doug. In a survey of some 300 Boston-area fifth and sixth graders, Schor found strong evidence of a causal relationship between heavier involvement in consumer culture and strained relationships with parents, greater feelings of boredom and physical pain, higher levels of depression and anxiety, and lower self-esteem.

This finding is troubling precisely because corporate advertisers, as Schor and others have amply documented, have become increasingly brazen in the past 10 to 15 years about marketing directly to children, with the explicit purpose of establishing brand identifications and consumer loyalty as early as possible. By age ten, the average American kid is aware of over 300 specific brand names. A particular goal of this marketing is to persuade children to nag their parents to buy them things. A recent study reveals that the average American child aged three to eight now nags his or her parents nearly five times a day for material goods. Furthermore, research shows that over 80% of parents respond positively to such nagging at least some of the time, and marketers have estimated that up to one-half of sales of popular products for kids are a direct result of children nagging their parents. Probably not coincidentally, since the 1970s, as the impact of commercial culture on childhood has increased, the observed mental and physical health outcomes of American children, including levels of depression, obesity, and attention deficit disorder, have worsened.

So maybe it's not good to be obsessed with consumer goods, or to be, consciously or subconsciously, the slave of some advertising executive who knows how to play on your insecurities, self-image, and aspirations. But isn't money, at some level, necessary to make us happy?

Here the answer is slightly more complicated, but a large body of research—much of it usefully summarized by political scientist Robert Lane in his 2000 book *The Loss of Happiness in Market Democracies*—suggests it is not at all inconsistent with the view Aristotle expressed over 2,000 years ago: we need some material goods to be happy, but not an excess of them. Consider evidence from the Social Capital Community Benchmark Survey, a survey of some 33,050 Americans conducted by the Saguaro Center for Civic Engagement at Harvard in 2000. Among many other topics, this survey asked people how happy they are, allowing researchers to assess the most important predictors of greater happiness. How does income stack up in importance compared to having friends, confidantes, and close family relationships, and to being an active member of the community?

The survey data suggest that holding other demographic factors equal, an individual who earns $30,000 to $50,000 a year, visits with relatives three times a month, has at least ten "close friends" and at least three people he or she can confide in, and belongs to a religious congregation as well as three other organizations has a 47.5% likelihood of self-reporting as "very happy."* In contrast, consider someone demographically alike in all other respects who earns over $100,000 a year, but visits with relatives just one time a month, has only one to two "close friends," has only one person to confide in, is not part of a religious congregation, and belongs to only one organization. That person—richer in income but poorer in social connections—is estimated to have just a 28.6% chance of feeling "very happy."

Now, it's true that higher income, while not connected at all to family visits, is somewhat correlated with having more friends and confidantes and even more strongly associated with increased group memberships. Nor can anyone deny that economic circumstances influence well-being: controlling for other factors, moving from $30,000-$50,000 to over $100,000 a year in income is associated with a substantial rise in the likelihood of being "very happy"—from 34.4% to 45.3%. But the projected increase in the likelihood of being "very happy" associated with moving from having just three to five friends and two confidantes to over ten friends and at least three confidantes is even more substantial (from 32.2% to 44.2%). For most people, making five new friends and developing one or two especially close friendships are more realistic goals than doubling their income. The evidence suggests that expanding social ties is also a better strategy for finding happiness— especially if the alternative, chasing after more income, comes at the cost of fewer friends and weaker social connections. Income matters in shaping subjective well-being, but social connections matter more.

It would be misleading to leave the story at that, however. So far we have only been discussing raw income figures. But a closer look reveals that what people value more than their raw income is a sense of being *satisfied* with their economic circumstances. When we include both measures in statistical models predicting individual happiness, economic satisfaction predominates; it's a far more powerful predictor of well-being than absolute income. *Controlling for income level,* individuals who

---

* In this analysis, I control for citizenship status, the language the survey was conducted in, years lived in the community, marital status, number of children at home, gender, age, race, educational attainment, employment status, commuting time, and region of the country. I deliberately exclude from the analysis several factors which predict happiness but which are themselves closely related to economic levels, so as not to underestimate the influence of income: these include personal health, satisfaction with the one's neighborhood, homeownership status, and other "neighborhood effects."

are "very satisfied," "somewhat satisfied," or "not at all satisfied" with their economic circumstances have sharply divergent chances of being very happy: 48.7%, 33.3%, and 20.8% respectively. In contrast, if we control for people's level of economic satisfaction, more income does relatively little to promote happiness: a leap from the $30,000–$50,000 income bracket to the over-$100,000 bracket implies an increase of just four percentage points in the predicted likelihood of being "very happy," from 34.8% to 38.9%. Put another way, a person earning $30,000 to $50,000 who reports being "very satisfied" with her financial condition has, controlling for other factors, a 48.8% likelihood of being "very happy," whereas a person earning over $100,000 who is only "somewhat satisfied" with her financial condition has just a 37.5% likelihood of being "very happy." How much money one earns is, in itself, not an overwhelmingly decisive factor driving individual well-being, but being satisfied with what one has certainly is.

What is it that allows people to be happy with what they have? It could be that people who are psychologically disposed to be happier also tend to look more positively on whatever economic circumstances they find themselves in. But it's equally if not more plausible to think that two other factors drive economic satisfaction: a sense of economic security—in other words, knowing that you will be able to sustain your current lifestyle in the future—and freedom from the compulsion to compare your own versus others' income and consumption. But as scholars like Jacob Hacker and Robert Frank have pointed out, recent political-economic trends in the United States have had precisely the effect of weakening economic security and encouraging social comparisons. In his recent book *Falling Behind*, Frank insightfully discusses how the explosion in consumption by the super-rich in the last 20 years has shaped the behavior of middle- and upper-middle-class households, who feel that they too should have a bigger house or, to take Frank's favorite illustration, a more expensive barbecue grill.

IF CONSUMING MORE DOESN'T MAKE US HAPPIER, WHAT'S THE POINT OF CAPITALISM?

This brings us back to Adam Smith, who anticipated much of this body of evidence when he described the poor man's son who forsakes enjoyment of life for a life of industry and self-advancement as suffering from a fundamental delusion. Yet this insight did not lead Smith to reject capitalism. On the contrary, he thought this deception had a socially productive purpose: namely, helping to fuel economic progress, the advancement of industry, and the gradual rise of living standards— not just the living standards of the rich, but the living standards of average working people as well.

Indeed, in the subsequent 200 years, capitalism—or more accurately, capitalism modified by a range of state interventions, public spending, social welfare programs, and labor laws—has been remarkably successful in lifting overall living standards in places like the United Kingdom and the United States (albeit with often enormous social costs borne by millions of nameless workers who labored for capitalist employers under horrific conditions, enforced by the threat of hunger, and in some cases literally at gunpoint). In the 20th century alone, per capita income in the United States increased eightfold and life expectancy rose from 49 to 77 years.

That's the good news. The bad news is, median wage growth has stalled in the United States in the last 30 years, and has gone backwards for the least educated Americans. Total hours worked per household have risen as women work longer hours without a corresponding reduction in men's work hours. The hope of a secure, stable job has all but disappeared—hence today's widespread feelings of economic insecurity and dissatisfaction across income brackets. More to the point, there is good reason to doubt that simply continuing to "grow the economy" is going to address any of these concerns—or make most people any happier.

Consider just how rich a society this is. The U.S. Gross Domestic Product now stands at $13.8 trillion. If it were divided equally, that would come to over $180,000 for a family of four, or about $125,000 in take-home pay assuming an effective tax rate of 30%. In other words, the U.S. economy is large enough to provide a very comfortable life for each and every American.

But it doesn't. Why not?

A skyrocketing degree of economic inequality is one reason. The median income for married couple households in 2006 was $70,000, with of course many families making far, far less. While the income and wealth of the top 1% spike to unimaginable levels, many Americans simply do not have enough money to get by. With inequality comes not just poverty, but also widening disparities in status which themselves help fuel ever-greater levels of consumption as people spend more and more to try to keep up with the (ever-richer) Joneses.

The second reason is the widespread fact of economic insecurity. People whose jobs, health coverage, wage levels, and pensions are fragile naturally feel pressure to accumulate and advance as far as they can, lest they fall behind and lose what they now have. And, every week, we read about workers and communities who do in fact lose what they have as layoffs and plant shutdowns are announced. As we have seen, survey data (as well Adam Smith's intuitions) suggest that what matters most for well-being is the sense that one has enough and can feel comfortable about the future—that is, the very thing that the American economy fails to provide to the vast majority of families.

This insecurity is most potent in blue-collar America, but the middle class does not escape it either. Consider the life pattern of the average white-collar American. To go to college and get ahead, you have to borrow money and incur debt; to pay off the debt, you're under pressure to land a high-paying job; when you start a family, financial responsibilities multiply: you take on a mortgage, begin paying for child care or else accept a drop in household income, and within a few years face the stark realization that unless you make enough to either pay for private education or live in a neighborhood with good public schools, your children's education will suffer; and by the time you are finally done paying your children's college costs, it's already past time to begin building a nest egg for retirement and a cushion against illness. At no point does it seem to most people prudent—or even possible—simply to get off the treadmill.

Little wonder, then, that the Harvard social capital survey found just 26% of Americans to be "very satisfied" with their economic status (including just 54% of those making over $100,000 a year). It is impossible to address the issue of runaway consumerism without also addressing the issue of economic security. Indeed, as Knox College psychologist Tim Kasser, author of *The High Price of Materialism*, notes, a host of studies by psychologists and others demonstrate a strong relationship between numerous kinds of insecurity, especially economic insecurity, and the development of a materialist outlook on life.

This brings us to the third major reason the U.S. economy fails to foster a comfortable life for most Americans: long hours and overwork. Stress, fatigue, and sleep deprivation have become hallmarks of the American way of life. Over three-quarters of Americans report feeling stressed at least "sometimes," with a full one-third saying they experience stress "frequently." (The figures are higher still for persons holding jobs and for parents.) Likewise, roughly one-half of all Americans—including three-fifths of employed workers, parents, and persons aged 18 to 49—say they do not have enough time to do what they would like to in daily life, such as spend time with friends. Harvard political scientist Robert Putnam reports that the percentage of Americans regularly eating dinner together declined by one-third between 1977 and 1999. Research by the Families and Work Institute indicates that almost two-thirds (63%) would like to work fewer hours. On average those questioned said they would reduce their work week by more than ten hours if they could. But what people want and what the political economy provides are two different things: in the past generation, the centuries-long trend towards reducing the length of the work week has come to a screeching halt.

So the U.S. economy, as presently constituted, produces tremendous inequality, insecurity, and overwork. Nor is there reason to think that growing from a $14 trillion to, say, a $20 or $25 trillion economy will change these destructive trends.

It doesn't have to be this way. There is no inherent reason why we could not cease to regard more income as a good in itself, but instead alter our political economy so that it provides what Americans really need and want: greater employment security, stronger protection against the pitfalls of poverty, and more free time. We could choose to have the public guarantee employment opportunities for every willing worker, to put a floor on income, to decommodify health care and education, to reduce the gross inequalities of income and status which themselves help fuel consumerism, and to take future productivity growth in the form of more time, not more stuff.

To be sure, doing so would not be easy, and would require substantial institutional changes, possibly even a shift to a system that, as economist Gar Alperovitz puts it, lies "beyond capitalism." Many careful analysts, including Alperovitz and Schor, have thought long and hard about just how that could happen; indeed, there has been a rich debate in the past 15 years about the long-term possibilities of alternative political-economic frameworks that would reshape the logic of our current system.

It would be very easy to dismiss these ideas as "crazy" or "utopian." But, I submit, the moral task Adam Smith set for capitalism—that of making it economically possible for each and every person to live a materially comfortable life—has been achieved, at least in the advanced industrialized countries. The acquisitive life that goes with capitalism Smith never endorsed as good in itself. Neither should we, especially given the unhealthy consequences of an excessive consumerism that is now warping children's lives from their earliest years, and given the potentially planet-melting consequences of a way of life based on continual increases in consumption and economic activity.

That wasn't what Adam Smith wanted. Nor was it what the most influential and pragmatic of 20th-century economists, John Maynard Keynes, the man many credit with saving capitalism from itself, wanted. In a famous but too often neglected essay called "Economic Possibilities for Our Grandchildren," Keynes looked to a time when at last it would be possible for humanity (at least in the affluent nations) to turn its attention away from acquisition and toward broader moral concerns—such as "how to use his freedom from pressing economic cares, how to occupy the leisure, which science and compound interest will have won for him, to live wisely and agreeably and well."

That time has not yet come. But the remaining barriers to it are political, not economic; and the great task of this century is to assure that our prodigious economic capacities are directed towards supplying the real goods of human life: material security, meaningful work, and plentiful time for the friends and family who are the most lasting source of human happiness.

Sources: Adam Smith, *The Theory of Moral Sentiments* (1759) (Liberty Fund, 1984); Juliet Schor, *Born to Buy: The Commercialized Child and the New Consumer Culture* (Scribner, 2004); Tim Kasser, *The High Price of Materialism* (MIT Press, 2002); "Half of Americans are Pressed for Time; A Third Are Stressed Out," *Gallup News Svc*, May 3, 2004; "No time for R&R," *Gallup News Svc*, May 11, 2004; "Who Dreams, Perchance to Sleep?" *Gallup News Svc*, Jan. 25, 2005; Robert Putnam, *Bowling Alone: The Collapse and Revival of American Community* (Simon & Schuster, 2000); J. Bond, E. Galinsky, and J. Swanberg, *The 1997 National Study of the Changing Workforce*, Families and Work Institute, 1998; Gar Alperovitz, *America Beyond Capitalism: Reclaiming Our Wealth, Our*

Liberty, and Our Democracy (Wiley, 2004); Jerome Segal, *Graceful Simplicity: Towards a Philosophy and Politics of Simple Living* (Henry Holt, 1999); Juliet Schor, *A Sustainable Economy for the 21st Century* (Open Media, 1995); John Maynard Keynes, *Essays in Persuasion* (W.W. Norton, 1963); Jacob S. Hacker, *The Great Risk Shift* (Oxford Univ. Press, 2006); Robert H. Frank, *Falling Behind: How Rising Inequality Harms the Middle Class* (Univ. of Calif. Press, 2007); Robert E. Lane, *The Loss of Happiness in Market Democracies* (Yale Univ. Press, 2000); Robert M. Biswas-Diener, "Material Wealth and Subjective Well-Being," in M. Eid and R. J. Larsen, eds., *The Science of Subjective Well-Being* (Guilford Press, 2008).

The fundamental contradiction between capitalism and nature has led Joel Kovel to develop the idea of eco-socialism, a socialism "animated by eco-centric values." In this interview by Larry Peterson he explains why capitalism is not sustainable, and why any socialist alternative must be sustainable in order to be relevant.

CLIMATE CHANGE AND ECOSOCIALISM

An Interview with Joel Kovel

March/April 2009

Dollars & Sense: Many people are confused by the range of estimates of the extent of the problem of climate change. In your view, how dire is the threat, and how much time do we have to confront the problem in a serious way?

Joel Kovel: To me, the overall problem—not simply of climate change, but the whole ecological crisis of which climate change comprises a major part—is the gravest threat ever faced by humanity. We had better learn to recognize that the world as it has been known has been fundamentally changed, and act accordingly. Even if the tendencies that have given rise to this are reversed tomorrow—actually quite inconceivable—we will be suffering the consequences for generations. At the other end, my best guess is that we have ten years to begin to make basic changes. Otherwise, tipping points will be passed, and civilization will go downhill very rapidly.

The basic principle is that everything in nature exists interconnectedly, something that humanity in the modern era has largely forgotten. A sign of that forgetting is the habit of reducing everything to the costs of everything, i.e., economic reductionism. I would argue that this is a manifestation of our whole estrangement from nature.

D&S: Some people claim that earlier predictions of environmental crisis have been shown to be remarkably wrongheaded. Couldn't emerging technology resolve the climate crisis, as it has seemed to head off ones people have predicted before?

JK: First of all, those predictions were not "remarkably wrongheaded"; they were only somewhat premature. Today, virtually all of the major predictions are being borne out. Julian Simon, a flamboyant believer in the sustainability of our society (he predicted that it could last 7 billion years!) crowed in the 70s and 80s about winning bets that prices of raw materials would drop over time. You don't see people making that claim any more, especially in the energy sector. Here a positive feedback loop emerges, as the perception of "peak oil" drives warfare, social unrest, and intensified ravaging of the environment: see what's happening in Northern Alberta to the oil sands; or what Chevron is doing in Ecuador; or the story in Niger, with uranium extraction, and so on. And the most comprehensive study, the UN's "Millennium Assessment Report" of 2005, concluded that the majority of planet earth's ecosystems were in rapid decay.

The point about technology pulling us out of this dilemma deserves special emphasis. Of course we can always benefit from better technology; but that doesn't mean that the technology now available is inadequate to address this problem. What's missing are the social conditions for contending with ecological crisis. I'm afraid that speaking of state and market as leading the way is all too often a reshuffling of the same old deck. We need to confront the really salient issue. Consider this: since 1957, society has tripled its output of atmospheric carbon. In the same period population has increased by a factor of 2.3—a serious problem, to be sure, but a substantially lesser one; from another angle, we can say that the average person is "responsible" for 1.3 times as much carbon per capita as was the case fifty years ago. Clearly, the responsibility for the increase lies with the economic system; indeed, it would take two billion more people consuming at 1957 rates to throw the same amount of carbon into the atmosphere as we do today. So the question is, really, what induces the insane and uncontrollable "growth complex" of material goods, which by any rational assessment is driving this crisis? And this points us in the direction of the capitalist system.

D&S: So will living standards have to fall? Will dyed-in-the-wool consumerist societies —not to men-tion resource-hungry developing ones—be able to make such a rapid and thorough transformation?

JK: We cannot begin to approach this question except through a confrontation with capitalism, since consumerism is strictly the reflex of capitalist overproduction. We need to change the "need structures" that are induced through mass culture and undergird consumerist addiction. In addition, ever-growing inequalities of wealth introduce widespread envy and material cravings into society. All of these tendencies of capitalism make it impossible for society to respect ecological limits.

Living standards as now constructed in the industrial countries will have to fall. However, the notion of "living standard" is relative to one's world-view and mode of social existence. From the earliest days people have been able to live remarkably integral and spiritually advanced lives with a drastically lower level of "things" than now obtains in the so-called advanced societies. And it should not be forgotten that we are spending more and more just to reverse the effects of previous consumption and its associated waste. Our challenge is to see if lives can be reconstructed within the context of overcoming ecological crisis. This is why I argue that building toward a society beyond capitalism is the necessary condition for sustainability.

D&S: How have you and others at *Capitalism Nature Socialism* developed an ecologically conscious version of Marxism?

JK: Jim O'Connor's idea of the Second Contradiction made an "Eco-Marxism" possible by allowing the categories of Marxism to be applied in a rigorous way to our interactions with the external, natural world. Following Karl Polanyi, Jim integrated these with traditional crisis theory, showing both the essential unity of all forms of capitalist exploitation, and also their crisis-ridden character. The Second Contradiction postulated that the drive toward surplus value and profit caused capital to discount, hence degrade, the "conditions of production," which were defined by Jim as nature, the workers themselves, and infrastructure. An unintended yet necessary consequence of this was to depress the rate of profit, just as exploitation of workers reduced their ability to buy the commodities they made.

My focus has been on the expansive dynamic of capital, which accounts for its unsustainability, and immediately for the phenomena of climate change. I see this as rooted, first of all, in the fundamental shift outlined by Marx between an economy centered about use values, and the capitalist alternative centered in exchange value. People in pre-capitalist markets sell commodities for money in order to obtain other commodities they can use. Those in capitalist markets advance money to produce commodities to exchange for more money. Marx makes the profound observation that the second circuit has no limit, because money, as pure number, has no limit, in contrast to commodities produced for use—a person can consume only so much. Hence the capitalist economy is disconnected from nature at its root, and is "free" to mutilate the ecosphere. That this concretely happens is due to associated features of capitalism, such as competition driven by private ownership of the means of production, the complicity of the capitalist state, and the lawless character of a society grounded in exploitation.

Capitalism Nature Socialism also gives major emphasis to ecofeminist work because of the centrality of gender in our relations with nature; and finally, to an openness to radical and ecologically rational alternatives to capitalism: ecosocialism.

D&S: What about the international geopolitical realities? How can we expect Western governments, with all their historical baggage regarding pollution (and so much else), to seriously engage with the developing world, much of which is ruled by authoritarian governments, and beholden to foreign and domestic elites?

JK: The international dimension is crucial insofar as the ecological crisis is manifestly planetary, in both its causes and its effects. The rate of change of key ecosystems quite precisely follows the path of what has been called "globalization," one of the chief features of which is expansion in trade. While capitalism is the root problem, the present neoliberal period of capitalism, which began in the 1970s, is the setting for the heightened and globalized exploitation of nature (and also of labor) that surfaces as ecological crisis, with climate change as a principal but by no means exclusive manifestation.

What we call "imperialism" is deeply implicated in the ecological crisis. Throughout history, ecological events, at times catastrophic as in pandemics, have been interwoven with the rest of the fabric. The epoch of Western domination was ushered in by the spread of European diseases that eliminated 90% of the indigenous population of the Americas. Hence the uneven distribution of ecologically induced suffering is anything but new. Nor should it be read as absolute, since what characterizes the current ecological crisis is the "globalization" of hazards as well as of finance and trade—that is to say, if the seas rise six meters, a great deal of very valuable property will be destroyed along with that of commoners.

One of the most ominous implications of the present crisis is a survivalist mentality, manifest from gated communities, to vicious crackdowns on "illegal aliens," to fundamentalist wars. Anything that severs the interconnections of an ecosystem hastens its disintegration; this is bound to be the fate of a humanity disintegrating into fragments according to the logic of imperialism and its associated splittings.

But the ecological crisis affords another path as well, which increasing numbers of people are taking. This involves finding and adopting a universalist ethic stemming from perception of our common fate and our unity with nature. It requires overcoming all forms of chauvinism, including those that hold the human species over the rest of nature. Its practical foundation, however, is in anti-imperialist politics.

D&S: A few months back the senior science advisor to the British government claimed that he would "lose credibility" with the very government that—with much fanfare—commissioned his group's study if he insisted that the government commit itself to acknowledging its policy implications. Is this emblematic of the politics of climate change worldwide?

JK: Unfortunately, yes. There are of course even more lurid stories that came out of the Bush administration, where climate officials circulated in and out of Exxon-

Mobil, and reputable scientists were routinely threatened and punished for speaking the truth about climate change.

There is a basic lesson to be learned: The ecological crisis poses a bigger threat to humanity than fascism. During World War II, in Britain and the United States, the ruling classes and the state collaborated in the biggest mobilization in human history to defeat the Axis. In that case the capitalists could see that a degree of suspension of the normal operations of the market, as through planning, rationing, price controls, etc., would gain them the prized control over the global economy once the war crisis was over; from another angle, they could see their way clear of the seemingly intractable depression that had haunted the 1930s.

In this case, resolution of climate change (not to mention the other features of ecological crisis) will require such deep and permanent cuts in the processes of accumulation as to bring the capitalist era to a close. For example, a young economist, Minqi Li, has recently demonstrated ["Climate Change, Limits to Growth, and the Imperative for Socialism," *Monthly Review*, July/August 2008] that all scenarios that hold down global warming below the threshold of positive feedback loops that accelerate climate change will require sustained contractions in world domes-tic product—in other words, an end to "growth," which means the end of capitalism. The big bourgeoisie knows this, which is why they act irresponsibly, typically sacrificing the future to the accumulation of wealth. If they behaved differently, they wouldn't have control over accumulation, and others would step forward to take control. As Marx wrote, the capitalist is the personification of capital.

D&S: What about the coverage of the issue in the media? More of the same?

JK: Absolutely the same principle holds for the corporate media, which have during the neoliberal era become absorbed into ever-greater conglomerations of capital. This has necessarily stifled the independent voices of the press, as we see in reporting of political races, the war in Iraq, and much else. Here, once more, the context is a threat to the capitalist system itself, and therefore the behavior is more extreme. Watch the Weather Channel or the robotic weather correspondents on news programs. Will they ever, in reporting the increasingly bizarre weather patterns that accompany climate change, suggest that these correspond to an ever-gathering crisis, much less suggest that there might be a structural dynamic driving that crisis?

Virtually every sane adult (and many more children than one would suspect) knows that something very fishy is going on in the sphere of climate. People tend to be understandably worried about this. Imagine what a threat to the system would result if they became at all enlightened, which is to say, able to recognize just how profound is the threat to their future and even more, to the future of their children—and also that there is a coherent explanation as to why this is happening, one implicating the very centers of capitalist power.

To secure capital's rule, it is necessary to keep people in the dark, or to be more exact, confused, distracted, and vaguely reassured. The media tends, therefore, to meet people halfway, then move them in the wrong direction. False prophets like Al Gore are praised for calling attention to the threat posed by the carbon economy, and the fact that Gore does not attend to the role played by the accumulation of capital is never brought forward. At the same time, the corporate image machine is geared up for greenwashing.

Unhappily, the job of mass deception is relatively easy, since with the stakes so high and given the inherent complexities and level of fear, it takes only a little uncertainty to slow down necessary action. The media system is very effective in doing this.

D&S: What about carbon trading/taxes, the switch to renewables, and nuclear power? Can they help even in the short term?

JK: There is a simple and effective touchstone for evaluating proposed solutions to the climate change crisis: do not look at the technical details but at the class forces in play, and always act so as to weaken the forces of capital. From this standpoint, some schemes are doomed from their inception, while the fate of others depends on the politics of their implementation.

In the first category belongs emissions trading, including the Kyoto Protocols and their so-called "Clean Development Mechanisms" in which projects in the Global South are used, like Papal indulgences, to permit the industrial North to keep putting CO_2 into the atmosphere. This sounds odd, and it is. To be blunt: Kyoto is set up to fail, except from the standpoint of a "success" that is also a failure, namely, the making of money from the licensing of pollution credits (because such money becomes capital, which must be invested to make more capital, which is to say, made to enter a fresh cycle of throwing carbon into the atmosphere). What dooms Kyoto is transparently that of being the scheme of climate control entrusted to capital. I am not sure whether capitalists know consciously that an effective program of containing climate change will bring down their system, but they certainly act on this basis.

(When I refer to "Kyoto," I follow a common practice of including both the formal documents and the mass of practices undertaken in their wake. The written protocol is vague about a lot of details and implications. However, the total regime signified by Kyoto is one in which the actors are exclusively allied with capital. Hence everything is interpreted to create credits rather than taxes and to allow these to become subject to new forms of wealth generation through speculation. The architects of the Kyoto Protocols rationalized this as necessary to induce capitalists to get on board. They have done so—on a vessel headed toward the rocks.)

Carbon taxes belong to the second category. In principle they have the potential to reduce carbon emissions. In practice, this depends on how they are written, who is made to pay, and who stands behind them. As is pretty much the case for all kinds of taxation, politics are the decisive factor.

Alternative energy is an absolute necessity, and also a political football. The reader had better disabuse her or himself of the notion that nuclear power will solve this crisis, despite all the cheerleading for it. Intractably dangerous, enormously destructive, and expensive to build and operate, nuclear power is also basically inadequate. An MIT report from 2003 [S. Ansolabehere et al., "The Future of Nuclear Power," Massachusetts Institute of Technology, July 2003] says that 1,000 to 1,500 new 1,000-megawatt reactors would have to be built by 2050 just to displace 15–25% of the expected growth in carbon emissions from electricity generation over that time.

Similar considerations hold for genuinely renewable energies like solar, wind, geothermal, tidal, etc., despite their clear superiority from an ecological perspective. The point deserves the utmost emphasis: there is no technological or administrative fix for the ecological crisis. An effective resolution requires social transformation, one overriding criterion of which must be to keep carbon in the ground in the first place, and whose overall goals include reducing the burden of society on nature and promoting the healing and restoration of damaged ecosystems.

This requires radically anti-capitalist ecopolitics, some goals of which in the case of climate would be:

- solidarity with popular struggles to block the extraction of carbon and uranium; these occur worldwide, from Nigeria to Ecuador to Australia to California, and they need to be coordinated as well as extended;
- free and universal public transportation (just like schools and health care);
- nationalization of the oil, coal, and gas industries;
- total mobilization to force worthy climate protocols in Copenhagen in December 2009, by direct action if necessary—as is almost certainly going to be the case. This may require as many as a million people in the streets.

These measures can be seen as the prefiguration of the World Social Forum movement's slogan, "Another world is possible."

D&S: How can we deal with other environmental issues—nanotechnology, and pollution of the oceans and of space, for example—when all our efforts would seem to have to be focused on climate change?

JK: We need the notion of an ecological crisis to grasp that there are a number of ecosystemic crises, each of which can wreak major havoc and all of which are interrelated and share the same susceptibility to the accumulative pressure of capital. This is why, by the way, it is better to think in terms of ecology than environment, since the notion of an environment does not carry an assumption that its parts are interrelated. Within an ecological way of looking at things, things are differentiated but internally related. The climate crisis is one cause of the increasingly grave and lethal water crisis, just as terrestrial water flows shape climate. The same goes for increasing food crises, where the diversion of crops for biofuel production is causing incipient famine, while biotechnology becomes a potentially deadly instrument of capital by recklessly interfering with the evolved checks and balances by means of which nature introduces a degree of stability and equilibrium.

The ecological perspective requires that we see ourselves as part of nature, including as organic bodies subject to disease. Pandemics are themselves ecological events, co-determined by pollution-induced immune system disturbances, and increasingly likely. This perspective demands a complete rethinking of human existence. It cannot be grasped by a purely economic analysis.

D&S: What if a socialist movement becomes viable—perhaps due in part to the social and economic breakdown that would inevitably accompany the rapid climate change some are forecasting only a few decades hence—and takes power only to find itself unable to meet basic needs due to the effects of climate change?

JK: Today, any viable socialist movement has to be ecologically rooted, or else it is irrelevant. I would define ecosocialism as the movement toward a society of freely associated labor animated by ecocentric values, that is, by an ethic that foregrounds the healing of nature. In contrast to earlier socialisms, which often sought to perfect capitalism while redistributing the social product, ecosocialism advances the notion of limits on growth, not as a restric-tion upon life but as the flourishing of ecosystems in a state of balance and vibrant evolution.

Any actual socialist movement that comes to a degree of power in the interim would obviously be only a partial realization of this goal. There is no use in lamenting this prospect. One simply does the best one can and accepts the result stoically. Of course a degree of coercion would be required, especially of residual capitalist class forces. At some point, for example, the government will just have to decree strict rationing, or redirect production by fiat, without letting "market forces" do it. This is what happened in the World Wars, and the ecological crisis is their equivalent in terms of emergency. That's what states are for, and in any predictable scenario short of complete chaos, we will not be able to immediately dispense with state power. Everything here depends on how deeply ecosocialist principles have been internalized, that is, on how democratic/nonviolent means and ends have been integrated.

Rosa Luxemburg said a century ago that the real choice was between "socialism and barbarism." This remains the choice, except that socialism has become ecosocialism; while barbarism now comes into focus as ecocatastrophe, fascism, and endless war, with the nuclear option stronger than ever. That is simply the history into which we have been thrown, and we have no option except to make the best of it.

CONTRIBUTORS

Randy Albelda is a professor of economics at the University of Massachusetts-Boston and a *Dollars & Sense* associate.

Gar Alperovitz is professor of political economy at the University of Maryland and president of the National Center for Economic and Security Alternatives.

David Bacon is a journalist and photographer covering labor, immigration, and the impact of the global economy on workers.

Peter Barnes is a successful entrepeneur who co-founded Working Assets and has served on several business boards. He is a senior fellow at the Tomales Bay Insitute.

Ravi Bhandari is the Chevron Endowed Chair of Economics and International Political Economy at Saint Mary's College of California.

Heather Boushey is a senior economist at the Center for American Progress.

Ben Collins is a member of the *Dollars & Sense* collective and a research analyst at KLD Research & Analytics, a sustainable investment research company.

Chuck Collins is a senior scholar at the Institute for Policy Studies and co-author of *The Moral Measure of the Economy* (Orbis, 2007) and *Economic Apartheid in America* (New Press, 2005).

James Cypher is profesor-investigador, Programa de Doctorado en Estudios del Desarrollo, Universidad Autónoma de Zacatecas, Mexico, and a *Dollars & Sense* associate.

Ryan A. Dodd is a Ph.D. student in economics and a research associate at the Center for Full Employment and Price Stability, both at the University of Missouri-Kansas City.

Michael Engel is an emeritus professor of political science at Westfield State College in Massachusetts. He is the author of *The Struggle for Control of Public Education* (Temple University, 2000).

Daniel Fireside is the book editor at *Dollars & Sense.*

Ellen Frank teaches economics at UMass Boston.

Amy Gluckman is co-editor of *Dollars & Sense.*

Kayty Himmelstein is a former *Dollars & Sense* intern.

Howard Karger is professor of social work at the University of Houston and the author of *Short-Changed: Life and Debt in the Fringe Economy* (Berret-Koehler, 2005).

David C. Korten is an author, political activist, and critic of corporate globalization. He is co-founder and board chair of the Positive Futures Network.

Alex Linghorn is currently a postgraduate at the School of Oriental and African Studies (SOAS), University of London, UK.

Meizhu Lui is former executive director of United For a Fair Economy.

Arthur MacEwan is an emeritus professor of economics at the University of Massachusetts-Boston. He is a *Dollars & Sense* associate and founding member of the magazine.

John Miller John Miller teaches economics at Wheaton College and is a member of the *Dollars & Sense* collective.

William Moseley is an assistant professor of geography and former coordinator of the African Studies program at Macalester College in Saint Paul, Minn.

Dedrick Muhammad is senior organizer and research fellow at the Institute for Policy Studies.

Rebecca Parrish is a former *Dollars & Sense* intern.

Adam Sacks is Executive Director of The Center for Democracy and the Constitution.

Adria Scharf is director of the Richmond Peace Education Center in Richmond, Va., and is a former co-editor of *Dollars & Sense.*

Michelle Sheehan is a former member of the *Dollars & Sense* collective.

David Swanson is a board member of the Progressive Democrats of America and is the Washington director of democrats.com.

Chris Tilly is director of the Institute for Research on Labor andEmployment and professor of Urban Planning at UCLA. He is a *Dollars &Sense* associate.

Ramaa Vasudevan is assistant professor at Colorado State University and is a member of the *Dollars & Sense* collective.

Jeannette Wicks-Lim is an assistant research professor at the Political Economy Research Institute, UMass-Amherst.

Thad Williamson is assistant professor at the Jepson School of Leadership Studies, University of Richmond and a former member of the *Dollars & Sense* collective.

Rick Wolff is professor of economics at UMass-Amherst.

Breinigsville, PA USA
02 September 2009
223472BV00003B/3/P

9 781878 585530